Puppet 2.7 Cookbook

Build reliable, scalable, secure, high-performance systems to fully utilize the power of cloud computing

John Arundel

[PACKT] open source *
PUBLISHING   community experience distilled

BIRMINGHAM - MUMBAI

Puppet 2.7 Cookbook

First published: October 2011

Production Reference: 1171011

Published by Packt Publishing Ltd.
Livery Place
35 Livery Street
Birmingham B3 2PB, UK.

ISBN 978-1-84951-538-2

www.packtpub.com

Cover Image by Sujay Gawand (sujay0000@gmail.com)

Credits

Author

John Arundel

Reviewers

Mark Phillips

Eric Stonfer

Acquisition Editors

Chaitanya Apte

Kartikey Pandey

Development Editor

Alina Lewis

Technical Editors

Priyanka S

Ankita Shashi

Project Coordinator

Michelle Quadros

Proofreader

Matthew Humphries

Indexer

Monica Ajmera

Graphics

Valentina Joseph D'silva

Production Coordinator

Prachali Bhiwandkar

Cover Work

Prachali Bhiwandkar

About the Author

John Arundel is a consultant engineer who helps people build better infrastructure. He uses automation and configuration management to make computer systems cheaper, faster, and more reliable. Formerly a senior enterprise systems engineer in the hosting division of US telco Verizon, he now runs his own company, Bitfield Consulting, and says he has never worked so hard in his life, or for less money.

Over the years John has worked with clients in the advertising and media industry, software, finance, retail, logistics, and even the emergency services, advising on architecture, automation, security, backups, resilience, performance, capacity planning, and regulatory compliance. He has been a member of the Puppet community since its earliest days, and organizes regular local sysadmin meetups and social events.

John holds a B.Sc.(Hons) in Computer Science, with a research interest in kernel resource scheduler design, and is a certified Sun Solaris administrator, LPI (Linux Professional Institute) graduate, and a member of the British Computer Society (MBCS). He is security-cleared to work on computer systems for the UK nuclear industry, which is probably nothing to worry about.

He has also worked as a software developer, both professionally and for the fun of it, contributing to several open source projects, and building a high-performance research chess engine. He blogs regularly at `http://bitfieldconsulting.com` on Puppet and system administration topics, is usually to be found on Twitter (`@bitfield`) complaining about things, and often speaks at technical user groups and conferences.

In his negligible spare time, John enjoys repairing Land Rovers, playing Go, and barbecuing. He lives in London and Cornwall.

My thanks go to Luke Kanies and the team at Puppet Labs; also to Ken Barber, Lindsay Holmwood, Gary Larizza, Stephen Nelson-Smith, R.I. Pienaar, Julian Simpson, Jordan Sissel, Cosimo Streppone, James Turnbull, and Dean Wilson, who all provided valuable contributions to the book, whether they know it or not; and for their brave self-sacrifice in the cause of proofreading, Ian Chilton, Kris Buytaert, Stefan Goethals, and Martin Brooks. A special mention goes to the regulars of channel #puppet, who often helped out when things didn't work the way they were supposed to, which was virtually all the time.

About the Reviewers

Mark Philips has had a varied career spanning Motor Manufacturer, Internet, Telco, and Finance industries over the last 17 years. Engineering for UNIX estates from a handful of hosts through to many thousands, Mark has strived to automate anything and everything that had to be carried out more than once. Discovering Puppet in early 2007 was a boon to achieving his idea of systems nirvana—simple centralized and automated configuration management.

Mark runs an IT consultancy company, VNTX Limited, specializing in UNIX installation, integration, automation, and performance tuning.

When he's not in front of a computer, Mark can be found out riding one of his bicycles—training for a race, or boring his ever patient wife talking about cycling.

Eric Stonfer is a 10 year veteran of systems administration, with an emphasis on automation and configuration systems, and has been using Puppet to manage thousands of servers for over 3 years. In his spare time Eric is an avid home brewer.

www.PacktPub.com

Support files, eBooks, discount offers and more

You might want to visit www.PacktPub.com for support files and downloads related to your book.

Did you know that Packt offers eBook versions of every book published, with PDF and ePub files available? You can upgrade to the eBook version at www.PacktPub.com and as a print book customer, you are entitled to a discount on the eBook copy. Get in touch with us at service@packtpub.com for more details.

At www.PacktPub.com, you can also read a collection of free technical articles, sign up for a range of free newsletters and receive exclusive discounts and offers on Packt books and eBooks.

http://PacktLib.PacktPub.com

Do you need instant solutions to your IT questions? PacktLib is Packt's online digital book library. Here, you can access, read and search across Packt's entire library of books.

Why Subscribe?

- ▶ Fully searchable across every book published by Packt
- ▶ Copy and paste, print and bookmark content
- ▶ On demand and accessible via web browser

Free Access for Packt account holders

If you have an account with Packt at www.PacktPub.com, you can use this to access PacktLib today and view nine entirely free books. Simply use your login credentials for immediate access.

Table of Contents

Preface

A revolution is coming to IT operations. Configuration management tools can build servers in seconds and automate your entire network. Tools like Puppet are essential to take full advantage of the power of cloud computing, and build reliable, scalable, secure, and high-performance systems.

This book takes you beyond the basics and explores the full power of Puppet, showing you in detail how to tackle a variety of real-world problems and applications. At every step, it shows you exactly what commands you need to type and includes complete code samples for every recipe.

It takes the reader from rudimentary knowledge of Puppet to a more complete and expert understanding of Puppet's latest and most advanced features, community best practices, writing great manifests, scaling and performance, and how to extend Puppet by adding your own providers and resources.

This book also includes real examples from production systems and techniques that are in use in some of the world's largest Puppet installations, including a distributed Puppet architecture and a high-performance Puppetmaster solution using Apache and Passenger.

Explore the power of Puppet with this practical guide to the world's most popular configuration management system.

What this book covers

Chapter 1, *Puppet Infrastructure* introduces some key techniques for managing your Puppet server and manifests, including version control, automated deployment, file serving, pre-signing and autosigning certificates, scaling with Passenger, and a distributed decentralized Puppet architecture using Git.

Chapter 2, Monitoring, Reporting, and Troubleshooting covers ways that Puppet can report information about what it's doing, and the status of your systems. This includes graphical and e-mail reports, log and debug messages, dependency graphing, testing and dry-running your manifests, using tags, run stages, and environments, and a guide to some of Puppet's more common error messages.

Chapter 3, Puppet Language and Style will show you examples of good programming style in Puppet and language constructs that can help you keep your code concise and readable, including conditionals, selectors, case statements, arrays, and regular expressions.

Chapter 4, Writing Better Manifests takes you through structuring your Puppet manifests using node and class inheritance, resource dependencies, and parameterized classes. You'll also see how to get data in and out of Puppet from the environment using CSV files and shell scripts.

Chapter 5, Working with Files and Packages covers powerful techniques for managing config files, including ERB templates, generating files from snippets, and using the Augeas tool. You'll also see how to use Puppet to install packages from APT repositories, and how to set up your own APT and Gem repositories.

Chapter 6, Users and Virtual Resources explains how virtual resources can help you manage different combinations of users and packages on different machines, and shows you how to use Puppet's resource scheduling and auditing features.

Chapter 7, Applications focuses on some specific applications that you may need to manage with Puppet, including complete recipes for Apache and Nginx, MySQL, Drupal, and Rails.

Chapter 8, Servers and Cloud Infrastructure extends the power of Puppet to managing virtual machines, both in the cloud and on your desktop, with recipes for Vagrant and EC2 instances. It also shows you how to set up a Nagios monitoring server, load balancing with HAProxy, firewalls with `iptables`, network filesystems with NFS, and high-availability services with Heartbeat.

Chapter 9, External Tools and the Puppet Ecosystem looks at the tools that have grown up around Puppet and help you integrate it with the rest of your network, including Puppet Dashboard, Foreman, and MCollective. It also introduces you to some advanced topics including writing your own resource types, providers, and external node classifiers.

What you need for this book

To run the examples in this book, you will need a computer with Ubuntu Linux 10.04 and Puppet installed, and an Internet connection. Though not strictly necessary, I also recommend an espresso machine or some other form of caffeinated beverage dispenser.

Who this book is for

The book assumes that the reader already has a working Puppet installation and perhaps has written some basic manifests or adapted some published modules. It also requires some experience of Linux systems administration, including familiarity with the command line, file system, and text editing. No programming experience is required.

Conventions

In this book, you will find a number of styles of text that distinguish between different kinds of information. Here are some examples of these styles, and an explanation of their meaning.

Code words in text are shown as follows: " You'll need a Puppetmaster and a set of existing manifests in /etc/puppet."

A block of code is set as follows:

```
#!/bin/sh

syntax_errors=0
error_msg=$(mktemp /tmp/error_msg.XXXXXX)

if git rev-parse --quiet --verify HEAD > /dev/null
then
    against=HEAD
```

Any command-line input or output is written as follows:

```
# puppet parser validate/etc/puppet/manifests/site.pp
err: Could not parse for environment production: Syntax error at end
of file at /etc/puppet/manifests/site.pp:3
```

New terms and **important words** are shown in bold. Words that you see on the screen, in menus or dialog boxes for example, appear in the text like this: "clicking the **Next** button moves you to the next screen".

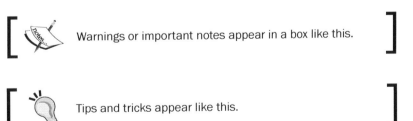

> Warnings or important notes appear in a box like this.

> Tips and tricks appear like this.

Reader feedback

Feedback from our readers is always welcome. Let us know what you think about this book—what you liked or may have disliked. Reader feedback is important for us to develop titles that you really get the most out of.

To send us general feedback, simply send an e-mail to feedback@packtpub.com, and mention the book title via the subject of your message.

If there is a book that you need and would like to see us publish, please send us a note in the **SUGGEST A TITLE** form on www.packtpub.com or e-mail suggest@packtpub.com.

If there is a topic that you have expertise in and you are interested in either writing or contributing to a book, see our author guide on www.packtpub.com/authors.

Customer support

Now that you are the proud owner of a Packt book, we have a number of things to help you to get the most from your purchase.

Downloading the example code

You can download the example code files for all Packt books you have purchased from your account at http://www.PacktPub.com. If you purchased this book elsewhere, you can visit http://www.PacktPub.com/support and register to have the files e-mailed directly to you.

Errata

Although we have taken every care to ensure the accuracy of our content, mistakes do happen. If you find a mistake in one of our books—maybe a mistake in the text or the code—we would be grateful if you would report this to us. By doing so, you can save other readers from frustration and help us improve subsequent versions of this book. If you find any errata, please report them by visiting http://www.packtpub.com/support, selecting your book, clicking on the **errata submission form** link, and entering the details of your errata. Once your errata are verified, your submission will be accepted and the errata will be uploaded on our website, or added to any list of existing errata, under the Errata section of that title. Any existing errata can be viewed by selecting your title from http://www.packtpub.com/support.

Piracy

Piracy of copyright material on the Internet is an ongoing problem across all media. At Packt, we take the protection of our copyright and licenses very seriously. If you come across any illegal copies of our works, in any form, on the Internet, please provide us with the location address or website name immediately so that we can pursue a remedy.

Please contact us at `copyright@packtpub.com` with a link to the suspected pirated material.

We appreciate your help in protecting our authors, and our ability to bring you valuable content.

Questions

You can contact us at `questions@packtpub.com` if you are having a problem with any aspect of the book, and we will do our best to address it.

1
Puppet Infrastructure

"Computers in the future may have as few as 1,000 vacuum tubes and weigh only 1.5 tons."— Popular Mechanics, 1949

In this chapter, we will cover:

- ▶ Using version control
- ▶ Using commit hooks
- ▶ Deploying changes with Rake
- ▶ Configuring Puppet's file server
- ▶ Running Puppet from cron
- ▶ Using autosign
- ▶ Pre-signing certificates
- ▶ Retrieving files from Puppet's filebucket
- ▶ Scaling Puppet using Passenger
- ▶ Creating a decentralized Puppet architecture

Some of the recipes in this book represent best practices as agreed upon by the Puppet community. Others are tips and tricks that will make it easier for you to work with Puppet, or introduce you to features that you may not have been previously aware of. Some recipes are short cuts which I wouldn't recommend you use as standard operating procedure, but may be useful in emergencies. Finally, there are some experimental recipes that you may like to try, but are only useful or applicable in very large infrastructures or otherwise unusual circumstances.

I hope that, by reading through and thinking about the recipes presented here, you will gain a deeper and broader understanding of how Puppet works and how you can use it to help you build better infrastructures. Only you can decide whether a particular recipe is appropriate for you and your organization, but I hope this collection will inspire you to experiment, find out more, and most of all—have fun using Puppet!

> You'll see that throughout the examples in this book, most of the commands are run as the `root` user. If you prefer to administer systems with a normal user account and `sudo`, please do it this way instead.

Because Linux distributions such as Ubuntu, Red Hat, and CentOS differ in the specific details of package names, configuration file paths, and many other things, I have decided that for reasons of space and clarity the best approach for this book is to pick one distribution (Ubuntu 10.04 Lucid) and stick with it. However, Puppet runs on almost every operating system there is, so you should have very little trouble adapting the recipes to your own favored OS and distribution.

At the time of writing this book, Puppet 2.7 was the latest stable version available, and consequently I have chosen that as the reference version of Puppet used. However, the syntax of Puppet commands changes every so often; so be aware that while older versions of Puppet are still perfectly usable, they may not support all of the features and syntax described in this book.

Using version control

"Unix was not designed to stop you from doing stupid things, because that would also stop you from doing clever things." —Doug Gwyn

Ever deleted something and wished you hadn't? The most important tip in this book is to put your Puppet manifests in a **version control system** such as Git or Subversion. Editing the manifests directly on the **Puppetmaster** is a bad idea, because your changes could get applied before you're ready. Puppet automatically detects any changes to manifest files, so you might find half-finished manifests being applied to your clients. This could have nasty results!

Instead, use version control (I recommend Git) and make the `/etc/puppet` directory on the Puppetmaster a checkout from your repository. This gives you several advantages:

▶ You don't run the risk of Puppet applying incomplete changes

▶ You can undo changes and revert to any previous version of your manifest

- You can experiment with new features using a branch, without affecting the master version used in production
- If several people need to make changes to the manifests, they can make them independently, in their own working copies, and then merge their changes later
- You can use the log feature to see what was changed, and when (and by whom).

Getting ready

You'll need a Puppetmaster and a set of existing manifests in /etc/puppet. If you don't have these already, refer to the Puppet documentation to find out how to install Puppet and create your first manifests.

To put your manifests under version control, you need to import the /etc/puppet directory from the Puppetmaster into your version control system, and make it a working copy. In this example, we'll use a **GitHub** account to store the Puppet configuration.

You'll need a GitHub account (it's free to sign up) and a repository. Follow the instructions at www.github.com to create one.

 You can download the example code files for all Packt books you have purchased from your account at http://www.PacktPub.com. If you purchased this book elsewhere, you can visit http://www.PacktPub.com/support and register to have the files e-mailed directly to you.

How to do it...

1. To turn the /etc/puppet directory on the Puppetmaster into a Git repository, run the following commands:

   ```
   root@cookbook:/etc/puppet# git init
   Initialized empty Git repository in /etc/puppet/.git/
   root@cookbook:/etc/puppet# git add manifests/ modules/
   root@cookbook:/etc/puppet# git commit -m "initial commit"
   [master (root-commit) c7a24cf] initial commit
    59 files changed, 1790 insertions(+), 0 deletions(-)
    create mode 100644 manifests/site.pp
    create mode 100644 manifests/utils.pp
   ...
   ```

2. Connect this to your GitHub repo and `push` as follows:

```
# git push -u origin master
Counting objects: 91, done.
Compressing objects: 100% (69/69), done.
Writing objects: 100% (91/91), 21.07 KiB, done.
Total 91 (delta 4), reused 0 (delta 0)
To git@github.com:bitfield/puppet-demo.git
 * [new branch]      master -> master
```

Branch master setup to track remote branch masters from the origin.

How it works...

You've created a "master" **repository** (usually known as a **repo** for short) at GitHub which contains your Puppet manifests. You can check out multiple copies of this in different places and work on them before committing your changes. For example, if you had a team of system admins, each of them could work on their own local copy of the repo.

The copy in `/etc/puppet` on the Puppetmaster is now just another working copy, slaved to the GitHub repo. When you decide that you want to tell Puppet about your changes, you can update this copy and it will pull the latest changes from GitHub.

There's more...

Now that you've set up version control, you can use the following workflow for editing your Puppet manifests:

1. Make your changes in the working copy using your favorite text editor.
2. Commit the changes and push them to the GitHub repo, as shown in the preceding text.
3. Update the Puppetmaster's working copy, using `git pull`.
    - ❏ Here is an example where we add a new file to the manifest, commit it, and then update the Puppetmaster's working copy. I've made some edits to the working copy on my laptop:

```
john@laptop:~$ cd puppet-work
john@laptop:~/puppet-work$ mkdir manifests
john@laptop:~/puppet-work$ touch manifests/nodes.pp
john@laptop:~/puppet-work$ git add manifests/nodes.pp
john@laptop:~/puppet-work$ git commit -m "adding nodes.pp"
[master 5c7b94c] adding nodes.pp
 0 files changed, 0 insertions(+), 0 deletions(-)
 create mode 100644 manifests/nodes.pp
```

```
john@laptop:~/puppet-work$ git push
Counting objects: 7, done.
Compressing objects: 100% (4/4), done.
Writing objects: 100% (4/4), 409 bytes, done.
Total 4 (delta 1), reused 0 (delta 0)
To git@github.com:bitfield/puppet-demo.git
   c7a24cf..b74d452  master -> master
```

❑ Now I'll update the working copy on the Puppetmaster:

```
root@cookbook:/etc/puppet# git pull
remote: Counting objects: 5, done.
remote: Compressing objects: 100% (2/2), done.
remote: Total 4 (delta 0), reused 0 (delta 0)
Unpacking objects: 100% (4/4), done.
From git@github.com:bitfield/puppet-demo.git
   26d668c..5c7b94c  master      -> origin/master
Updating 26d668c..5c7b94c
Fast-forward
0 files changed, 0 insertions(+), 0 deletions(-)
create mode 100644 manifests/nodes.pp
```

❑ You can automate this process by using a tool such as **Rake**.

See also

▶ *Deploying changes with Rake* in this chapter

▶ *Creating a decentralized Puppet architecture* in this chapter

▶ *Using commit hooks* in this chapter

Using commit hooks

It would be nice if we knew there was a syntax error in the manifest before we even committed it. You can have Puppet check the manifest using the `puppet parser validate` command:

```
# puppet parser validate/etc/puppet/manifests/site.pp
err: Could not parse for environment production: Syntax error at end of
file at /etc/puppet/manifests/site.pp:3
```

This is especially useful because a mistake anywhere in the manifest will stop Puppet from running on any node, even on nodes that don't use that particular part of the manifest. So checking in a bad manifest can cause Puppet to stop applying updates to production for some time, until the problem is discovered, and this could potentially have serious consequences.

The best way to avoid this is to automate the syntax check by using a **pre-commit hook** in your version control repo.

How to do it...

If you are using Git for version control, you can add a script, `.git/hooks/pre-commit` that syntax checks all files about to be committed. This example is taken from the Puppet Labs wiki:

```sh
#!/bin/sh

syntax_errors=0
error_msg=$(mktemp /tmp/error_msg.XXXXXX)

if git rev-parse --quiet --verify HEAD > /dev/null
then
    against=HEAD
else
    # Initial commit: diff against an empty tree object
    against=4b825dc642cb6eb9a060e54bf8d69288fbee4904
fi

# Get list of new/modified manifest and template files to check (in
git index)
for indexfile in `git diff-index --diff-filter=AM --name-only --cached
$against | egrep '\.(pp|erb)'`
do
    # Don't check empty files
    if [ `git cat-file -s :0:$indexfile` -gt 0 ]
    then
        case $indexfile in
            *.pp )
                # Check puppet manifest syntax
                git cat-file blob :0:$indexfile | puppet parser
                validate --ignoreimport > $error_msg ;;
            *.erb )
                # Check ERB template syntax
                git cat-file blob :0:$indexfile | erb -x -T - | ruby
                -c 2> $error_msg > /dev/null ;;
        esac
        if [ "$?" -ne 0 ]
        then
            echo -n "$indexfile: "
            cat $error_msg
            syntax_errors=`expr $syntax_errors + 1`
        fi
```

```
    fi
done

rm -f $error_msg

if [ "$syntax_errors" -ne 0 ]
then
    echo "Error: $syntax_errors syntax errors found, aborting commit."
    exit 1
fi
```

How it works...

The commit hook script will prevent you from committing any files with syntax errors:

```
# git commit -m "spot the deliberate mistake" manifests/site.pp
err: Could not parse for environment production: Syntax error at end of
file; expected '}' at /etc/puppet/manifests/site.pp:3
manifests/site.pp: Error: 1 syntax errors found, aborting commit.
```

There's more...

You can find this script, and more details about it, on the Puppet Labs wiki: http://
projects.puppetlabs.com/projects/1/wiki/Puppet_Version_Control

You can use a similar update hook to prevent broken manifests from being pushed to the Puppetmaster: see the wiki page for details.

See also

▶ *Using version control* in this chapter

Deploying changes with Rake

Like everyone who makes his living with a keyboard, I hate unnecessary typing. If you are using the workflow described in the section on using version control, you can add some automation to make this process a little easier. There are several tools that can run commands for you on remote servers, including Capistrano and Fabric, but for this example we'll use Rake.

If you don't have Rake installed already, run the following command:

```
apt-get install rake
```

You'll need a working Internet connection.

How to do it...

1. Create a file in the top level of your Puppet working copy named `Rakefile` that looks like this:

    ```
    PUPPETMASTER = 'cookbook'
    SSH = 'ssh -t -A'

    task :deploy do
        sh "git push"
        sh "#{SSH} #{PUPPETMASTER} 'cd /etc/puppet && sudo git pull'"
    end
    ```

2. When you make changes in your working copy of the Puppet manifests, you can simply run:

    ```
    $ rake deploy
    ```

3. Rake will take care of updating the Git repo and refreshing the Puppetmaster's working copy for you:

    ```
    $ git push
    Counting objects: 4, done.
    Delta compression using 2 threads.
    Compressing objects: 100% (3/3), done.
    Writing objects: 100% (3/3), 452 bytes, done.
    Total 3 (delta 0), reused 0 (delta 0)
    To ssh:/ /git@cookbook.bitfieldconsulting.com/var/git/cookbook
        561e5a6..a8b8c76  master -> master
    ssh -A -l root cookbook 'cd /etc/puppet && git pull'
    From ssh://cookbook.bitfieldconsulting.com/var/git/cookbook
        561e5a6..a8b8c76  master       -> origin/master
    Updating 561e5a6..a8b8c76
    Fast-forward
     Rakefile |    6 ++++++
     1 files changed, 6 insertions(+), 0 deletions(-)
     create mode 100644 Rakefile
    ```

4. You can also add a Rake task to run Puppet on the client machine:

```
task :apply => [:deploy] do
    client = ENV['CLIENT']
    sh "#{SSH} #{client} 'sudo puppet agent --test'" do |ok,
    status|
        puts case status.exitstatus
            when 0 then "Client is up to date."
            when 1 then "Puppet couldn't compile the manifest."
            when 2 then "Puppet made changes."
            when 4 then "Puppet found errors."
        end
    end
end
```

5. When you want to test your changes on the client machine, run the following command:

   rake CLIENT=cookbook apply

6. Replace `cookbook` with the name of the client machine, or set the `CLIENT` environment variable so that Rake knows which machine to run Puppet on.

   info: Caching catalog for cookbook

   info: Applying configuration version '1292865016'

   info: Creating state file /var/lib/puppet/state/state.yaml

   notice: Finished catalog run in 0.03 seconds

7. If you want to see what changes Puppet would make, without actually changing anything, use the `--noop` flag:

```
task :noop => [:deploy] do
    client = ENV['CLIENT']
    sh "#{SSH} #{client} 'sudo puppet agent --test --noop'"
end
```

8. Now you can run:

   $ rake noop

   This will show you a preview of the changes.

How it works...

A `Rakefile` consists of a series of tasks, identified by the `task` keyword. The task definition is a set of steps, in this case the sequence of shell commands required to push your manifest changes to the master repo, and update the Puppetmaster's working copy.

Tasks can be linked, so that one depends on the other. For example, in our `Rakefile` the `apply` task is linked to `deploy`, so that whenever you run `rake apply`, Rake will make sure the `deploy` task is done first, and the `apply` task next.

There's more...

You can extend this `Rakefile` to automate more tasks, including running a syntax check on the Puppet manifests before updating them, and even bootstrapping a new machine with Puppet. Rake is a powerful tool and can be a big help in managing a large network with Puppet.

See also

- ▶ *Using version control* in this chapter
- ▶ *Creating a decentralized Puppet architecture* in this chapter
- ▶ *Using commit hooks* in this chapter

Configuring Puppet's file server

Deploying configuration files is one of the most common uses of Puppet. Most non-trivial services need some kind of configuration file, and you can have Puppet push it to the client using a `file` resource as shown in the following code:

```
file { "/opt/nginx/conf.d/app_production.conf":
    source => "puppet:///modules/app/app_production.conf",
}
```

The `source` parameter works like this: the first part after `puppet:///` is assumed to be the name of a **mount point**, and the remainder is treated as a path to the file as shown.

```
puppet:///<mount point>/<path>
```

Usually the value of `<mount point>` is `modules`, as in the preceding example. In this case, Puppet will look for the file in:

```
manifests/modules/app/files/app_production.conf
```

`modules` is a mount point that Puppet treats specially: it expects the next path component to be the name of a module, and it will then look in the module's `files` directory for the remainder of the path.

However, Puppet lets you create custom mount points, which can have individual access control settings, and can be mapped to different locations on the Puppetmaster. In this recipe we'll see how to create and configure these custom mount points.

How to do it...

1. Add a stanza to the Puppetmaster's `fileserver.conf`, with the name of your mount point in square brackets, and the path where Puppet should look for data, as shown:

```
[san]
      path /mnt/san/mydata/puppet
```

2. In your manifest, specify a file source using your mount point name as follows:

```
source => "puppet:///san/admin/users.htpasswd",
```

and Puppet will convert this to the path:

```
/mnt/san/mydata/puppet/admin/users.htpasswd
```

One good reason to create a custom mount point like this is to add some security. Let's say you have a top-secret password file which should only be deployed to the web server, and no other machine needs it. If someone can run Puppet on any machine that has a valid certificate to access the Puppetmaster, there's nothing to stop them executing a manifest like this:

```
file { "/home/cracker/goodstuff/passwords.txt":
    source => "puppet:///web/passwords.txt",
}
```

They can easily retrieve the secret data. Indeed, anyone who can check out the Puppet repo or who has an account on the Puppetmaster could access this file. One way to avoid this is to put secret data into a special mount point with access control.

3. Add `allow` and `deny` parameters to your mount point definition in `fileserver.conf` like this:

```
[secret]
      /data/secret
      allow web.example.com
      deny *
```

How it works...

In this case, only `web.example.com` can access the file. The default is to deny all access, so the `deny *` line isn't strictly necessary, but it's good style to make it explicit. The web server can then use a `file` resource as shown in the following code:

```
file { "/etc/passwords.txt":
    source => "puppet:///secret/passwords.txt",
}
```

If this manifest is executed on `web.example.com`, it will work, but on any other clients, it will fail.

There's more...

You can also specify an IP address instead of a hostname, optionally using (**CIDR**) **Classless Inter-Domain Routing** (slash) notation or wildcards, as follows:

```
allow 10.0.55.0/24
allow 192.168.0.*
```

See also

▶ *Using modules section in Chapter 3*

▶ *Distributing directory trees section in Chapter 6*

▶ *Using multiple file sources section in Chapter 6*

Running Puppet from cron

Is your Puppet sleeping on the job? By default, when you run the Puppet agent on a client, it will become a daemon (background process), waking up every 30 minutes to check for any manifest updates and apply them (optionally after a randomized delay using the splay setting in puppet.conf). If you want more control over when Puppet runs, you can trigger it using cron instead.

For example, if you have many Puppet clients, you may want to deliberately stagger the Puppet run times to spread the load on the Puppetmaster. A simple way to do this is to set the minute or hour of the cron job time using a hash of the client hostname.

How to do it...

Use Puppet's inline_template function, which allows you to execute Ruby code:

```
cron { "run-puppet":
    command => "/usr/sbin/puppet agent --test",
    minute  => inline_template("<%= hostname.hash.abs % 60 %>"),
}

service { "puppet":
    ensure => stopped,
    enable => false,
}
```

How it works...

Because each hostname produces a unique hash value, each client will run Puppet at a different minute past the hour. This hashing technique is useful for randomizing any `cron` jobs to improve the odds that they won't interfere with each other.

There's more...

You may find that running Puppet as a daemon leaks memory over time, or that occasionally Puppet can get into a stuck state when communicating with the master. Running Puppet from `cron` should also fix these problems.

There are other ways to trigger Puppet runs, including the **MCollective** tool, which we'll cover in detail elsewhere in this book.

See also

- ▶ *Efficiently distributing cron jobs section* in *Chapter 6*
- ▶ *Using embedded Ruby section* in *Chapter 3*
- ▶ *Using MCollective section* in *Chapter 9*

Using autosign

In cryptography, as in life, you have to be careful what you sign. Normally, when you introduce a new client to the Puppetmaster, you need to generate a certificate request on the client, and then sign it on the master. However, you can skip this step by enabling **autosigning**.

How to do it...

Create the file `/etc/puppet/autosign.conf` on the Puppetmaster with the following contents: `*.example.com`

How it works...

Puppet checks any incoming certificate requests to see if they match a line from `autosign.conf`. Any certificate requests from clients with a hostname matching `*.example.com` will be automatically signed by the Puppetmaster.

Important: This is a potential security problem, since it amounts to trusting any client that can connect to the Puppetmaster. For this reason, autosigning is not recommended. If you do use it, make sure that the Puppetmaster is protected by a firewall that allows only approved clients or IP ranges to connect. A more secure approach is **pre-signing**.

See also

▶ *Pre-signing certificates* in this chapter

Pre-signing certificates

Because of the security implications, it's best to avoid using autosign if you can help it. In general, if you want to automate adding a large number of clients, it's better to pre-generate the certificates on the Puppetmaster and then push them to the client as part of the build process. You can use `puppet cert --generate <hostname>` to do this.

How to do it...

1. Generate a pre-signed certificate for `client1.example.com` with the following command:

    ```
    puppet cert --generate client1.example.com
    ```

    Puppet will now generate and sign a client certificate in the name of `client1.example.com`.

2. Transfer the three required files; the private key, the client certificate, and the CA certificate, to the new client. These are found in the following locations:

    ```
    /etc/puppet/ssl/private_keys/client1.example.com.pem
    /etc/puppet/ssl/certs/client1.example.com.pem
    /etc/puppet/ssl/certs/ca.pem
    ```

    Transfer these to the corresponding directories on the client, and it will then be authenticated without the certificate request step. Note that the location of Puppet's SSL certs varies according to the `ssldir` setting in `puppet.conf`.

See also

Using autosign in this chapter

Retrieving files from Puppet's filebucket

"A Freudian slip is when you say one thing, but mean your mother."—Anon

We all make mistakes; that's why pencils have erasers. Whenever Puppet changes a file on the client, it keeps a backup copy of the previous version. We can see this process in action if we make a change, however small, to an existing file:

```
# puppet agent --test
info: Caching catalog for cookbook
info: Applying configuration version '1293459139'
--- /etc/sudoers     2010-12-27 07:12:20.421896753 -0700
+++ /tmp/puppet-file20101227-1927-13hjvy6-0 2010-12-27 07:13:21.645702932
-0700
@@ -12,7 +12,7 @@

 # User alias specification
-User_Alias SYSOPS = john
+User_Alias SYSOPS = john,bob


info: FileBucket adding /etc/sudoers as {md5}
c07d0aa2d43d58ea7b5c5307f532a0b1
info: /Stage[main]/Admin::Sudoers/File[/etc/sudoers]: Filebucketed /etc/
sudoers to puppet with sum c07d0aa2d43d58ea7b5c5307f532a0b1
notice: /Stage[main]/Admin::Sudoers/File[/etc/sudoers]/content: content
changed '{md5}c07d0aa2d43d58ea7b5c5307f532a0b1' to '{md5}0d218c16bd31206e
312c885884fa947d'
notice: Finished catalog run in 0.45 seconds
```

The part we're interested in is this line:

```
info: /Stage[main]/Admin::Sudoers/File[/etc/sudoers]: Filebucketed /etc/
sudoers to puppet with sum c07d0aa2d43d58ea7b5c5307f532a0b1
```

Puppet creates an MD5 hash of the file's contents and uses this to create a **filebucket** path, based on the first few characters of the hash. The filebucket is where Puppet keeps backup copies of any files that it replaces, and it's located by default in `/var/lib/puppet/clientbucket`.

```
# ls /var/lib/puppet/clientbucket/c/0/7/d/0/a/a/2/
c07d0aa2d43d58ea7b5c5307f532a0b1
contents  paths
```

As you just saw, the `# ls` command listed the filenames. You will see two files in the bucket location: `contents` and `paths`. The `contents` file contains, as you might expect, the original contents of the file. The `paths` file contains its original path.

It's easy to find the file if you know its content hash (as we did in this case). If you don't, it's helpful to create a table of contents of the whole filebucket by building an index file.

How to do it...

1. Create the index file using the following command:

   ```
   # find /var/lib/puppet/clientbucket -name paths -execdir cat {}
   \; -execdir pwd \; -execdir date -r {} +"%F %T" \; -exec echo \; >
   bucket.txt
   ```

2. Search the index file to find the file you're looking for:

   ```
   # cat bucket.txt
   ```

   ```
   /etc/sudoers
   ```

   ```
   /var/lib/puppet/clientbucket/c/0/7/d/0/a/a/2/
   c07d0aa2d43d58ea7b5c5307f532a0b1
   ```

   ```
   2010-12-27 07:13:21
   ```

   ```
   /etc/sudoers
   ```

   ```
   /var/lib/puppet/clientbucket/1/0/9/0/e/2/8/a/1090e28a70ebaae872c2e
   c78894f49eb
   ```

   ```
   2010-12-27 07:12:20
   ```

3. To retrieve the file once you know its bucket path, just copy the `contents` file to the original filename:

   ```
   # cp /var/lib/puppet/clientbucket/1/0/9/0/e/2/8/a/1090e28a70ebaae8
   72c2ec78894f49eb/contents /etc/sudoers
   ```

How it works...

The script will create a complete list of files in the filebucket, showing the original name of the file, the bucket path, and the modification date (in case you need to retrieve one of several previous versions of the file). Once you know the bucket path, then you can copy the file back into place.

There's more...

You can have Puppet create backup copies of the file in its original location, rather than in the filebucket. To do this, use the `backup` parameter in your manifest:

```
file { "/etc/sudoers":
    mode    => "440",
    source => "puppet:///modules/admin/sudoers",
    backup => ".bak",
}
```

Now, if Puppet replaces the file, it will create a backup version in the same location with the extension `.bak`. To make this the default policy for all files, use:

```
File {
    backup => ".bak",
}
```

To disable backups altogether, use the following code:

```
        backup => false,
```

Scaling Puppet using Passenger

If your Puppet infrastructure's starting to creak at the seams, the culprit could be the Puppetmaster's web server. Puppet ships with a simple web server called **Webrick** to handle client connections to the Puppetmaster. Webrick is not really considered suitable for using Puppet in production; with more than a few servers as it can bring the Puppetmaster to its knees.

Mongrel is sometimes suggested as an alternative as it is a little better than Webrick, but not much. In order to scale Puppet to hundreds of servers, the preferred approach is to switch to a high-performance web server such as Apache using the **Passenger** (`mod_rails`) extension.

Puppet comes with the necessary configuration to run under Passenger, so all you need to do is install Apache and Passenger, and add a suitable virtual host. The following example uses Ubuntu 10.04. You can find instructions on the Puppet Labs website for how to do the same in Red Hat Linux, CentOS, and other distributions at `http://projects.puppetlabs.com/projects/1/wiki/Using_Passenger`.

Getting ready

It will be helpful if you have available the source **tarball** for the version of Puppet you're running, because it provides several template files and configuration snippets which you can use to set up Passenger. For example, if you're running Puppet 2.7.1, download this file: `http://puppetlabs.com/downloads/puppet/puppet-2.7.1.tar.gz`.

If you are using a different version, you will find a suitable download link at
`http://puppetlabs.com`. Unpack the source tarball with:

```
tar xzf puppet-2.7.1.tar.gz
```

How to do it...

1. Install Apache and Passenger, plus associated dependencies:

    ```
    # apt-get install apache2 libapache2-mod-passenger rails
    librack-ruby libmysql-ruby
    # gem install rack
    ```

2. Create the necessary directories for Passenger to find the Puppet configuration:

    ```
    /etc/puppet/rack
    /etc/puppet/rack/public
    ```
    These directories should be owned by `root` and set mode `0755`.

3. Create the `config.ru` file which will tell Passenger how to start the Puppet
    application. You can use the example file provided with the Puppet distribution:

    ```
    # cp /tmp/puppet-2.7.1/ext/rack/files/config.ru /etc/puppet/rack/
    ```
    ```
    # chown puppet /etc/puppet/rack/config.ru
    ```
    For Puppet 2.7.1, it has the following contents:

    ```
    # a config.ru, for use with every rack-compatible webserver.
    # SSL needs to be handled outside this, though.

    # if puppet is not in your RUBYLIB:
    # $:.unshift('/opt/puppet/lib')

    $0 = "master"

    # if you want debugging:
    # ARGV << "--debug"

    ARGV << "--rack"
    require 'puppet/application/master'
    # we're usually running inside a Rack::Builder.new {} block,
    # therefore we need to call run *here*.
    run Puppet::Application[:master].run
    ```

4. You now need to create a virtual host for Apache to listen on the correct port and send requests to the Puppet application. Again, you can use the example provided with the Puppet distribution:

```
# cp /tmp/puppet-2.7.1/ext/rack/files/apache2.conf /etc/apache2/
sites-available/puppetmasterd
```

```
# a2ensite puppetmasterd
```

The file contents will look something like this:

```
# you probably want to tune these settings
PassengerHighPerformance on
PassengerMaxPoolSize 12
PassengerPoolIdleTime 1500
# PassengerMaxRequests 1000
PassengerStatThrottleRate 120
RackAutoDetect Off
RailsAutoDetect Off

Listen 8140

<VirtualHost *:8140>
  SSLEngine on
  SSLProtocol -ALL +SSLv3 +TLSv1
  SSLCipherSuite ALL:!ADH:RC4+RSA:+HIGH:+MEDIUM:-LOW:-SSLv2:-EXP

  SSLCertificateFile     /etc/puppet/ssl/certs/cookbook.
  bitfieldconsulting.com.pem
  SSLCertificateKeyFile  /etc/puppet/ssl/private_keys/cookbook.
  bitfieldconsulting.com.pem
  SSLCertificateChainFile /etc/puppet/ssl/ca/ca_crt.pem
  SSLCACertificateFile   /etc/puppet/ssl/ca/ca_crt.pem
  # If Apache complains about invalid signatures on the CRL, you
  can try disabling
  # CRL checking by commenting the next line, but this is not
  recommended.
  SSLCARevocationFile    /etc/puppet/ssl/ca/ca_crl.pem
  SSLVerifyClient optional
  SSLVerifyDepth  1
  SSLOptions +StdEnvVars

  DocumentRoot /etc/puppet/rack/public/
  RackBaseURI /
  <Directory /etc/puppet/rack/>
    Options None
    AllowOverride None
    Order allow,deny
    allow from all
  </Directory>
</VirtualHost>
```

5. Edit this file to set the values of the `SSLCertificateFile` and `SSLCertificateKeyFile` to your own certificates (it's easiest to create these certificates if you've already run Puppet at least once).

6. You will also need to enable Passenger and `mod_ssl` in Apache:

```
# a2enmod passenger ssl
```

7. Add the following lines to your `/etc/puppet/puppet.conf`:

```
ssl_client_header = SSL_CLIENT_S_DN
ssl_client_verify_header = SSL_CLIENT_VERIFY
```

8. Stop your existing Puppetmaster if it is running.

9. Start Apache as follows:

```
# /etc/init.d/apache2 restart
```

10. If everything has worked, you will be able to run Puppet as usual:

```
# puppet agent --test
info: Caching catalog for cookbook.bitfieldconsulting.com
info: Applying configuration version '1294145142'
notice: Finished catalog run in 0.25 seconds
```

How it works...

Instead of using Puppet's built-in web server, which is rather slow and can only handle one connection at a time, you'll now be using the high-performance multi-threaded Apache web server. Puppet is embedded as an application using the Rack framework, which is much more efficient. You should find that you can handle many more clients and more frequent Puppet runs using the "Apache + Passenger" configuration, and that the impact on server memory and performance is less than using the standard Puppetmaster daemon.

There's more...

Here is an example Puppet manifest that will implement the preceding steps for you (on an Ubuntu system):

```
class puppet::passenger {
    package { [ "apache2-mpm-worker",
                "libapache2-mod-passenger",
                "librack-ruby",
                "libmysql-ruby" ]:
        ensure => installed,
    }
```

```
service { "apache2":
    enable  => true,
    ensure  => running,
    require => Package["apache2-mpm-worker"],
}

package { "rack":
    provider => gem,
    ensure   => installed,
}

file { [ "/etc/puppet/rack",
         "/etc/puppet/rack/public" ]:
    ensure => directory,
    mode   => "755",
}

file { "/etc/puppet/rack/config.ru":
    source => "puppet:///modules/puppet/config.ru",
    owner  => "puppet",
}

file { "/etc/apache2/sites-available/puppetmasterd":
    source => "puppet:///modules/puppet/puppetmasterd.conf",
}

file { "/etc/apache2/sites-enabled/puppetmasterd":
    ensure => symlink,
    target => "/etc/apache2/sites-available/puppetmasterd",
}

exec { "/usr/sbin/a2enmod ssl":
    creates => "/etc/apache2/mods-enabled/ssl.load",
}
}
```

Once you're up and running with Passenger, you can use the following command to restart the Puppetmaster application:

```
# service apache2 restart
```

To monitor that Passenger is running, check for the process named `ApplicationPoolServerExecutable`.

You can also load-balance Passenger instances in the same way that you would for a regular web application.

For more details, or if you run into problems, consult the **Puppet-on-Passenger** documentation at: http://projects.puppetlabs.com/projects/1/wiki/Using_Passenger

See also

▶ *Creating decentralized Puppet architecture* in this chapter

Creating decentralized Puppet architecture

"I have the world's largest collection of seashells. I keep it scattered around the beaches of the world... perhaps you've seen it." —Steven Wright

Some systems—notably the Mafia—run best when they're decentralized. The most common way to use Puppet is to run a Puppetmaster server, which Puppet clients can then connect to and receive their manifests from. However, you can run `puppet apply` directly on a manifest file to have it executed as shown in the following command line. (You'll normally want to use the `-v` switch to enable verbose mode, so you can see what's happening):

```
# puppet apply -v manifest.pp
info: Applying configuration version '1294313350'
```

You can even supply a manifest directly on the command line:

```
# puppet apply -e "file { '/tmp/test': ensure => present }"
notice: /Stage[main]//File[/tmp/test]/ensure: created
```

In other words, if you can arrange to distribute a suitable manifest file to a client machine, you can have Puppet execute it directly without the need for a central Puppetmaster. This removes the performance bottleneck of a single master server, and also eliminates a single point of failure. It also avoids having to sign and exchange SSL certificates when provisioning a new client machine.

There are many ways you could deliver the manifest file to the client, but Git (or another version control system such as Mercurial, or Subversion) does most of the work for you. You can edit your manifests in a local working copy, commit them to Git and push them to a central repo, and from there they can be automatically distributed to the client machines.

Getting ready

If your Puppet manifests aren't already in Git, follow the steps in *Using version control for your Puppet manifests* in this chapter.

How to do it...

1. Make a bare clone of your Puppet repo on the client as follows:

```
# git clone --bare ssh://git@repo.example.com/var/git/puppet
```

2. Copy the contents of this repo into your `/etc/puppet/` directory using the following command:

    ```
    # git archive --format=tar HEAD | (cd /etc/puppet && tar xf -)
    ```

3. Run Puppet on your `site.pp` file:

    ```
    # puppet apply -v /etc/puppet/manifests/site.pp

    info: Applying configuration version '1294313353'
    ```

    Once this is working, the next step is to have the configuration repo automatically push out changes to the clients. With Git, you can do this using remotes, like so:

    ```
    # git remote add web ssh://git@web1.example.com/etc/puppet
    ```

    If you have multiple client machines, you can add more URLs to the same remote:

    ```
    # git remote set-url --add webs ssh:// git@web2.example.com/etc/
    puppet
    ```

    ```
    # git remote set-url --add webs ssh:// git@web3.example.com/etc/
    puppet

    ...
    ```

    or simply edit the Git configuration file (`.git/config`) like this:

    ```
    [remote "web"]
        url = ssh:// git@web1.example.com/etc/puppet
        url = ssh://git@web2.example.com/etc/puppet
        url = ssh://git@web3.example.com/etc/puppet
        ...
    ```

4. Now you can push to any client machine, or group of machines, from the repo server with the following command:

    ```
    # git push web
    ```

5. The final step is to have the client machine update its `/etc/puppet` directory whenever it receives a push from the repo server. You can do this using a Git post-receive hook. In your bare repo, create the file `hooks/post-receive` and make it executable (mode `0755`):

    ```
    #!/bin/sh
    git archive --format=tar HEAD | (cd /etc/puppet && tar xf -)
    ```

How it works...

Instead of contacting the Puppetmaster to receive their compiled manifest, each client compiles its own from a local copy of the manifest source. This is updated every time you push updates from the Git server (or from your working checkout). This is more efficient with respect to network bandwidth, as clients don't have to contact the Puppetmaster on every run. It also eliminates a single point of failure, as clients can be updated from anywhere.

Using a decentralized Puppet architecture based on Git as outlined here gives you a great deal of flexibility. You can configure access controls and permissions using SSH keys, and allow each client machine or group only as much access as it needs. Manifests for a database server group, for example, can be made available only to those machines that need it.

While it requires some extra work to set up, and is not necessary for most small organizations, this way of deploying Puppet gives you extra flexibility and control for the most demanding environments.

There's more...

If you want to have Puppet apply the changes every time they are pushed, you can edit the `post-receive` script to do this, or take any other action you want. Alternatively, you could run Puppet manually, or from `cron` as described earlier in this chapter—just run `puppet apply`.

There are a few disadvantages to using a Git-based architecture: you can't use advanced Puppet features such as external node classifiers or stored configurations. However, when you need to scale to a large number of nodes, this is the simplest way to do it.

You can find a more detailed discussion of this architecture in Stephen Nelson-Smith's article at `http://bitfieldconsulting.com/scaling-puppet-with-distributed-version-control`.

See also

- ▶ *Scaling Puppet using Passenger* in this chapter
- ▶ *Using version control* in this chapter

2
Monitoring, Reporting, and Troubleshooting

"Found problem more than one. However, this does not mean that relevant part is thing by mistake. Could be fertilized by special purpose in other application program."—Error message

In this chapter, we will cover the following topics:

- ► Generating reports
- ► E-mailing log messages containing specific tags
- ► Creating graphical reports
- ► Producing automatic HTML documentation
- ► Drawing dependency graphs
- ► Testing your Puppet manifests
- ► Doing a dry run
- ► Detecting compilation errors
- ► Understanding Puppet errors
- ► Logging command output
- ► Logging debug messages
- ► Inspecting configuration settings
- ► Using tags
- ► Using run stages
- ► Using environments

We've all had the experience of sitting in an exciting presentation about some new technology, and then rushing home to play with it. Of course, once you start experimenting with it, you immediately run into problems. What's going wrong? Why doesn't it work? How can I see what's happening under the hood? This chapter will help you answer some of these questions, and give you the tools to solve common Puppet problems. We'll also see how you can generate useful reports on your Puppet infrastructure, and how Puppet can help you monitor and troubleshoot your network as a whole.

Generating reports

"What the world really needs is more love and less paperwork."—Pearl Bailey

Truth is often the first casualty of large infrastructures. If you're managing a lot of machines, Puppet's reporting facility can give you some valuable information on what's actually happening out there.

How to do it...

To enable reports, just add the following to a client's `puppet.conf`:

```
report = true
```

How it works...

With reporting enabled, Puppet will generate a report file on the Puppetmaster, containing data such as the following:

- ▶ Time required to fetch configuration from the Puppetmaster
- ▶ Total time of the run
- ▶ Log messages output during the run
- ▶ List of all resources in the client's manifest
- ▶ Whether Puppet changed each resource
- ▶ Whether a resource was out of sync with the manifest

By default, these reports are stored in `/var/lib/puppet/reports`, but you can specify a different destination using the `reportdir` option. You can either create your own scripts to process these reports (which are in the standard **YAML** format), or use a tool such as **Puppet Dashboard** to get a graphical overview of your network.

There's more...

A few tips for getting the best from Puppet's reports are explained in the following text.

Enabling reports on the command line

If you just want one report, or you don't want to enable reporting for all clients, you can add the `--report` switch to the command line when you run Puppet manually:

```
# puppet agent --test --report
```

You can also see some statistics about a Puppet run by supplying the `--summarize` switch as follows:

```
# puppet agent --test --summarize
info: Retrieving plugin
info: Caching catalog for cookbook.bitfieldconsulting.com
info: Applying configuration version '1306169315'
notice: Finished catalog run in 0.58 seconds
Changes:
Events:
Resources:
            Total: 7
Time:
  Config retrieval: 3.65
        Filebucket: 0.00
          Schedule: 0.00
```

Logging Puppet messages to syslog

Puppet can also send its log messages to the Puppetmaster's **syslog**, so that you can analyze them with standard syslog tools. To enable this, set the following option in the Puppetmaster's `puppet.conf`:

```
    [master]
    reports = store,log
```

The default report type is `store` (it writes the reports to `/var/lib/puppet/reports`), and `log` tells Puppet to also send messages to the syslog.

See also

▶ *Creating graphical reports* in this chapter

▶ *Logging debug messages* in this chapter

▶ *Using Puppet Dashboard* in *Chapter 9*

E-mailing log messages containing specific tags

If, like most sysadmins, you feel like you don't get enough e-mail, you'll be looking for a way to generate more. Another type of Puppet report is called `tagmail`. This will e-mail the log messages to any address you specify.

How to do it...

1. Add `tagmail` to the comma-separated list of reports in `puppet.conf`:

   ```
   [master]
   reports = store,tagmail
   ```

2. Add some **tags** and associated e-mail addresses in the file `/etc/puppet/tagmail.conf`. For example, this line will e-mail all log messages to me:

   ```
   all: john@example.com
   ```

3. When Puppet runs, you will get an e-mail that looks like the following:

   ```
   From: report@cookbook.bitfieldconsulting.com
   Subject: Puppet Report for cookbook.bitfieldconsulting.com
   To: john@example.com

   Mon Jan 17 08:42:30 -0700 2011 //cookbook.bitfieldconsulting.com/
   Puppet (info): Caching catalog for cookbook.bitfieldconsulting.com
   Mon Jan 17 08:42:30 -0700 2011 //cookbook.bitfieldconsulting.com/
   Puppet (info): Applying configuration version '1295278949'
   ```

How it works...

Puppet looks at each line in `tagmail.conf` and sends any messages matching the tag to the e-mail address specified. The special tag `all` matches all messages. The tag `err` matches errors as shown in the following code snippet:

```
err: john@example.com
```

You can list as many rules as you like in the `tagmail.conf` file, and Puppet will send e-mails for all rules that match. In the following example, errors go to one address, and web server related messages go to another:

```
err: puppetmaster@example.com
webserver: webteam@example.com
```

There's more...

The `tagmail` reports are a powerful feature which you may need to experiment with a bit so that you can get the most out of them. I have given a few tips to help you in the following text.

What are tags?

Tags are explained in more detail later in this book, but for reporting purposes, it's enough to know that a **tag** can be the name of a node or a class. For example, the tag `webserver` is matched if a machine includes the class `webserver`. You can also add a tag explicitly, using the `tag` function as follows:

```
class exim {
    tag("email")
    service { "exim4":
        ensure => running,
        enable => true,
    }
}
```

Specifying multiple tags, or excluding tags

You can specify a comma-separated list of tags in `tagmail.conf`, and also exclude certain tags by using an exclamation point (`!`).

```
all, !webserver: puppetmaster@example.com
```

Sending reports to multiple e-mail addresses

You can send messages to multiple, comma-separated e-mail addresses as shown in the following code-snippet:

```
err: puppetmaster@example.com, sysadmin@example.com
```

See also

- ▶ *Generating reports* in this chapter
- ▶ *Creating graphical reports* in this chapter
- ▶ *Using tags* in this chapter

Creating graphical reports

Let's face it, bosses like pretty pictures. Puppet can produce report data in a form suitable for processing by the **RRD** (**Round-Robin Database**) graph library, to produce a graphical representation of metrics such as the runtime on each client.

Getting ready

You will need to install the RRD tools and libraries for Ruby on your system. For Ubuntu, run the following command:

```
# apt-get install rrdtool librrd-ruby
```

How to do it...

Add the `rrdgraph` report type to your `puppet.conf` as follows:

```
reports = store,rrdgraph
```

How it works...

For each run, Puppet will record data in the client's RRD directory (the default is `/var/lib/puppet/rrd/<clientname>`). It will create graphs in a PNG format for events, resources, and retrieval time, while the raw data is available to you in the `.rrd` files if you want to process it further using third-party RRD tools.

There's more...

For more detailed reporting and graphing, you can use Puppet Dashboard.

See also

▶ *Using Puppet dashboard* in *Chapter 9*

Producing automatic HTML documentation

> *"An expert is someone who is one page ahead of you in the manual."—David Knight*

Like most engineers, I never read the manual, unless and until the product actually catches fire. However, as your manifests get bigger and more complex, it can be helpful to create HTML documentation for your nodes and classes using Puppet's automatic documentation tool, `puppet doc`.

How to do it...

Run `puppet doc` over your manifest as follows:

```
puppet doc --all --outputdir=/var/www/html/puppet --mode rdoc
--manifestdir=/etc/puppet/manifests/
```

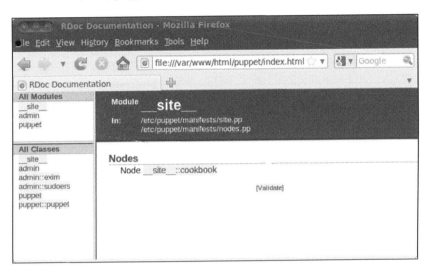

How it works...

`puppet doc` creates a structured HTML documentation tree in `/var/www/html/puppet` similar to that produced by **RDoc**, the popular Ruby documentation generator. This makes it easier to understand how different parts of the manifest relate to one another, as you can click on an included class name and see its definition.

There's more...

`puppet doc` will generate basic documentation of your manifests as they are at present. However, you can include more useful information by adding comments to your manifest files, using the standard RDoc syntax. Here's an example of some documentation comments added to a class:

```
class puppet {
    # This class sets up the Puppet client.
    #
    # ==Actions
    # Install a cron job to run Puppet.
    #
    # ==Requires
```

```
# * Package["puppet"]
#
cron { "run-puppet":
    command => "/usr/sbin/puppet agent --test >/dev/null 2>&1",
    minute  => inline_template("<%= hostname.hash.abs % 60 %>"),
}
}
```

Your comments are added to the documentation for each class in the resulting HTML files as shown in the following screenshot:

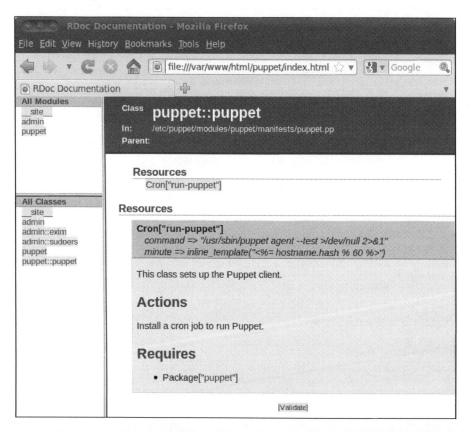

Drawing dependency graphs

Dependencies can get complicated quickly, and it's easy to end up with a **circular dependency** (where A depends on B which depends on A) which will cause Puppet to complain and stop work. Fortunately, Puppet's --graph option makes it easy to generate a diagram of your resources and the dependencies between them, which can be a big help in fixing such problems.

Getting ready...

Install the `graphviz` package to view the diagram files as shown in the following code snippet:

```
# apt-get install graphviz
```

How to do it...

1. Create the file `/etc/puppet/modules/admin/manifests/ntp.pp` with the following code containing a circular dependency:

```
class admin::ntp {
    package { "ntp":
      ensure => installed,
      require => File["/etc/ntp.conf"],
    }

    service { "ntp":
      ensure  => running,
      require => Package["ntp"],
    }

    file { "/etc/ntp.conf":
      source  => "puppet:///modules/admin/ntp.conf",
      notify  => Service["ntp"],
      require => Package["ntp"],
    }
}
```

2. Copy your existing `ntp.conf` file into Puppet:

```
# cp /etc/ntp.conf /etc/puppet/modules/admin/files
```

3. Include this class on a node:

```
node cookbook {
   include admin::ntp
}
```

4. Run Puppet as follows:

```
# puppet agent --test
info: Retrieving plugin
info: Caching catalog for cookbook.bitfieldconsulting.com
err: Could not apply complete catalog: Found 1 dependency cycle:
(File[/etc/ntp.conf] => Package[ntp] => File[/etc/ntp.conf]);
try using the '--graph' option and open the '.dot' files in
OmniGraffle or GraphViz
notice: Finished catalog run in 0.42 seconds
```

5. Run Puppet with the `--graph` option as suggested:

   ```
   # puppet agent --test --graph
   ```

6. Check that the graph files have been created:

   ```
   # ls /var/lib/puppet/state/graphs/
   expanded_relationships.dot  relationships.dot  resources.dot
   ```

7. Create a graphic of the relationships graph:

   ```
   # dot -Tpng -o relationships.png /var/lib/puppet/state/graphs/
   relationships.dot
   ```

8. View the graphic with the following command:

   ```
   # eog relationships.png
   ```

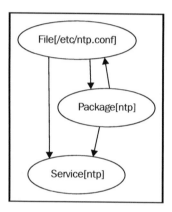

How it works...

When you run puppet `--graph` (or enable the graph option in puppet.conf) Puppet will generate three graphs in **DOT** format (a graphics language).These are as follows:

► `resources.dot`: shows the hierarchical structure of your classes and resources, but without dependencies

► `relationships.dot`: shows the dependencies between resources as arrows, as in the preceding example

► `expanded_relationships.dot`: is a more detailed version of the relationships graph

The dot tool (part of the graphviz package) will convert these to an image format such as PNG for viewing.

In the relationships graph, each resource in your manifest is shown as a balloon, with arrowed lines connecting them to indicate the dependencies. You can see that in our example, the dependencies between `File["/etc/ntp.conf"]` and `Package["ntp"]` form a circle.

To fix the circular dependency problem, all you need to do is remove one of the dependency lines and thus break the circle.

There's more...

Resource and relationship graphs can be useful even when you don't have a bug to find. If you have a very complex network of classes and resources, studying the resources graph can help you see where to simplify things. Similarly, when dependencies become too complicated to understand from reading the manifest, the graphs can be a much more useful form of documentation.

Testing your Puppet manifests

"If all else fails, immortality can always be assured by spectacular error."
—J.K. Galbraith

Trouble has a way of sneaking up on you like a bug on a windshield. The standard checks provided by monitoring tools like **Nagios** don't always cover everything you want to monitor. While metrics such as load average and disk space can be useful problem indicators', I like to be able to get higher-level information about the applications and services my machines provide.

For example, if you are running a web application, it's not enough to know that the web server is listening to connections on port 80 and responding with an `HTTP 200 OK` status. It could just be returning the default Apache welcome page.

If your web application is an online store, for example, you might want to check the following:

► Do we see expected text in the returned page (for example, "Welcome to FooStore")?

► Can we log in as a user (if the application supports sessions)?

► Can we search for a product and see the expected result?

► Is the response time satisfactory?

This kind of monitoring—focusing on the behavior of the application, rather than operational metrics of the server itself—is sometimes called **behavior-driven monitoring**.

Just as developers often use behavior-driven tests to verify that the application does what it should when they make code changes, you can use behavior-driven monitoring to monitor it continuously in production.

In fact, thanks to a tool called cucumber-nagios, you can run the same tests the developers use. Lindsay Holmwood's wrapper for the popular **Cucumber** testing framework lets you run Cucumber-based tests under Nagios as though they were standard Nagios metrics.

Getting ready

1. To install cucumber-nagios, you will need a few dependencies first. If you are on Ubuntu or Debian, you will probably need to install **RubyGems** from source, as cucumber-nagios needs RubyGems 1.3.6 or higher. Download the **tarball** from the RubyGems site: http://rubygems.org/pages/download. Unpack it and run ruby setup.rb to build and install the package.

2. Next, you need to install a few more dependencies:

   ```
   # apt-get install ruby1.8-dev libxml2-dev
   ```

3. Finally, you can install cucumber-nagios itself as follows:

   ```
   # gem install cucumber-nagios
   ```

How to do it...

1. Once RubyGems and all its dependencies have been installed, you can start writing Cucumber tests. To do this, first use cucumber-nagios to help create a project directory with everything you will need:

   ```
   # cucumber-nagios-gen project mytest
   Generating with project generator:
           [ADDED]    features/steps
           [ADDED]    features/support
           [ADDED]    .gitignore
           [ADDED]    .bzrignore
           [ADDED]    lib/generators/feature/%feature_name%.feature
           [ADDED]    Gemfile
           [ADDED]    bin/cucumber-nagios
           [ADDED]    lib/generators/feature/%feature_name%_steps.rb
           [ADDED]    README
   Your new cucumber-nagios project can be found in /root/mytest.

   Next, install the necessary RubyGems with:
           bundle install
   Your project has been initialized as a git repository.
   ```

2. It's a good idea to run `bundle install` inside the project directory, as `cucumber-nagios` advises you to do. This will bundle all the dependencies for `cucumber-nagios` inside the directory. Then you can move the project directory to any machine and it will work.

```
# cd mytest
# bundle install
```

3. Now we can start writing a test. As an example, let's test the home page on Google:

```
# cucumber-nagios-gen feature www.google.com home
Generating with feature generator:
[ADDED] features/www.google.com/home.feature
[ADDED] features/www.google.com/steps/home_steps.rb
```

4. If you edit the `home.feature` file, you will find that `cucumber-nagios` has generated a basic initial test for you:

```
Feature: www.google.com
  It should be up

  Scenario: Visiting home page
    When I go to "http://www.google.com"
    Then the request should succeed
```

You can run this from the project directory as follows:

```
# cucumber --require features features/www.google.com/home.feature
Feature: www.google.com
  It should be up


  Scenario: Visiting home page                    # features/www.google.
  com/home.feature:4
    When I go to "http://www.google.com" # features/steps/http_
    steps.rb:11
    Then the request should succeed       # features/steps/http_
    steps.rb:64


1 scenario (1 passed)
2 steps (2 passed)
0m0.176s
```

5. Assuming this works (if it doesn't, call Google), all you need to do to make this feature a Nagios check is to run it with `cucumber-nagios` instead of `cucumber`:

```
# bin/cucumber-nagios features/www.google.com/home.feature
CUCUMBER OK - Critical: 0, Warning: 0, 2 okay | passed=2;
failed=0; nosteps=0; total=2; time=0
```

How it works...

Any script can be a Nagios monitoring plugin; it just has to return the appropriate exit status (0 for OK, 1 for warning, and 2 for critical). `cucumber-nagios` wraps Cucumber tests to do this, and also prints out useful information which Nagios will report via the alert or the web interface.

There's more...

By itself, this doesn't do anything very useful. However, Cucumber lets you write quite sophisticated interaction scripts with websites: you can fill in form fields, search, click buttons, match text on the page, and so on. Whatever features of your web application or service you want to monitor; first figure out what a user would do in a web browser, then automate those steps with Cucumber to create the monitoring script.

You can find out more about how to write tests for `cucumber-nagios` on the Cucumber website: `http://cukes.info/`

Doing a dry run

> *"No alarms and no surprises."—Radiohead*

I hate surprises. Sometimes your Puppet manifest doesn't do exactly what you expected, or perhaps someone else has checked in changes you didn't know about. Either way, it's good to know exactly what Puppet is going to do before it does it.

For example, if it would update a config file and restart a production service this could result in unplanned downtime. Also, sometimes manual configuration changes are made on a server which Puppet would overwrite.

To avoid these problems, you can use Puppet's **dry run** mode (also called **noop** mode, for **no operation**).

How to do it...

Run Puppet with the `--noop` switch:

```
# puppet agent --test --noop
info: Connecting to sqlite3 database: /var/lib/puppet/state/
clientconfigs.sqlite3
info: Caching catalog for cookbook.bitfieldconsulting.com
info: Applying configuration version '1296492323'
--- /etc/exim4/exim4.conf    2011-01-17 08:13:34.349716342 -0700
```

```
+++ /tmp/puppet-file20110131-20189-127zyug-0    2011-01-31
09:45:27.792843709 -0700
```

```
@@ -1,4 +1,5 @@
 #########
+# allow spammers to use our host as a relay
 #########
```

notice: /Stage[main]/Admin::Exim/File[/etc/exim4/exim4.conf]/content: is {md5}02798714adc9c7bf82bf18892199971a, should be {md5}6f46256716c0937f3b6 ffd6776ed059b (noop)

info: /Stage[main]/Admin::Exim/File[/etc/exim4/exim4.conf]: Scheduling refresh of Service[exim4]

notice: /Stage[main]/Admin::Exim/Service[exim4]: Would have triggered 'refresh' from 1 events

notice: Finished catalog run in 0.90 seconds

How it works...

In `noop` mode, Puppet does everything it would normally, with the exception of actually making any changes to the machine. It tells you what it would have done, and you can compare this with what you expected to happen. If there are any differences, double-check the manifest or the current state of the machine.

In the preceding example, note that Puppet warns us it would have restarted the `exim` service, due to a config file update. This may or may not be what we want, but it's useful to know in advance. I make it a rule, when applying any non-trivial changes on production servers, to run Puppet in `noop` mode first, and verify what's going to happen.

There's more...

You can also use dry run mode as a simple auditing tool. It will tell you if any changes have been made to the machine since Puppet last applied its manifest. Some organizations require all config changes to be made with Puppet, which is one way of implementing a change control process. Unauthorized changes can be detected using Puppet in the dry run mode where you can then decide whether to merge the changes back into the Puppet manifest, or undo them.

See also

- ▶ *Auditing resources* in *Chapter 6*

Detecting compilation errors

"My mechanic told me, 'I couldn't repair your brakes, so I made your horn louder.'"—Steven Wright

Usually, when there's a problem, we'll want to stop and fix it before continuing. However, when running in daemon mode, Puppet will ignore any compilation errors in the manifest and just apply the last known working version from its cache. This behavior is governed by the `usecacheonfailure` config setting, and its default setting, `true`:

```
# puppet --genconfig |grep usecacheonfailure
  # usecacheonfailure = true
```

It's worth noting that when you apply manifests by hand using `puppet agent --test`, this doesn't happen: Puppet will complain and refuse to do anything if there is an error in the manifest. That's because the `--test` switch is shorthand for the following options:

```
# puppet agent --onetime --verbose --ignorecache --no-daemonize --no-usecacheonfailure
```

Because `usecacheonfailure` is on when Puppet runs as a daemon, sometimes you won't notice mistakes in a manifest for a while, as Puppet keeps on silently running an old version of the manifest instead of complaining.

How to do it...

If you want to change this behavior, set the following value in `puppet.conf`:

```
    usecacheonfailure = false
```

How it works...

With this option set, Puppet will immediately complain about errors and refuse to run until they are corrected.

Understanding Puppet errors

Stop! Error time. Puppet's error messages can be confusing, and sometimes don't contain much helpful information about how to actually resolve the problem.

How to do it...

Often the first step is simply to search the web for the error message text and see what explanations you can find for the error, along with any helpful advice about fixing it. Here are some of the most common puzzling errors, with possible explanations:

▶ `Could not evaluate: Could not retrieve information from source(s)`

This means you specified a `source` parameter for a file and Puppet couldn't find it. Check that the file is present and has been checked in, and also that the source path is correct.

▶ `change from absent to file failed: Could not set 'file on ensure: No such file or directory`

This is often caused by Puppet trying to write a file to a directory that doesn't exist. Check that the directory either exists already or is defined in Puppet, and that the file resource require the directory (so that the directory is always created first).

▶ `undefined method `closed?' for nil:NilClass`

This unhelpful error message is roughly translated as "something went wrong". It tends to be a catch-all error caused by many different problems, but you may be able to determine what is wrong from the name of the resource, the class, or the module. One trick is to add the `--debug` switch, to get more useful information:

```
# puppet agent --test --debug
```

If you check your Git history to see what was touched in the most recent change, this may be another way to identify what's upsetting Puppet.

▶ `Could not parse for environment --- "--- production": Syntax error at end of file at line 1`

This can be caused by mistyping command line options: for example, if you type `puppet -verbose` instead of `puppet --verbose`. That kind of error can be hard to see.

▶ `Could not request certificate: Retrieved certificate does not match private key; please remove certificate from server and regenerate it with the current key`

Either the node's SSL host key has changed, or Puppet's SSL directory has been deleted, or you are trying to request a certificate for a machine with the same name as an existing node. Generally, the simplest way to fix this is to remove Puppet's SSL directory from the client machine (usually this is `/etc/puppet/ssl`) and run `puppet cert --clean <nodename>` on the Puppetmaster. Then run Puppet again, and it should generate a certificate request correctly.

► `Could not retrieve catalog from remote server: wrong header line format`

This usually indicates an error in compiling a template. You'll see this kind of error if you have a typo in your ERB syntax, such as in the following code snippet:

```
rails_env <%!= app_env %>
```

► `Duplicate definition: X is already defined in [file] at line Y; cannot redefine at [file] line Y`

This one has caused me some confusion in the past. Puppet's complaining about a duplicate definition, and normally if you have two resources with the same name, Puppet will helpfully tell you where they are both defined. But in this case, it's indicating the same file and line number for both. How can one resource be a duplicate of itself?

The answer is: if it's a `define`. If you create two instances of a `define`, you'll also have two instances of all the resources contained within the `define`, and they need to have distinct names. For example:

```
define check_process() {
    exec { "is-process-running?":
        command => "/bin/ps ax |/bin/grep ${name} >/tmp/
        pslist.${name}.txt",
    }
}

check_process { "exim": }
check_process { "nagios": }
```

```
# puppet agent --test
info: Retrieving plugin
err: Could not retrieve catalog from remote server: Error 400 on
SERVER: Duplicate definition: Exec[is-process-running?] is already
defined in file /etc/puppet/manifests/nodes.pp at line 22; cannot
redefine at /etc/puppet/manifests/nodes.pp:22 on node cookbook.
bitfieldconsulting.com
warning: Not using cache on failed catalog
err: Could not retrieve catalog; skipping run
```

Because the `exec` resource is named `is-process-running?` and this stays the same no matter what you pass to the `define`, Puppet will refuse to create two instances of it. The solution is to include the name of the instance in the title of each resource, as follows:

```
exec { "is-process-${name}-running?":
    command => "/bin/ps ax |/bin/grep ${name} >/tmp/
    pslist.${name}.txt",
}
```

Logging command output

"Computer says no."—Little Britain

Detailed feedback on problems can be helpful. When you use `exec` resources to run commands on the node, it's not always easy to find out why they haven't worked. Puppet will give you an error message if a command returns a non-zero exit status. The error will be similar to the following:

```
err: /Stage[main]//Node[cookbook]/Exec[this-will-fail]/returns: change
from notrun to 0 failed: /bin/ls file-that-doesnt-exist returned 2
instead of one of [0] at /etc/puppet/manifests/nodes.pp:10
```

Often we would like to see the actual output from the command that failed, rather than just the numerical exit status. You can do this with the `logoutput` parameter.

How to do it...

Define an `exec` resource with the `logoutput` parameter as follows:

```
exec { "this-will-fail":
    command  => "/bin/ls file-that-doesnt-exist",
    logoutput => on_failure,
}
```

How it works...

Now, if the command fails, Puppet will also print its output:

```
notice: /Stage[main]//Node[cookbook]/Exec[this-will-fail]/returns: /bin/
ls: cannot access file-that-doesnt-exist: No such file or directory

err: /Stage[main]//Node[cookbook]/Exec[this-will-fail]/returns: change
from notrun to 0 failed: /bin/ls file-that-doesnt-exist returned 2
instead of one of [0] at /etc/puppet/manifests/nodes.pp:11
```

There's more...

You can set this to be the default for all `exec` resources by defining the following:

```
Exec {
    logoutput => on_failure,
}
```

If you want to see the command output whether it succeeds or fails, use the following:

```
logoutput => true,
```

Logging debug messages

The truth will make you free. It can be very helpful when debugging problems if you can print out information at a certain point in the manifest. This is a good way to tell, for example, if a variable isn't defined or has an unexpected value. Sometimes it's useful just to know that a particular piece of code has been run. Puppet's `notify` resource lets you print out such messages.

How to do it...

Define a `notify` resource in your manifest at the point you want to investigate:

```
notify { "Got this far!": }
```

How it works...

When this resource is compiled Puppet will print out the message:

notice: Got this far!

There's more...

If you're the kind of brave soul who likes experimenting, and I hope you are, you'll probably find yourself using debug messages a lot to figure out why your code doesn't work. So knowing how to get the most out of Puppet's debugging features can be a great help. Some of these uses are explained in the following text.

Printing out variable values

You can reference variables in the message:

```
notify { "operatingsystem is $operatingsystem": }
```

Puppet will interpolate the values in the printout:

notice: operatingsystem is Ubuntu

Printing the full resource path

For more advanced debugging, you may want to use the parameter `withpath` to see in which class the `notify` message was executed:

```
notify { "operatingsystem is $operatingsystem":
    withpath => true,
}
```

Now the notify message will be prefixed with the complete resource path as shown in the following code snippet:

```
notice: /Stage[main]/Nagios::Target/Notify[operatingsystem is Ubuntu]/
message: operatingsystem is Ubuntu
```

Logging messages on the Puppetmaster

Sometimes you just want to log a message on the Puppetmaster, without generating extra output on the client. You can use the `notice` function to do this:

```
notice("I am running on node $fqdn")
```

Now when you run Puppet, you will not see any output on the client, but on the Puppetmaster a message like this will be sent to the syslog:

```
Jan 31 11:51:38 cookbook puppet-master[22640]: (Scope(Node[cookbook])) I
am running on node cookbook.bitfieldconsulting.com
```

Inspecting configuration settings

Pop quiz, hotshot!. You already know that Puppet's configuration settings are stored in `puppet.conf`, but any parameter not mentioned in that file will take a default value. How can you see the value of any configuration parameter, regardless of whether or not it's explicitly set in `puppet.conf`? The answer is to use Puppet's `--genconfig` switch.

How to do it...

Run the following command:

```
# puppet --genconfig
```

How it works...

This will output every configuration parameter and its value (and there are lots of them). It does, however, include helpful comments explaining what each parameter does.

To find the specific value you're interested in, you can use `grep` in the following manner:

```
# puppet --genconfig |grep "reportdir ="
    reportdir = /var/lib/puppet/reports
```

Using tags

Tag, you're it! Sometimes one Puppet class needs to know about another— or, at least, to know whether or not it's present. For example, a class that manages the firewall may need to know whether the node is a web server.

Puppet's `tagged` function will tell you whether a named class or resource is present in the catalog for this node. You can also apply arbitrary tags to a node or class and check for the presence of these tags.

How to do it...

1. To help you find out if you're running on a particular node or class of node, all nodes are automatically tagged with the node name and the names of any parent nodes it inherits from.

    ```
    node bitfield_server {
        include bitfield
    }

    node cookbook inherits bitfield_server {
        if tagged("cookbook") {
            notify { "this will succeed": }
        }
        if tagged("bitfield_server") {
            notify { "so will this": }
        }
    }
    ```

2. To help you tell whether a particular class is included on this node, all nodes are automatically tagged with the names of all the classes they include, and their parent classes.

    ```
    include apache::port8000

    if tagged("apache::port8000") {
        notify { "this will succeed": }
    }

    if tagged("apache") {
        notify { "so will this": }
    }
    ```

3. If you want to set an arbitrary tag on a node, use the `tag` function:

```
tag("old-slow-server")
if tagged("old-slow-server") {
    notify { "this will succeed": }
}
```

4. If you want to set a tag on a particular resource, use the `tag` **metaparameter**:

```
file { "/etc/ssh/sshd_config":
    source => "puppet:///modules/admin/sshd_config",
    notify => Service["ssh"],
    tag    => "security",
}
```

5. You can also use tags to determine which parts of the manifest to apply. If you use the `--tags` option on the Puppet command-line, only those classes or resources tagged with specific tags will be applied. For example, if you want to update only the `exim` configuration, but not run any other parts of the manifest, use the following command:

```
# puppet agent --test --tags exim
```

There's more...

You can use tags to create a collection of resources. For example if some service depends on a large number of file snippets, you can use the following:

```
class firewall::service {
    service { "firewall":
        ...
    }

    File <| tag == "firewall-snippet" |> ~> Service["firewall"]
}

class myapp {
    file { "/etc/firewall.d/myapp.conf":
        tag => "firewall-snippet",
        ...
    }
}
```

Here, we've specified that the `firewall` service should be notified if any `file` resource tagged `firewall-snippet` is updated. All we need to do to add a firewall config snippet for any particular app or service is to tag it `firewall-snippet`, and Puppet will do the rest.

Although we could add `notify => Service["firewall"]` to each snippet resource, if our definition of the `firewall` service were ever to change we would have to hunt down and update all the snippets accordingly. The tag lets us encapsulate the logic in one place, making future maintenance and refactoring much easier.

Using run stages

"What do you get when you play country music backwards? You get your girl back, your dog back, your pick-up back, and you stop drinking."—Louis Saaberda

It's important to do things in the right order. A common requirement is to apply a certain resource before all others (for example, installing a package repository), or after all others (for example, deploying an application once its dependencies are installed). Puppet's **run stages** allow you to do this.

How to do it...

1. Add the following to your manifest:

    ```
    class install_repos {
        notify { "This will be done first": }
    }

    class deploy_app {
        notify { "This will be done last": }
    }

    stage { "first": before => Stage["main"] }
    stage { "last": require => Stage["main"] }

    class { "install_repos": stage => "first" }
    class { "deploy_app": stage => "last" }
    ```

2. Run Puppet as follows:

    ```
    # puppet agent --test
    info: Retrieving plugin
    info: Caching catalog for cookbook.bitfieldconsulting.com
    info: Applying configuration version '1303127505'
    notice: This will be done first
    notice: /Stage[first]/Beginning/Notify[This will be done first]/
    message: defined 'message' as 'This will be done first'
    notice: This will be done last
    notice: /Stage[last]/End/Notify[This will be done last]/message:
    defined 'message' as 'This will be done last'
    notice: Finished catalog run in 0.59 seconds
    ```

How it works...

1. We declared the classes for the things we want done first and last.

```
class install_repos {
    notify { "This will be done first": }
}

class deploy_app {
    notify { "This will be done last": }
}
```

2. Then we created a run stage named `first`:

```
stage { "first": before => Stage["main"] }
```

The parameter `before` specifies that everything in stage `first` must be done before anything in stage `main` (the default stage).

3. Then we created a run stage named `last`:

```
stage { "last": require => Stage["main"] }
```

The parameter `require` specifies that stage `main` must be completed before any resource in stage `last`.

4. Finally, we included the two classes `install_repos` and `deploy_app`, specifying that they should be part of stages `first` and `last` respectively:

```
class { "install_repos": stage => "first" }
class { "deploy_app": stage => "last" }
```

Note that we used the keyword `class`, rather than `include`, just like when we were passing parameters to classes. You can think of `stage` as a parameter that can always be passed to any class.

5. Puppet will now apply the stages in the following order:

    i. first

    ii. main

    iii. last

There's more...

In fact, you can define as many run stages as you like, and set up any ordering for them. This can simplify a complicated manifest, which would otherwise require a lot of explicit dependencies between resources, to a great extent. If you can divide all the resources into groups A and B, and everything in A must be done before B, it's a prime candidate for using run stages.

Gary Larizza has written a helpful introduction to using run stages, with some real-world examples, at `http://glarizza.posterous.com/using-run-stages-with-puppet`.

Using environments

> *A Zen student went up to a hot dog vendor and said: "Make me one with everything."—Joke*

Context is important. If you want to test Puppet manifests before putting them into production, you can use Puppet's **environment** feature to do this. This lets you apply a different manifest depending on the environment setting of the client machine. For example, you might define the following environments:

- `development`
- `staging`
- `production`

You can set up environments in your `puppet.conf` file. In this example, we'll add a `development` environment, pointing to a different set of manifests.

How to do it...

Add the following lines to `puppet.conf`:

```
[development]
manifest = /etc/puppet/env/development/manifests/site.pp
modulepath = /etc/puppet/env/development/modules:/etc/puppet/modules
```

How it works...

You can put your environment manifests anywhere you like, as long as you set the `manifest` parameter to point to the top-level `site.pp` file. In this example we've put the manifests for this environment in `/etc/puppet/env/development`. Similarly, you need to set `modulepath` to the location of your modules directory for that environment.

In the preceding example, the `modulepath` also includes `/etc/puppet/modules`; this is so that if Puppet doesn't find a module in your `development` environment, it will also look for it in the default environment. This means you only need to put the modules you're working on into the `development` environment.

The default environment is `production`, so if you run Puppet without specifying an environment, that's what you'll get.

There's more...

If you are using a version control system such as Git, your environments can be Git branches. Once you have finished testing and staging a new module, you can merge it into the Git master branch for use in production. You can read more about this strategy for using environments in R.I. Pienaar's article: `http://www.devco.net/archives/2009/10/10/puppet_environments.php`.

You can specify the environment of a client machine in several ways. You can use the `--environment` switch when running Puppet as follows:

```
# puppet agent --test --environment=development
```

Alternatively, you can specify it in the client's `puppet.conf`:

```
[main]
environment=development
```

If you are using an external node classifier script (described elsewhere in this book), this can also specify the client's environment.

You can also have a different `fileserver.conf` for each environment (see the section on configuring Puppet's file server). To do this, set the variable `fileserverconfig` for each environment in the Puppetmaster's `puppet.conf` file as follows:

```
[development]
fileserverconfig = /etc/puppet/fileserver.conf.development

[production]
fileserverconfig = /etc/puppet/fileserver.conf.production
```

For more information, see the Puppet Labs page on using environments: `http://projects.puppetlabs.com/projects/1/wiki/Using_Multiple_Environments`

See also

- ▶ *Using version control* in *Chapter 1*
- ▶ *Using modules* in *Chapter 3*
- ▶ *Using an external node classifier* in *Chapter 9*

3
Puppet Language and Style

"Computer language design is just like a stroll in the park. Jurassic Park, that is."
—Larry Wall

In this chapter we will cover the following topics:

- ▶ Using community Puppet style
- ▶ Using modules
- ▶ Using standard naming conventions
- ▶ Using embedded Ruby
- ▶ Writing manifests in pure Ruby
- ▶ Iterating over multiple items
- ▶ Writing powerful conditional statements
- ▶ Using regular expressions in if statements
- ▶ Using selectors and case statements
- ▶ Testing if values are contained in strings
- ▶ Using regular expression substitutions

"Elegance is not a dispensable luxury, but a factor that decides between success and failure."—Edsger W. Dijkstra

In this chapter you'll learn to write elegant Puppet manifests. By elegant in this context I mean readable, efficient, and consistent code which conforms to community usage.

We'll look at how to organize and structure your code into modules following community conventions, so that other people will find it easy to read and maintain your code. I'll also show you some powerful features of the Puppet language which will let you write concise, yet expressive, manifests.

Using community Puppet style

> *"A society made up of individuals who were all capable of original thought would probably be unendurable." —H. L. Mencken*

Sometimes going along with the crowd is a good idea. If other people need to read or maintain your manifests, or if you want to share code with the community, it's a good idea to follow the existing style conventions as closely as possible.

How to do it...

1. Always quote your resource names; for example, use `package { "exim4":` and not `package { exim4:`

   Some characters like hyphens and spaces can confuse Puppet's parser, and to be on the safe side it's wise to put all names consistently in double quotes.

2. Always quote parameter values that are not reserved words in Puppet; for example:

   ```
   name => "Nucky Thompson",

   mode => "0700",

   owner => "deploy",
   ```

   but

   ```
   ensure => installed,

   enable => true,

   ensure => running,
   ```

   Always include curly braces ({ }) around variable names when referring to them in strings. For example:

   ```
   source => "puppet:///modules/webserver/${brand}.conf",
   ```

   Otherwise Puppet's parser has to guess which characters should be part of the variable name and which belong to the surrounding string. Curly braces make it explicit.

3. Always end lines that declare parameters with a comma, even if it is the last parameter:

```
service { "memcached":
    ensure => running,
    enable => true,
}
```

Very often, when you edit the file, you'll want to append an extra parameter to it and forget to add the necessary comma!

4. When declaring a resource with a single parameter, make the declaration on one line and with no trailing comma as follows:

```
package { "puppet": ensure => installed }
```

5. Where there is more than one parameter, give each parameter its own line:

```
package { "rake":
    ensure   => installed,
    provider => gem,
    require  => Package["rubygems"],
}
```

When declaring **symlinks**, use `ensure => link` as follows:

```
file { "/etc/php5/cli/php.ini":
    ensure => link,
    target => "/etc/php.ini",
}
```

6. To make the code easier to read, line up the parameter arrows in line with the longest parameter, as shown in the following code:

```
file { "/var/www/${app}/shared/config/rvmrc":
    owner   => "deploy",
    group   => "deploy",
    content => template("rails/rvmrc"),
    require => File["/var/www/${app}/shared/config"],
}
```

The arrows should be aligned for each resource, but not across the whole file; otherwise it can make it difficult for you to cut and paste code from one file to another.

There's more...

The Puppet community maintains a style guide document on the Puppet Labs site:
`http://projects.puppetlabs.com/projects/puppet/wiki/Style_Guide`

Tim Sharpe has written a `puppet-lint` tool that you can use to check your manifests for style guide compliance. Run `gem install puppet-lint` to use it, or have a look at `https://github.com/rodjek/puppet-lint` for more details.

Using modules

Shamed by your Puppet code? Do people blench and look away when they see your manifests? One of the most important things you can do to make your Puppet manifests clearer and more maintainable is to organize them into **modules**.

A module is simply a way of grouping related things; for example, a `webserver` module might include everything necessary to be a webserver such as Apache configuration files, virtual host templates, and the Puppet code necessary to deploy these.

Separating things into modules makes it easier to re-use and share code; it's also the most logical way to organize your manifests. In this example we'll create a module to manage `memcached`, a memory caching system commonly used with web applications.

How to do it...

1. Find your `modulepath`; this is set in puppet.conf but the default value is `/etc/puppet/modules`. If you are using version control for your Puppet manifests, as I recommend you do, then use the directory in your working copy which will be deployed to `/etc/puppet/modules` instead.

    ```
    # puppet --genconfig |grep modulepath
    modulepath = /etc/puppet/modules:/usr/share/puppet/modules
    ```

    Create a subdirectory in the module path named `memcached`:

    ```
    # cd /etc/puppet/modules
    # mkdir memcached
    ```

    Inside this, create manifests and `files` directories:

    ```
    # cd memcached
    # mkdir manifests files
    ```

    In the `manifests` directory, create another file `init.pp` with the following contents:

    ```
    class memcached {
        package { "memcached":
            ensure => installed,
        }
    ```

```
    file { "/etc/memcached.conf":
        source => "puppet:///modules/memcached/memcached.conf",
    }

    service { "memcached":
        ensure  => running,
        enable  => true,
        require => [ Package["memcached"],
                     File["/etc/memcached.conf"] ],

    }
}
```

Changing to the `files` directory, create the file `memcached.conf` with the following contents:

```
-m 64
-p 11211
-u nobody
-l 127.0.0.1
```

2. To use your new module, add this to your node definition:

```
node cookbook {
    include memcached
}
```

3. Run Puppet to test the new configuration:

```
# puppet agent --test

info: Retrieving plugin

info: Caching catalog for cookbook.bitfieldconsulting.com

info: Applying configuration version '1300361964'

notice: /Stage[main]/Memcached/Package[memcached]/ensure: ensure
changed 'purged' to 'present'

...

info: /Stage[main]/Memcached/File[/etc/memcached.conf]:
Filebucketed /etc/memcached.conf to puppet with sum a977521922a151
c959ac953712840803

notice: /Stage[main]/Memcached/File[/etc/memcached.conf]/content:
content changed '{md5}a977521922a151c959ac953712840803' to '{md5}
f5c0bb01a24a5b3b86926c7b067ea6ba'

notice: Finished catalog run in 20.68 seconds
```

4. Check that the new service is running:

```
# service memcached status

 * memcached is running
```

How it works...

Modules have a specific directory structure. Not all of these directories need to be present, but if they are, this is how they should be organized:

```
MODULEPATH/
    MODULE_NAME/
        files/
        templates/
        manifests/

            ...

        README
```

The `memcached` class is defined in the file `memcached.pp`, which will be imported by Puppet automatically. Now we can include it on nodes:

```
include memcached
```

Inside the `memcached` class, we refer to the `memcached.conf` file:

```
file { "/etc/memcached.conf":
    source => "puppet:///modules/memcached/memcached.conf",
}
```

As we saw in the section on Puppet's file server and custom mount points, the `source` parameter in the preceding code tells Puppet to look for the file in the following path:

```
MODULEPATH/
    memcached/
        files/
            memcached.conf
```

There's more...

Learn to love modules, because they'll make your Puppet life a lot easier. They're not complicated. However, practice and experience will help you judge when things should be grouped into modules, and how best to arrange your module structure. Some tips which may help you on the way, have been explained in the following text.

Templates

If you need to use a template as part of the module, place it in the `MODULE_NAME/templates` directory and refer to it as follows:

```
file { "/etc/memcached.conf":
    content => template("memcached/memcached.conf"),
}
```

Puppet will look for the file in:

```
MODULEPATH/
    memcached/
        templates/
            memcached.conf
```

Facts, functions, types, and providers

Modules can also contain custom facts, custom functions, custom types, and providers. For more information about these, see the chapter on external tools and the Puppet ecosystem.

puppet-module

You can also use the `puppet-module` gem to generate the directory layout for new modules, rather than doing it by hand. See the section *Using public modules* in *Chapter 9* for more details.

Third-party modules

You can download modules provided by other people and use them in your own manifests just like the modules you create. For more on this, see the section *Using public modules* in *Chapter 9*.

Module organization

For more details on how to organize your modules, go to the Puppet Labs site: `http://docs.puppetlabs.com/guides/modules.html`.

See also

- ▶ *Configuring Puppet's file server* in *Chapter 1*
- ▶ *Creating custom Facter facts* in *Chapter 9*
- ▶ *Using public modules* in *Chapter 9*
- ▶ *Creating your own resource types* in *Chapter 9*
- ▶ *Creating your own providers* in *Chapter 9*

Using standard naming conventions

"There are only two hard problems in computer science: cache invalidation, naming things, and off-by-one errors."— Phil Karlton

Choosing appropriate and informative names for your modules and classes will be a big help when it comes to maintaining your code. This is even more true if other people need to read and work on your manifests.

How to do it...

1. Name modules after the software or service they manage: for example, `apache` or `haproxy`.

    Name classes within modules after the function or service they provide to the module: for example, `apache::vhosts` or `rails::dependencies`.

    If a class within a module disables the service provided by that module, name it as `disabled`. For example, a class that disables Apache should be named `apache::disabled`.

2. If a node provides multiple services, have the node definition include one module or class named for each service. For example:

    ```
    node server014 inherits server {
        include puppet::server
        include mail::server
        include repo::gem
        include repo::apt
        include zabbix
    }
    ```

3. The module that manages users should be named `user`.

4. Within the `user` module, declare your virtual users within the class `user::virtual`.

5. Within the `user` module, subclasses for particular groups of users should be named after the group such as `user::sysadmins`, or `user::contractors`.

6. When you need to override a class for some specific node or service, inherit that class and prefix the name of the subclass with the node. For example, if your node `cartman` needs a special SSH configuration, and you want to override the `ssh` class, do it as follows:

    ```
    class cartman_ssh inherits ssh {
        [ override config here ]
    }
    ```

7. When using Puppet to deploy configuration files for different services, name the file after the service, but with a suffix indicating what kind of file it is. For example:

    ❑ Apache init script—`apache.init`

    ❑ Log rotation configuration snippet for Rails—`rails.logrotate`

    ❑ Nginx vhost file for `mywizzoapp`—`mywizzoapp.vhost.nginx`

    ❑ MySQL configuration for standalone server—`standalone.mysql`

    If you need to manage, for example, different Ruby versions, name the class after the version it is responsible for, such as `ruby192` or `ruby186`.

There's more...

The Puppet community maintains a set of best practice guidelines for your Puppet infrastructure which includes some hints on naming: `http://projects.puppetlabs.com/projects/1/wiki/Puppet_Best_Practice`.

Some people prefer to include multiple classes on a node by using a comma-separated list, rather than separate `include` statements. For example:

```
node server014 inherits server {
    include puppet::server,
            mail::server,
            repo::gem,
            repo::apt,
            zabbix
}
```

This is a matter of style, but I prefer to use separate `include` statements, one to a line, because it makes it easier to copy and move around class inclusions between nodes without having to tidy up the commas and indentation every time.

I mentioned inheritance in a couple of the preceding examples. If you're not sure what this is, don't worry: I'll explain it in detail in the next chapter.

Using embedded Ruby

"Ruby, like fire, is a very useful friend, and a very dangerous enemy."—Mikkel Bruun

Templates are a powerful way of using embedded Ruby to help build configuration files dynamically and iterate over arrays. However, you can embed Ruby in your manifests directly without having to use a separate file, by calling the `inline_template` function.

How to do it...

Pass your Ruby code to `inline_template` within the Puppet manifest as follows:

```
cron { "nightly-job":
    command => "/usr/local/bin/nightly-job",
    hour => "0",
    minute => inline_template("<%= hostname.hash.abs % 60 %>"),
}
```

How it works...

Anything inside the string passed to `inline_template` is executed as if it were an ERB template. That is, anything inside the `<%=` and `%>` delimiters will be executed as Ruby code, and the rest will be treated as a string.

See also

▶ *Using ERB templates* in *Chapter 5*

▶ *Using array iteration in templates* in *Chapter 5*

Writing manifests in pure Ruby

¿ Hablas español? Learning languages can be fun, but not everyone wants to do it. Puppet has sometimes been criticized for requiring you to write manifests in its own dedicated configuration language, rather than an existing general-purpose language such as Ruby.

Not everyone considers this a drawback. The computer scientist Dennis Ritchie remarked:

> *"A language that doesn't have everything is actually easier to program in than some that do."*

Whatever your views, this criticism no longer applies—Puppet has experimental support for writing manifests in Ruby, which is quite usable in production even though it is still at a fairly early stage. You can mix and match Ruby and Puppet files within your manifests; Puppet will determine the language based on the file extension: `.rb` for Ruby files, `.pp` for Puppet files.

The **domain-specific language** (**DSL**) for writing manifests in Ruby looks very similar to the standard Puppet language. In the following example I'll show you how to turn a typical Puppet manifest into Ruby. The original manifest in Puppet's language is as follows:

```
class admin::exim {
    package { "exim4": ensure => installed }

    service { "exim4":
        ensure  => running,
        require => Package["exim4"],
    }

    file { "/etc/exim4/exim4.conf":
        content => template("admin/exim4.conf"),
        notify  => Service["exim4"],
        require => Package["exim4"],
    }
}
```

How to do it...

Create the file `/etc/puppet/modules/admin/manifests/exim.rb` with the following contents:

```ruby
hostclass "admin::exim" do
    package "exim4", :ensure => :installed

    service "exim4",
        :ensure  => :running,
        :require => "Package[exim4]"

    file "/etc/exim4/exim4.conf",
        :content => template(["admin/exim4.conf"]),
        :notify  => "Service[exim4]",
        :require => "Package[exim4]"
end
```

Include this class on a node and run Puppet.

How it works...

1. The keyword hostclass declares a class, just like class in Puppet: `hostclass admin::exim do`

2. We then have a `do ... end` block which is the equivalent of curly braces in Puppet.

3. Resources are declared by calling a function named after the resource type: for example, `package` or `service`: `package "exim4", :ensure => :installed`

4. Parameters are passed to the function as a comma-separated list, with the parameter names quoted or given a leading colon to make them a Ruby symbol:`:ensure  => :running,`

    Again built-in Puppet names such as `:installed` or `:running` are Ruby symbols.

5. When we need to refer to resources to indicate a relationship, as with `:require`, the resource identifier is given as a string with the resource type capitalized and the name in square brackets: `require => "Package[exim4]"`

    We can call a function like template by just using its name and round brackets, and passing its arguments as an array delimited by square brackets:`:content => template(["admin/exim4.conf"]),`.

There's more...

The Ruby DSL is at an early stage. It's fun to experiment with, but unless there are really compelling reasons for using Ruby, I'd stick to the standard Puppet language for now. It's quite possible that in the future the Ruby DSL will become widely used, but in the meantime, you'll find life easier without it. If you do want to use it, however, the following text contains a couple of handy hints.

Variables

While you can use Ruby variables just as you normally would in a Ruby program, you can access your Puppet variables by using `scope.lookupvar` as follows:

```
notice( "I am running on node %s" % scope.lookupvar("fqdn") )
```
gives:

notice: I am running on node cookbook.bitfieldconsulting.com

To set a variable so that it is in scope within your Puppet manifest, use `scope.setvar` as follows:

```
require 'time'
scope.setvar("now", Time.now)
notice( "At the third stroke, the time sponsored by Bitfield
Consulting will be: %s" % scope.lookupvar("now") )
```
The preceding code results in the following:

notice: At the third stroke, the time sponsored by Bitfield Consulting will be: Wed Mar 23 05:58:16 -0600 2011

Documentation

You can find more about how to use the Ruby DSL, including more advanced topics such as virtual resources and collections, on the Puppet Labs site: `http://projects.puppetlabs.com/projects/1/wiki/Ruby_Dsl`.

Ken Barber has supplied some syntax examples giving a direct comparison between Puppet and Ruby DSL constructs at `https://github.com/bobsh/puppet-rubydsl-examples`.

Finally, James Turnbull has written a blog post showing a more advanced use of Ruby to connect to a MySQL server: `http://www.puppetlabs.com/blog/using-ruby-in-the-puppet-ruby-dsl/`.

Iterating over multiple items

It's one darned thing after another! **Arrays** are a powerful feature in Puppet; wherever you want to perform the same operation on a list of things, an array may able to help. You can create an array just by putting its contents in square brackets:

```
$lunch = [ "franks", "beans", "mustard" ]
```

How to do it...

Add the following code to your manifest:

```
$packages = [ "ruby1.8-dev",
              "ruby1.8",
              "ri1.8",
              "rdoc1.8",
              "irb1.8",
              "libreadline-ruby1.8",
              "libruby1.8",
              "libopenssl-ruby" ]

package { $packages: ensure => installed }
```

Run Puppet, and note that each package should now be installed.

How it works...

Where Puppet encounters an array as the name of a resource, it creates a resource for each element in the array. In the preceding example, a new `package` resource is created for each of the packages in the `$packages` array, with the same parameters (`ensure => installed`). This is a very compact way of instantiating lots of similar resources.

There's more...

If you thought arrays were exciting, wait till you hear about hashes.

Hashes

A **hash** is like an array, but each of the elements can be stored and looked up by name. For example:

```
$interface = { name => 'eth0',
               address => '192.168.0.1' }
```

```
notice("Interface ${interface[name]} has address
${interface[address]}")

Interface eth0 has address 192.168.0.1
```

Hash values can be anything that you can assign to a variable: strings, function calls, expressions, or even other hashes or arrays.

Creating arrays with the split function

You can declare literal arrays using square brackets, as follows:

```
define lunchprint() {
    notify { "Lunch included $name": }
}

$lunch = [ "egg", "beans", "chips" ]
lunchprint { $lunch: }

Lunch included egg
Lunch included beans
Lunch included chips
```

But Puppet can also create arrays for you from strings, using the `split` function, as follows:

```
$menu = "egg beans chips"
$items = split($menu, ' ')
lunchprint { $items: }

Lunch included egg
Lunch included beans
Lunch included chips
```

Note that `split` takes two arguments; the first being the string it has to split. The second is the character to split on; in this example, a single space. As Puppet works its way through the string, when it encounters a space, it will interpret it as the end of one item and the beginning of the next. So, given the string `"egg beans chips"`, this will be split into three items.

The character to split on can be any character, or a string:

```
$menu = "egg and beans and chips"
$items = split($menu, ' and ')
```

It can also be a regular expression; for example, a set of alternatives separated by a | (pipe) character:

```
$lunch = "egg:beans,chips"
$items = split($lunch, ':|,')
```

Writing powerful conditional statements

Life is full of choices. Puppet's `if` statement allows you to change the manifest based on the value of a variable or an expression. With it, you can apply different resources or parameter values depending on certain facts about the node such as the operating system, or the memory size. You can also set variables within the manifest that can change the behavior of included classes. For example, nodes in data center A might need to use different DNS servers as compared to nodes in data center B, or you might need to include one set of classes for an Ubuntu system, and a different set for other systems.

How to do it...

Add the following code to your manifest:

```
if $lsbdistid == "Ubuntu" {
    notice("Running on Ubuntu")
} else {
    notice("Non-Ubuntu system detected. Please upgrade to Ubuntu
immediately.")
}
```

How it works...

Puppet treats whatever follows the `if` keyword as an expression and evaluates it. If the expression is evaluated as `true`, Puppet will execute the code within the curly braces.

Optionally, you can add an `else` branch, which will be executed if the expression is evaluated as `false`.

There's more...

You can write very complicated `if` statements in Puppet, but I recommend you don't. Very often, it's better to change your design (for example, using a template) rather than use `if`. While looking through some of my production manifests for examples, I was surprised to find that I haven't used `if` at all in many thousands of lines of code. Still, your mileage may vary, so here are some more tips on using `if`.

elsif

You can add further tests using the `elsif` keyword, as follows:

```
if $lsbdistid == "Ubuntu" {
    notice("Running on Ubuntu")
} elsif $lsbdistid == "Debian" {
    notice("Close enough...")
```

```
} else {
    notice("Non-Ubuntu system detected. Please upgrade to Ubuntu
immediately.")
}
```

Comparisons

You can check if two values are equal using the == syntax, as in our example:

```
if $lsbdistid == "Ubuntu" {
    ...
}
```

Or, you can check if they are not equal using != as follows:

```
if $lsbdistid != "CentOS" {
    ...
}
```

You can also compare numeric values using < and > as follows:

```
if $uptime_days > 365 {
    notice("Really .. there have been kernel security patches out
there for ages, you will so be Owned!")
}
```

To test if a value is greater (or less) than or equal to another value, use <= or >=:

```
if $lsbmajdistrelease <= 9 {
    ...
}
```

Combining expressions

You can put together the kind of simple expressions described in the preceding code snippets into more complex, logical expressions using and, or, and not as follows:

```
if ($uptime_days > 365) and ($lsbdistid == "Ubuntu") {
    ...
}

if ($role == "webserver") and ( ($datacenter == "A") or ($datacenter
== "B") ) {
    ...
}
```

See also

▶ *Using regular expressions in if statements* in this chapter

▶ *Testing if values are contained in strings* in this chapter

▶ *Using selectors and case statements* in this chapter

Using regular expressions in if statements

"Some people, when confronted with a problem think; 'I know, I'll use regular expressions.' Now they have two problems."—Jamie Zawinski

Another kind of expression you can test in if statements and other conditionals is the **regular expression**. A regular expression is a powerful way of comparing strings using pattern matching.

How to do it...

Add the following to your manifest:

```
if $lsbdistdescription =~ /LTS/ {
    notice("Looks like you are using a Long Term Support version of
    Ubuntu.")
} else {
    notice("You might want to upgrade to a Long Term Support version
    of Ubuntu...")
}
```

How it works...

Puppet treats the text supplied between the forward slashes as a regular expression that specifies what the text to be matched is. If the match as a whole succeeds, the if expression will be true and so the code between the first set of curly braces will be executed.

If you wanted instead to do something and the text does not match, use !~ rather than =~ as shown in the following code snippet:

```
if $lsbdistdescription !~ /LTS/ {
```

There's more...

As Jamie Zawinski hinted, regular expressions are very powerful, but can be difficult to understand and debug. If you find yourself using a regular expression so complex that you can't see what it does at a glance, think about simplifying your design to make it easier. However, one particularly useful feature of regular expressions is the ability to capture patterns.

Capturing patterns

You can not only match text using a regular expression, but also capture the matched text and store it in a variable:

```
$input = "Puppet is better than manual configuration"
if $input =~ /(.*) is better than (.*)/ {
    notice("You said '$0'. Looks like you're comparing $1 to $2!")
}
```

You said 'Puppet is better than manual configuration'. Looks like you're comparing Puppet to manual configuration!

The variable `$0` stores the whole matched text (assuming the overall match succeeded). If you put brackets around any part of the regular expression, that creates a **group** and any matched groups will also be stored in variables. The first matched group will be `$1`, the second `$2`, and so on, as in the preceding example.

Regular expression syntax

Puppet uses a subset of Ruby's regular expression syntax, so the following link may be helpful if you're not already familiar with regular expressions: `http://gnosis.cx/publish/programming/regular_expressions.html`.

See also

▶   *Using regular expression substitutions* in this chapter

Using selectors and case statements

"Smarts is the most exclusive club in town. Everyone welcome."—Sign

Sometimes it's important to be selective. Although you could write any conditional statement using `if`, Puppet provides a couple of extra forms to help you express conditionals more easily such as the selector and the case statement.

How to do it...

1. Add the following to your manifest:

```
$systemtype = $operatingsystem ? {
    "Ubuntu" => "debianlike",
    "Debian" => "debianlike",
    "RedHat" => "redhatlike",
    "Fedora" => "redhatlike",
    "CentOS" => "redhatlike",
    default  => "redhatlike",
}

notify { "You have a ${systemtype} system": }
```

2. Next, add the following to your manifest:

```
class debianlike {
    notify { "Special manifest for Debian-like systems": }
}

class redhatlike {
    notify { "Special manifest for RedHat-like systems": }
}

case $operatingsystem {
    "Ubuntu",
    "Debian": {
        include debianlike
    }
    "RedHat",
    "Fedora",
    "CentOS": {
        include redhatlike
    }
}
```

How it works...

Our example demonstrates both the selector and the `case` statement, so let's see in detail how each of them works.

▶ **Selector**

   In the first example, we used a selector (the `?` operator) to choose a value for the `$systemtype` variable depending on the value of `$operatingsystem`. This is similar to the ternary operator in C or Ruby, but instead of choosing between two possible values, you can have as many values as you like.

Puppet will compare the value of $operatingsystem to each of the possible values we have supplied such as Ubuntu, Debian, and so on. These values could be regular expressions (for a partial string match, or to use wildcards, for example), but in our case we have just used literal strings. As soon as it finds a match, the selector expression returns whatever value is associated with the matching string. If the value of $operatingsystem is Fedora, for example, the selector expression will return the string redhatlike and so this will be assigned to the variable $systemtype.

▶ **Case** statement

Unlike selectors, the case statement does not return a value. case statements are handy when you want to execute different code depending on the value of some expression. In our second example, we used the case statement to include either the class debianlike, or the class redhatlike, depending on the value of $operatingsystem.

Again, Puppet compares the value of $operatingsystem to a list of potential matches. These could be regular expressions, or strings, or as in our example, comma-separated lists of strings. When it finds a match, the associated code between curly braces is executed. So if the value of $operatingsystem is Ubuntu, then the code include debianlike will be executed.

There's more...

Once you've got to grips with basic use of selectors and case statements, you may find the following tips useful.

Regular expressions

As with if statements, you can use regular expressions with selectors and case statements, and you can also capture the values of matched groups and refer to them using $1, $2, and so on.

```
case $lsbdistdescription {
    /Ubuntu (.+)/: {
        notify { "You have Ubuntu version $1": }
    }
    /CentOS (.+)/: {
        notify { "You have CentOS version $1": }
    }
}
```

Defaults

Both selectors and `case` statements let you specify a `default` value, which is chosen if none of the other options match:

```
$lunch = "Sausage and chips"
$lunchtype =  $lunch ? {
    /chips/ => "unhealthy",
    /salad/ => "healthy",
    default => "unknown",
}

notify { "Your lunch was ${lunchtype}": }
```

Your lunch was unhealthy

Testing whether values are contained in strings

Want to know what's in and what's out? Puppet's `in` keyword can help, with expressions such as the following:

```
if "foo" in $bar
```

This will be evaluated as `true` if the string `foo` is a substring of $bar. If $bar is an array, and if `foo` is an element of the array, the expression is `true`. If $bar is a hash, the expression is `true` if `foo` is one of the keys of $bar.

How to do it...

1. Add the following code to your manifest:

```
if $operatingsystem in [ "Ubuntu", "Debian" ] {
    notify { "Debian-type operating system detected": }
} elsif $operatingsystem in [ "RedHat", "Fedora", "SuSE", "CentOS"
] {
    notify { "RedHat-type operating system detected": }
} else {
    notify { "Some other operating system detected": }
}
```

2. Run Puppet:

```
# puppet agent --test
Debian-type operating system detected
```

There's more...

`in` expressions can be used not just for `if` statements or other conditionals, but anywhere an expression can be used. For example, you can assign the result to a variable as follows:

```
$debianlike = $operatingsystem in [ "Debian", "Ubuntu" ]

if $debianlike {
    $ntpservice = "ntp"
} else {
    $ntpservice = "ntpd"
}
```

Using regular expression substitutions

"Change is inevitable, except from vending machines."—Robert C. Gallagher

Puppet's `regsubst` function provides an easy way to manipulate text, search and replace within strings, or extract patterns from strings. We commonly need to do this with data obtained from a fact for example, or from external programs.

In this example we'll see how to use `regsubst` to extract the first three octets of an IP address (the network part, assuming it's a Class C address).

How to do it...

1. Add the following to your manifest:
   ```
   $class_c = regsubst($ipaddress, "(.*)\..*", "\1.0")
   notify { $ipaddress: }
   notify { $class_c: }
   ```

2. Run Puppet:
   notice: 10.0.2.15

   notice: 10.0.2.0

How it works...

`regsubst` takes at least three parameters: `source`, `pattern`, and `replacement`. In our example, we specified the source string as `$ipaddress`, which happens to be:

```
10.0.2.15
```

We also specified the `pattern` as `(.*)\..*` and the replacement as `\1.0`

The `pattern` will match the whole IP address, capturing the first three octets in round brackets. The captured text will be available as `\1` for use in the `replacement` string.

The whole of the matched text (in this case the whole string) is replaced with `replacement`. This is `\1` (the captured text from the `source` string) followed by the string `.0`, which evaluates to: `10.0.2.0`

There's more...

`pattern` can be any regular expression, using the same (Ruby) syntax as regular expressions in `if` statements.

See also

▶ *Importing dynamic information* in *Chapter 4*

▶ *Getting information about the environment* in *Chapter 4*

▶ *Using regular expressions in if statements* in this chapter

4
Writing Better Manifests

"There are only two kinds of programming languages: those people always bitch about and those nobody uses."—Bjarne Stroustrup

In this chapter we will cover the following topics:

- ▶ Using arrays of resources
- ▶ Using define resources
- ▶ Using dependencies
- ▶ Using node inheritance
- ▶ Using class inheritance and overriding
- ▶ Passing parameters to classes
- ▶ Writing reusable, cross-platform manifests
- ▶ Getting information from the environment
- ▶ Importing dynamic information
- ▶ Importing data from CSV files
- ▶ Passing arguments to shell commands

Your Puppet manifest is the living documentation for your entire infrastructure. Keeping it tidy and well organized is a great way to make it easier to maintain and understand. Puppet gives you a number of tools to do this, including the following:

- ▶ Arrays
- ▶ Defines
- ▶ Dependencies
- ▶ Inheritance
- ▶ Class parameters

We'll see how to use all of these and more. As you read through the chapter, try out the examples, and look through your own manifests to see where these features might help you simplify and improve your Puppet code.

Using arrays of resources

Anything you can do to a resource, you can do to an array of resources. Use this idea to re-factor your manifests to make them shorter and clearer.

How to do it...

1. Identify a class in your manifest where you have several instances of the same kind of resource—for example, packages:

```
package { "sudo" : ensure => installed }
package { "unzip" : ensure => installed }
package { "locate" : ensure => installed }
package { "lsof" : ensure => installed }
package { "cron" : ensure => installed }
package { "rubygems" : ensure => installed }
```

2. Group them together and replace them with a single `package` resource using an array as follows:

```
package { [ "cron",
            "locate",
            "lsof",
            "rubygems"
            "screen",
            "sudo"
            "unzip" ] :
    ensure => installed,
}
```

How it works...

Most of Puppet's resource types can accept an array instead of a single name, and will create one instance for each of the elements in the array. All the parameters you provide for the resource (for example, `ensure => installed`) will be assigned to each of the new resource instances.

See also

▶ *Iterating over multiple items* in *Chapter 3*

Using define resources

"Girl number twenty unable to define a horse!" said Mr. Gradgrind.—Charles Dickens, 'Hard Times'

Unless you know how to define what you want, you won't get it. In the preceding example, we saw how to reduce redundant code by grouping identical resources into arrays. However, this technique is limited to resources where all the parameters are the same. When you have a set of resources that have some parameters in common and some different, you need to use a `define` resource to group them together.

How to do it...

1. Add the following to your manifest:

```
define tmpfile() {
    file { "/tmp/$name":
        content => "Hello, world",
    }
}

tmpfile { ["a", "b", "c"]: }
```

2. Run Puppet:

```
notice: /Stage[main]//Node[cookbook]/Tmpfile[a]/File[/tmp/a]/
ensure: defined content as '{md5}bc6e6f16b8a077ef5fbc8d59d0b931b9'

notice: /Stage[main]//Node[cookbook]/Tmpfile[b]/File[/tmp/b]/
ensure: defined content as '{md5}bc6e6f16b8a077ef5fbc8d59d0b931b9'

notice: /Stage[main]//Node[cookbook]/Tmpfile[c]/File[/tmp/c]/
ensure: defined content as '{md5}bc6e6f16b8a077ef5fbc8d59d0b931b9'
```

How it works...

You can think of a **define** as being like a cookie-cutter. It describes a pattern that Puppet can use to create lots of similar resources. Any time you declare a `tmpfile` instance in your manifest, Puppet will insert all the resources contained in the `tmpfile` definition.

In our example, the definition of `tmpfile` contains a single `file` resource, whose `content` is "Hello, world", and whose `path` is /tmp/${name}. If you declared an instance of `tmpfile` with the name `foo` as follows:

```
tmpfile { "foo": }
```

then, Puppet would create a file with the path /tmp/foo. In other words, ${name} in the definition will be replaced by the name of any actual instance that Puppet is asked to create. It's almost as though we created a new kind of resource: a `tmpfile`, which has one parameter: its name.

Just like with regular resources, we don't have to pass just one name: we can provide an array of names and Puppet will create a number of `tmpfile` instances, as in the preceding example.

There's more...

In the preceding example, we created a `define` where the only parameter that varies between instances is the name. But we can add whatever parameters we want, so long as we declare them in the definition:

```
define tmpfile( $greeting ) {
    file { "/tmp/$name":
        content => $greeting,
    }
}
```

and pass values to them when we declare an instance of the resource as follows:

```
tmpfile{ "foo": greeting => "Hello, world" }
```

You can declare multiple parameters as a comma-separated list:

```
define webapp( $domain, $path, $platform ) {
    ...
}

webapp { "mywizzoapp":
    domain   => "mywizzoapp.com",
    path     => "/var/www/apps/mywizzoapp",
    platform => "Rails",
}
```

This is a powerful technique for abstracting out everything that's common to certain resources, and keeping it in one place so that you **Don't Repeat Yourself**. In the preceding example, there might be many individual resources contained within `webapp`: packages, config files, source code checkouts, virtual hosts, and so on. But all of them are the same for every instance of `webapp` except the parameters we provide. These might be referenced in a template, for example, to set the domain for a virtual host.

Using dependencies

"Remove wrapper, open mouth, insert muffin, eat."—Instructions on 7-11 muffin packaging

To make sure things happen in the right order, you can specify in Puppet that one resource depends on another; for example, you need to install package X before you can start the service it provides, so you would mark the service as dependent on the package. Puppet will sort out the required order to meet all the dependencies.

In some configuration management systems, resources are applied in the order you write them - in other words, the ordering is implicit. That's not the case with Puppet, where resources are applied in a more or less random (but consistent) order unless you state an explicit ordering using dependencies. Some people prefer the implicit approach, because you can write the resource definitions in the order that they need to be done, and that's the way they'll be executed.

On the other hand, in many cases the ordering of resources doesn't matter. With an implicit-style system, you can't tell whether resource B is listed after resource A because B depends on A, or because it just happens to have been written in that order. That makes refactoring more difficult, as moving resources around may break some implicit dependency.

Puppet makes you do a little more work by specifying the dependencies up front, but the resulting code is clearer and easier to maintain. Let's look at an example.

How to do it...

1. Create a new file `/etc/puppet/modules/admin/manifests/ntp.pp` with the following contents:

```
class admin::ntp {
    package { "ntp":
        ensure => installed,
    }

    service { "ntp":
        ensure   => running,
```

```
                require => Package["ntp"],
        }

        file { "/etc/ntp.conf":
            source  => "puppet:///modules/admin/ntp.conf",
            notify  => Service["ntp"],
            require => Package["ntp"],
        }
    }
```

2. Copy your existing `ntp.conf` file into Puppet as follows:

   # cp /etc/ntp.conf /etc/puppet/modules/admin/files

3. Add the `admin::ntp` class to your server in `nodes.pp`:

```
node cookbook {
    include admin::ntp
}
```

4. Now remove the existing `ntp.conf` file:

   # rm /etc/ntp.conf

5. Run Puppet:

   # puppet agent --test

   info: Retrieving plugin

   info: Caching catalog for cookbook.bitfieldconsulting.com

   info: Applying configuration version '1302960655'

   notice: /Stage[main]/Admin::Ntp/File[/etc/ntp.conf]/ensure: defined content as '{md5}3386aaad98dd5e0b28428966dac9e1f5'

   info: /Stage[main]/Admin::Ntp/File[/etc/ntp.conf]: Scheduling refresh of Service[ntp]

   notice: /Stage[main]/Admin::Ntp/Service[ntp]: Triggered 'refresh' from 1 events

   notice: Finished catalog run in 2.36 seconds

How it works...

This example demonstrates two kinds of dependencies: `require`, and `notify`. In the first case, the `ntp` service requires the `ntp` package to be applied first:

```
service { "ntp":
    ensure  => running,
    require => Package["ntp"],
}
```

In the second case, the NTP config file is set to `notify` the `ntp` service; in other words, if the file changes, Puppet should restart the `ntp` service to pick up its new configuration:

```
file { "/etc/ntp.conf":
    source  => "puppet:///modules/admin/ntp.conf",
    notify  => Service["ntp"],
    require => Package["ntp"],
}
```

This implies that the service depends on the file as well as on the package, and so Puppet will be able to apply all three resources in the correct order as follows:

```
Package["ntp"] -> File["/etc/ntp.conf"] ~> Service["ntp"]
```

In fact, this is another way to specify the same dependency chain. Adding the preceding line to your manifest will have the same effect as the `require` and `notify` parameters in our example (the `->` means `require`, while `~>` means `notify`). However, I prefer to use `require` and `notify` because the dependencies are defined as part of the resource, so it's easier to see what's going on. For complex chains of dependencies, though, you may want to use the `->` notation instead.

There's more...

You can also specify that a resource depends on a certain class:

```
require => Class["my-apt-repo"]
```

You can specify dependencies not just between resources and classes, but between **collections**:

```
Yumrepo <| |> -> Package <| provider == yum |>
```

is a powerful way to express that all `yumrepo` resources should be applied before all `package` resources whose `provider` is `yum`.

 Historical note: In versions of Puppet prior to 2.7, the catalog was applied in a non-deterministic way, which means that resources could be applied in a different order every time Puppet runs. This could cause some interesting issues, as a Puppet manifest that worked without errors on one machine could fail on another. This is no longer the case, and as Puppet Labs put it, Puppet will now "either succeed reliably, or fail reliably". If you are using an earlier version and having this problem, upgrading should fix it.

Using node inheritance

It's a brave (or foolish) sysadmin who puts all her servers in one basket. Let's say you have dedicated servers hosted with three different providers: WreckSpace, GoDodgy, and VerySlow. They have different data centers and geographical locations, so you will need to make small modifications to your config for servers hosted with each provider. You have several different types of servers, but they are distributed randomly across the three providers.

One way to implement this in Puppet would be to set a variable in the node definition that tells the node where it is:

```
node webserver127 {
    $provider = "VerySlow"
    include admin::basics
    include admin::ssh
    include admin::ntp
    include puppet::client
    include backup::client
    include webserver
}
node loadbalancer5 {
    $provider = "WreckSpace"
    include admin::basics
    include admin::ssh
    include admin::ntp
    include puppet::client
    include backup::client
    include loadbalancer
}
```

As you can see, this results in a lot of duplication. It would be much easier if we simply defined a kind of node that is a `WreckSpace` server, for example, and then we could create nodes which **inherit** from that node, including only the classes that determine what it does: `loadbalancer` or `webserver`.

How to do it...

1. Create a base class for all your nodes, which contains only the classes that every node has as follows:

```
node server {
    include admin::basics
    include admin::ssh
    include admin::ntp
    include puppet::client
    include backup::client
}
```

2. Create three different subclasses of this `server` node, each with the appropriate `provider` variable:

```
node wreckspace_server inherits server {
    $provider = "WreckSpace"
}

node gododgy_server inherits server {
    $provider = "GoDodgy"
}

node veryslow_server inherits server {
    $provider = "VerySlow"
}
```

3. Now, let's say you need to create a new web server in `VerySlow`. To do this, just inherit from `veryslow_server`:

```
node webserver904 inherits veryslow_server {
    include webserver
}
```

How it works...

When one node inherits from another, it picks up the entire configuration that the parent node had. You can then add anything which makes this particular node different.

You can have a node inherit from a node that inherits from another node, and so on. You can't inherit from more than one node though—so you can't have, for example:

```
node movable_server inherits gododgy_server, veryslow_server,
wreckspace_server {
    # This won't work
}
```

There's more...

Just as with a normal node definition, you can specify a list of node names that will all inherit the same definition:

```
node webserver1, webserver2, webserver3 inherits wreckspace_server {
    ...
}
```

Alternatively, you can also have a regular expression that will match multiple servers:

```
node /webserver\d+.veryslow.com/ inherits veryslow_server {
    ...
}
```

See also

▶ *Using class inheritance and overriding* in this chapter

Using class inheritance and overriding

Just as nodes can inherit from other nodes, to save you duplicating lots of stuff for nodes that are very similar, the same idea works for classes.

For example, imagine you have a class `apache` which manages the Apache web server, and you want to set up a new Apache machine but with a slightly different config file - perhaps listening on a different port.

You could duplicate the whole of the `apache` class, except for the config file. Alternatively, you could take the config file out of the `apache` class and create two new classes, each of which includes the base `apache` class and adds a different version of the config file.

A cleaner way is to inherit from the `apache` class, but override just the config file.

Getting ready...

1. Create the directory structure for a new `apache` module:

   ```
   # mkdir /etc/puppet/modules/apache
   # mkdir /etc/puppet/modules/apache/manifests
   # mkdir /etc/puppet/modules/apache/files
   ```

2. Create the file /etc/puppet/modules/apache/manifests/init.pp with the following contents:

   ```
   class apache {
       package { "apache2-mpm-worker": ensure => installed }

       service { "apache2":
           enable  => true,
           ensure  => running,
           require => Package["apache2-mpm-worker"],
       }

       file { "/etc/apache2/ports.conf":
           source => "puppet:///modules/apache/port80.conf.apache",
           notify => Service["apache2"],
       }
   }
   ```

3. Install the Apache package, if it's not already present, and copy the included `ports.conf` file into Puppet:

```
# apt-get install apache2-mpm-worker
# cp /etc/apache2/ports.conf /etc/puppet/modules/apache/files/
port80.conf.apache
```

4. Add the `apache` class to a node as follows:

```
node cookbook {
    include apache
}
```

5. Run Puppet to verify that the manifest works.

How to do it...

1. Create a new version of `port80.conf.apache` named `port8000.conf.apache` with the following changes:

```
NameVirtualHost *:8000
Listen 8000
```

2. Now add a new file `/etc/puppet/modules/apache/manifests/port8000.pp` with the following contents:

```
class apache::port8000 inherits apache {
    File["/etc/apache2/ports.conf"] {
        source => "puppet:///modules/apache/port8000.conf.apache",
    }
}
```

3. Change your node to include the `apache::port8000` class instead of `apache`:

```
node cookbook {
    include apache::port8000
}
```

4. Run Puppet to check that it makes the required changes:

```
# puppet agent --test
info: Retrieving plugin
info: Caching catalog for cookbook.bitfieldconsulting.com
info: Applying configuration version '1302970905'
--- /etc/apache2/ports.conf 2010-11-18 14:16:23.000000000 -0700
+++ /tmp/puppet-file20110416-6165-pzeivi-0   2011-04-16
10:21:47.204294334 -0600
@@ -5,8 +5,8 @@
 # Debian etch). See /usr/share/doc/apache2.2-common/NEWS.Debian.
```

```
gz and
  # README.Debian.gz

-NameVirtualHost *:80

-Listen 80

+NameVirtualHost *:8000

+Listen 8000


<IfModule mod_ssl.c>
      # If you add NameVirtualHost *:443 here, you will also have
to change
```

info: FileBucket adding /etc/apache2/ports.conf as {md5}38b31d2032
6f3640a8dfbe1ff5d1c4ad

info: /Stage[main]/Apache/File[/etc/apache2/ports.conf]:
Filebucketed /etc/apache2/ports.conf to puppet with sum
38b31d20326f3640a8dfbe1ff5d1c4ad

notice: /Stage[main]/Apache/File[/etc/apache2/ports.conf]/content:
content changed '{md5}38b31d20326f3640a8dfbe1ff5d1c4ad' to '{md5}4
1d9d446f779c55f13c5fe5a7477d943'

info: /Stage[main]/Apache/File[/etc/apache2/ports.conf]:
Scheduling refresh of Service[apache2]

notice: /Stage[main]/Apache/Service[apache2]: Triggered 'refresh'
from 1 events

notice: Finished catalog run in 4.85 seconds

How it works...

Let's take another look at the new class:

```
class apache::port8000 inherits apache {
    File["/etc/apache2/ports.conf"] {
        source => "puppet:///modules/apache/port8000.conf.apache",
    }
}
```

You can see that after the class name we have `inherits apache`. This will make the class an exact copy of `apache`, except for the changes that follow.

The following code snippet:

```
File["/etc/apache2/ports.conf"] {
```

specifies that we want to make changes to the `file` resource named /etc/apache2/ports.conf in the parent class (note that `File` is capitalized, meaning that we're referring to an existing resource rather than defining a new one).

The following code snippet:

```
source => "puppet:///modules/apache/port8000.conf.apache",
```

means that we are going to override the `source` parameter of the parent class's resource with a new value. The result will be exactly the same as if we had copied the whole class definition from `apache` but changed the value of `source`:

```
class apache {
    package { "apache2-mpm-worker": ensure => installed }

    service { "apache2":
        enable  => true,
        ensure  => running,
        require => Package["apache2-mpm-worker"],
    }

    file { "/etc/apache2/ports.conf":
        source => "puppet:///modules/apache/port8000.conf.apache",
        notify => Service["apache2"],
    }
}
```

There's more...

Overriding inherited classes may seem complicated at first. Once you get the idea, though, it's actually quite simple. It's a great way to make your manifests more readable because it removes lots of duplication, and focuses only on the parts that differ. Here are some more ways to use overriding.

Undefining parameters

Sometimes you don't want to change the value of a parameter, you just want to remove its value altogether. To do this, use the value `undef`. The result will be as though the parameter had never been defined in the first place.

```
class apache::norestart inherits apache {
    File["/etc/apache2/ports.conf"] {
        notify => undef,
    }
}
```

Adding extra values using the +> operator

Similarly, instead of replacing a value, you may want to add more values to those defined in the parent class. The **plusignment** operator +> will do this:

```
class apache::ssl inherits apache {
    file { "/etc/ssl/certs/cookbook.pem":
        source => "puppet:///modules/apache/cookbook.pem",
    }

    Service["apache2"] {
        require +> File["/etc/ssl/certs/cookbook.pem"],
    }
}
```

The +> operator adds a value (or an array of values surrounded by square brackets) to the value defined in the parent class. In this case, what we end up with is the equivalent of this:

```
service { "apache2":
    enable  => true,
    ensure  => running,
    require => [ Package["apache2-mpm-worker"], File["/etc/ssl/certs/
    cookbook.pem"] ],
}
```

Disabling resources

One of the most common uses for inheritance and overrides is to disable services or other resources:

```
class apache::disabled inherits apache {
    Service["apache2"] {
        enable  => false,
        ensure  => stopped,
    }
}
```

See also

- ▶ *Using node inheritance* in this chapter
- ▶ *Passing parameters to classes* in this chapter
- ▶ *Using standard naming conventions* in *Chapter 3*

Passing parameters to classes

Sometimes it's very useful to **parameterize** some aspect of a class. For example, you might need to manage different versions of a gem package, and rather than making separate classes for each that differ only in the version number, or using inheritance and overrides, you can pass in the version number as a parameter.

How to do it...

1. Declare the parameter as part of the class definition as follows:

```
class eventmachine( $version ) {
    package { "eventmachine":
        provider => gem,
        ensure   => $version,
    }
}
```

2. Then use the following syntax to include the class on a node:

```
class { "eventmachine": version => "0.12.8" }
```

How it works...

The class definition:

```
class eventmachine( $version ) {
```

is just like a normal class definition except it specifies that the class takes one parameter: $version. Inside the class, we've defined a package resource as follows:

```
package { "eventmachine":
    provider => gem,
    ensure   => $version,
}
```

This is a gem package, and we're requesting to install version $version.

When you include the class on a node, instead of the usual syntax:

```
include eventmachine
```

there's a class statement as follows:

```
class { "eventmachine": version => "0.12.8" }
```

This has the same effect, but also sets a value for the parameter $version.

There's more...

You can specify multiple parameters for a class:

```
class mysql( $package, $socket, $port ) {
```

and supply them in the same way:

```
class { "mysql":
    package => "percona-sql-server-5.0",
    socket  => "/var/run/mysqld/mysqld.sock",
    port    => "3306",
}
```

You can also give default values for some of your parameters:

```
class mysql( $package, $socket, $port = "3306" ) {
```

or all, as shown in the following code snippet:

```
class mysql(
    package = "percona-sql-server-5.0",
    socket  = "/var/run/mysqld/mysqld.sock",
    port    = "3306" ) {
```

Unlike a `define`, only one instance of a parameterized class can exist on a node. So where you need to have several different instances of the resource, use a `define` instead.

See also

- ▶ *Using node inheritance* in this chapter
- ▶ *Using class inheritance and overriding* in this chapter

Writing reusable, cross-platform manifests

Every system administrator dreams of a unified, homogeneous infrastructure, of identical machines all running the same version of the same OS. As in other areas of life, however, the reality is often messy and doesn't conform to the plan.

You are probably responsible for a bunch of assorted servers of varying age and architecture, running different kernels from different OS distributions, often scattered across different data centers and ISPs.

This situation should strike terror into the hearts of sysadmins of the "SSH in a `for` loop" persuasion, because executing the same commands on every server can have different, unpredictable, and even dangerous results.

We should certainly strive to bring older servers up to date and get everything as far as possible working on a single reference platform to make administration simpler, cheaper, and more reliable. But until we get there, Puppet makes coping with heterogeneous environments slightly easier.

How to do it...

1. If you have servers in different data centers that need slightly different network configuration, for example, use the node inheritance technique to encapsulate the differences:

```
node wreckspace_server inherits server {
        include admin::wreckspace_specific
}
```

2. Where you need to apply the same manifest to servers with different OS distributions, the main differences will probably be the names of packages and services, and the location of config files. Try to capture all these differences into a single class, using selectors to set global variables:

```
$ssh_service = $operatingsystem? {
    /Ubuntu|Debian/ => "ssh",
    default         => "sshd",
}
```

Then you needn't worry about the differences in any other part of the manifest; when you refer to something, use the variable in confidence that it will point to the right thing in each environment:

```
  service { $ssh_service:
      ensure => running,
  }
```

3. Often we need to cope with mixed architectures; this can affect the paths to shared libraries, and also may require different versions of packages. Again, try to encapsulate all the required settings in a single `architecture` class which sets global variables:

```
$libdir = $architecture ? {
    x86_64  => "/usr/lib64",
    default => "/usr/lib",
}
```

Then you can use these wherever an architecture-dependent value is required, in your manifests or even in templates:

```
; php.ini
[PHP]
; Directory in which the loadable extensions (modules) reside.
extension_dir = <%= libdir %>/php/modules
```

How it works...

The advantage of this approach (which could be called "top-down") is that you only need to make your choices once. The alternative, bottom-up approach, would be to have a selector or `case` statement everywhere a setting is used:

```
service { $operatingsystem? {
    /Ubuntu|Debian/ => "ssh",
    default         => "sshd" }:
    ensure => running,
}
```

This not only results in lots of duplication, but makes the code harder to read. And when a new operating system is added to the mix, you'll need to make changes throughout the whole manifest, instead of just in one place.

There's more...

If you are writing a module for public distribution (for example on Puppet Forge), you can make it much more valuable by making it as cross-platform as possible. As far as you can, test it on lots of different distributions, platforms, and architectures, and add the appropriate variables so it works everywhere.

If you use a public module and adapt it to your own environment, consider updating the public version with your changes if you think they might be helpful to other people.

Even if you are not thinking of publishing a module, bear in mind that it may be in production use for a long time and may have to adapt to many changes in the environment. If it's designed to cope with this from the start, it'll make life easier for you - or whoever ends up maintaining your code.

> *"Always code as if the guy who ends up maintaining your code will be a violent psychopath who knows where you live."—Dave Carhart*

See also

▶ *Using node inheritance* in this chapter

▶ *Using class inheritance and overriding* in this chapter

▶ *Using public modules* in *Chapter 9*

Getting information about the environment

"In Paris they simply stared when I spoke to them in French. I never did succeed in making those idiots understand their language."—Mark Twain

Local knowledge can be very useful. Often in a Puppet manifest, you need to know some local information about the machine you're on. **Facter** is the tool that accompanies Puppet to provide a standard way of getting information ('facts') from the environment about things like:

- ▶ Operating system
- ▶ Memory size
- ▶ Architecture
- ▶ Processor count

To see a complete list of the facts available on your system, run the command: `# facter`

While it can be handy to get this information from the command line, the real power of Facter lies in being able to access these facts in your Puppet manifests.

How to do it...

1. Reference a Facter fact in your manifest like any other variable as follows:

```
notify { "This is $operatingsystem version
$operatingsystemrelease, on $architecture architecture, kernel
version $kernelversion": }
```

2. When Puppet runs, it will fill in the appropriate values for the current node:

```
notice: This is Ubuntu version 10.04, on i386 architecture,
kernel version 2.6.32
```

How it works...

Facter provides an abstraction layer for Puppet, and a standard way for manifests to get information about their environment. When you refer to a fact in a manifest, Puppet will query Facter to get the current value, and insert it into the manifest.

There's more...

You can also use facts in **ERB** templates. For example, you might want to insert the node's hostname into a file, or change a config setting for an application based on the memory size of the node. When you use fact names in templates, remember that they don't need a dollar sign, because this is Ruby, not Puppet:

```
$KLogPath <%= case kernelversion when "2.6.31" then "/var/run/rsyslog/
kmsg" else "/proc/kmsg" end %>
```

See also

▶ *Creating custom Facter facts* in *Chapter 9*

Importing dynamic information

Even though some system administrators like to wall themselves off from the rest of the office using piles of old printers, we all need to exchange information with other departments from time to time. For example, you may need to insert data into your Puppet manifests which is derived from some outside source. The `generate` function is very useful for this.

Getting ready...

Create the script `/usr/local/bin/latest-puppet.rb` on the Puppetmaster with the following contents:

```
#!/usr/bin/ruby

require 'open-uri'

page = open("http://www.puppetlabs.com/misc/download-options/").read
print page.match(/stable version is ([\d\.]*)/)[1]
```

How to do it...

1. Add the following to your manifest:

    ```
    $latestversion = generate("/usr/local/bin/latest-puppet.rb")
    notify { "The latest stable Puppet version is ${latestversion}.
    You're using ${puppetversion}.": }
    ```

2. Run Puppet:

    ```
    # puppet agent --test
    notice: The latest stable Puppet version is 2.6.5. You're
    using 2.6.3.
    ```

How it works...

The `generate` function runs the specified script or program on the Puppetmaster (not the client) and returns the result - in this case, the version number of the latest stable Puppet release.

I don't recommend you run this script in production, as Puppet Labs have a habit of rearranging their web site, but you get the idea. Anything a script can do, print, fetch, or calculate - for example the results of a database query - can be brought into your manifest using `generate`.

It's worth remembering that, just as with embedded Ruby calls in templates, the `generate` function is run on the Puppetmaster and not on the node that is running Puppet. I once made this mistake by calling `/bin/hostname` in a template and finding to my surprise that all my nodes were apparently named `puppet`.

When you need to get information specifically about the node, this is best done with a custom fact.

There's more...

If you need to pass arguments to the executable called by `generate`, add them as extra arguments to the function call as follows:

```
$latestpuppet = generate("/usr/local/bin/latest-version.rb", "puppet")
$latestmc = generate("/usr/local/bin/latest-version.rb",
"mcollective")
```

Puppet will try to protect you from malicious shell calls by restricting the characters you can use in a call to `generate`, so shell pipelines aren't allowed, for example. The simplest and safest thing to do is to put all your logic into a script and then call that script.

See also

► *Creating custom Facter facts* in *Chapter 9*
► *Importing data from CSV files* in this chapter

Importing data from CSV files

Want to know something? When you need to look up some value in a table, you could do it with lengthy `case` statements or selectors, but a neater way is to use the `extlookup` function. This queries an external CSV file on the Puppetmaster and returns the matching piece of data.

Grouping all such data into a single file and moving it outside the Puppet manifests makes it easier to maintain, as well as easier to share with other people: a development team can manage the things Puppet needs to know about their application, for example, by deploying a suitable CSV file as part of the release. Puppet just needs to know where to find the file, and `extlookup` will do the rest.

Getting ready...

1. Create the file `/var/www/apps/common.csv` with the following contents:

```
path,/var/www/apps/%{name}
railsversion,3
domain,www.%{name}.com
```

2. Create the file `/var/www/apps/myapp.csv` with the following contents:

```
railsversion,2
```

How to do it...

1. Add the following to your manifest:

```
$extlookup_datadir = "/var/www/apps/"
$extlookup_precedence = [ "%{name}", "common" ]

class app( $name ) {
    $railsversion = extlookup("railsversion")
    $path = extlookup("path")
    $domain = extlookup("domain")
    notify { "App data: Path ${path}, Rails version
    ${railsversion}, domain ${domain}": }
}

class { "app": name => "myapp" }
```

2. Run Puppet:

```
# puppet agent --test
info: Retrieving plugin
info: Caching catalog for cookbook.bitfieldconsulting.com
info: Applying configuration version '1303129760'
notice: App data: Path /var/www/apps/myapp, Rails version 2,
domain www.myapp.com
notice: /Stage[main]/App/Notify[App data: Path /var/www/apps/
myapp, Rails version 2, domain www.myapp.com]/message: defined
'message' as 'App data: Path /var/www/apps/myapp, Rails version 2,
domain www.myapp.com'
notice: Finished catalog run in 0.58 seconds
```

How it works...

1. The first thing we do is define the variable $extlookup_datadir, which tells extlookup what directory to look for data files in. You would normally set this in site.pp or wherever you define global variables:

   ```
   $extlookup_datadir = "/var/www/apps/"
   ```

2. Then, we tell extlookup what data files to look at, in order of precedence:

   ```
   $extlookup_precedence = [ "%{name}", "common" ]
   ```

   This can be an array of any length. When we make an extlookup query, Puppet will try each of the files in order until it finds one that has the requested value. The file names can contain variables. In this example, we've used %{name}, so we're expecting a variable called $name to be set when we call extlookup and Puppet will use its value as the first filename to look for.

3. Next, inside the app class, we call extlookup to get a value:

   ```
   $railsversion = extlookup("railsversion")
   ```

   The extlookup machinery now looks for a CSV file to read the data from. It looks in the $extlookup_datadir directory (in this case /var/www/apps) for a file named %{name}.csv (in this case myapp.csv). So it reads the file /var/www/apps/myapp.csv which contains railsversion,2

   We've found the required value (2), so extlookup returns it.

4. The next extlookup call isn't so lucky:

   ```
   $path = extlookup("path")
   ```

   Again, extlookup looks first in myapp.csv, but it doesn't find a value matching path. So it moves on to the next file listed in $extlookup_precedence, which is common.csv:

   ```
   path,/var/www/apps/%{name}
   railsversion,3
   domain,www.%{name}.com
   ```

   Thankfully, this does match, so Puppet returns the value /var/www/apps/%{name}, which in this case evaluates to /var/www/apps/myapp.

You can see that this allows us to have a set of default values in common.csv that each app may choose to override in its own myapp.csv file. extlookup will keep on querying the files listed in $extlookup_precedence until it finds the value requested. As myapp.csv is listed first, any setting in it will take precedence over settings in common.csv.

There's more...

You can also specify default values in the `extlookup` call, to be used if no suitable data is found in the CSV files:

```
$path = extlookup("path", "/var/www/misc")
```

You can also specify a CSV file to be consulted first, before anything in `$extlookup_precedence`:

```
$path = extlookup("path", "/var/www/misc", "paths")
```

This will look in `paths.csv` for the data, and if it doesn't find it, will move on to the files listed in `$extlookup_precedence` as usual.

The values in your CSV files can also refer to variables, as we did here:

```
domain,www.%{name}.com
```

You can use any variable that's in scope, including Facter facts:

```
domain,%{fqdn}
```

R.I. Pienaar's article "Complex data and Puppet" is an excellent introduction to `extlookup`: `http://www.devco.net/archives/2009/08/31/complex_data_and_puppet.php`.

Jordan Sissel has written about configuring your whole infrastructure using `extlookup`: `http://sysadvent.blogspot.com/2010/12/day-12-scaling-operability-with-truth.html`.

See also

- ▶ *Importing dynamic information* in this chapter
- ▶ *Creating custom Facter facts* in *Chapter 9*

Passing arguments to shell commands

If you need to insert values into a command line, they often need to be quoted, especially if they contain spaces. The `shellquote` function will take any number of arguments, including arrays, and quote each of the arguments and return them all as a space-separated string that you can pass to commands.

In this example, we would like to set up an `exec` resource which will rename a file, but both the source and the target name contain spaces, so they need to be correctly quoted in the command line.

How to do it...

1. Add the following to your manifest:

```
$source = "Hello Jerry"
$target = "Hello... Newman"
$argstring = shellquote( $source, $target )
$command = "/bin/mv ${argstring}"
notify { $command: }
```

2. Run Puppet:

notice: /bin/mv "Hello Jerry" "Hello... Newman"

How it works...

1. First we define the `$source` and `$target` variables, which are the two filenames we want to use in the command line as follows:

```
$source = "Hello Jerry"
$target = "Hello... Newman"
```

2. Then we call `shellquote` to concatenate these variables into a quoted, space-separated string.

```
$argstring = shellquote( $source, $target )
```

3. Then we put together the final command line:

```
$command = "/bin/mv ${argstring}"
```

4. The result is:

/bin/mv "Hello Jerry" "Hello... Newman"

5. This command line can now be run with an `exec` resource. What would happen if we didn't use `shellquote`?

```
$source = "Hello Jerry"
$target = "Hello... Newman"
$command = "/bin/mv ${source} ${target}"
notify { $command: }
```

notice: /bin/mv Hello Jerry Hello... Newman

This won't work because `mv` expects space-separated arguments, so will interpret this as a request to move three files `Hello`, `Jerry`, and `Hello...` into a directory named `Newman`, which probably isn't what we want.

5
Working with Files and Packages

"If builders built buildings the way programmers wrote programs, then the first woodpecker that came along would destroy civilization."—Gerald Weinberg

In this chapter we will cover the following topics:

- ▶ Making quick edits to config files
- ▶ Using Augeas to automatically edit config files
- ▶ Building config files using snippets
- ▶ Using ERB templates
- ▶ Using array iteration in templates
- ▶ Installing packages from a third-party repository
- ▶ Setting up an APT package repository
- ▶ Setting up a gem repository
- ▶ Building packages automatically from source
- ▶ Comparing package versions

Almost everything you'll do as a Puppet administrator involves either files or packages. They are the most important kinds of resources in Puppet and this chapter will help you to understand them thoroughly, and learn some useful features and patterns to help you make better use of them.

In this chapter we'll see how to make small edits to files, how to make larger changes in a structured way using the **Augeas** tool, how to construct files from concatenated snippets, and how to generate files from templates. We'll also learn how to install packages from additional repositories, and how to create those repositories.

Making quick edits to config files

Did you know Puppet can do micro-surgery? Often we don't want to have to put a whole config file into Puppet just to add one setting—especially if the file is managed by someone else and we can't overwrite it. What would be useful is a simple recipe to add a line to a config file if it's not already present: for example, adding a module name to /etc/modules to tell the kernel to load that module at boot.

You can use an exec resource to do jobs like this: this example shows how to use exec to append a line to a text file.

How to do it...

1. Create the file /etc/puppet/manifests/utils.pp with the following content:

```
define append_if_no_such_line($file, $line) {
    exec { "/bin/echo '$line' >> '$file'":
        unless => "/bin/grep -Fx '$line' '$file'",
    }
}
```

2. Add this line to /etc/puppet/manifests/site.pp:

```
import "utils.pp"
```

3. Now add this to your manifest:

```
append_if_no_such_line { "enable-ip-conntrack":
    file => "/etc/modules",
    line => "ip_conntrack",
}
```

4. Run Puppet:

```
# puppet agent --test
info: Retrieving plugin
info: Caching catalog for cookbook.bitfieldconsulting.com
info: Applying configuration version '1303649606'
notice: /Stage[main]//Node[cookbook]/Append_if_no_such_
line[enable-ip-conntrack]/Exec[/bin/echo 'ip_conntrack' >> '/etc/
modules']/returns: executed successfully
notice: Finished catalog run in 1.22 seconds
```

How it works...

The `exec` resource will append the specified text in `$line` to the file `$file`, provided it's not already present:

```
exec { "/bin/echo '$line' >> '$file'":
  unless => "/bin/grep -Fx '$line' '$file'",
```

This `append_if_no_such_line` resource is now available for you to use in your manifest. In this example, we've used it to ensure that the `/etc/modules` file (which specifies what kernel modules to load at boot time) contains the following line:

```
ip_conntrack
```

There's more...

You can use similar `define` functions to perform other minor operations on text files. For example, the following code snippet will enable you to search and replace within a file:

```
define replace_matching_line( $match, $replace ) {
  exec { "/usr/bin/ruby -i -p -e 'sub(%r{$match}, \"$replace\")'
  $name":
    onlyif => "/bin/grep -E '$match' $name",
    logoutput => on_failure,
  }
}

replace_matching_line { "/etc/apache2/apache2.conf":
    match   => "LogLevel .*",
    replace => "LogLevel debug",
}
```

See also

▶ *Using Augeas to automatically edit config files* in this chapter

Using Augeas to automatically edit config files

Of course, the great thing about standards is that there are so many of them. Sometimes it seems like every application config file format is slightly different, and writing regular expressions to parse and modify all of them can be a tiresome business.

Thankfully, Augeas is here to help. Augeas is a tool which aims to simplify working with different config file formats, by presenting them all as a simple tree of values. Puppet's Augeas support allows you to create `augeas` resources which can make the required config changes intelligently and automatically.

Getting ready...

Before we can use Augeas, we need to install it. The following Puppet code will add Augeas to your setup.

1. Create the file `/etc/puppet/modules/admin/manifests/augeas.pp` with the following contents:

```
class admin::augeas {
    package { [ "augeas-lenses",
                "augeas-tools",
                "libaugeas0",
                "libaugeas-ruby1.8" ]:
        ensure => "present"
    }
}
```

2. Include the following class on a node:

```
node cookbook {
    include admin::augeas
}
```

3. Run Puppet:

```
# puppet agent --test
info: Retrieving plugin
info: Caching catalog for cookbook.bitfieldconsulting.com
info: Applying configuration version '1303657095'
notice: /Stage[main]/Admin::Augeas/Package[augeas-tools]/ensure:
ensure changed 'purged' to 'present'
notice: Finished catalog run in 21.96 seconds
```

How to do it...

1. Create the file `/etc/puppet/modules/admin/manifests/ipforward.pp` with the following contents:

```
class admin::ipforward {
    augeas { "enable-ip-forwarding":
        context => "/files/etc/sysctl.conf",
```

```
            changes => [
                "set net.ipv4.ip_forward 1",
            ],
        }
    }
```

2. Include this class on a node:

```
node cookbook {
    include admin::augeas
    include admin::ipforward
}
```

3. Run Puppet:

 # puppet agent --test

info: Retrieving plugin

info: Caching catalog for cookbook.bitfieldconsulting.com

info: Applying configuration version '1303729376'

notice: /Stage[main]/Admin::Ipforward/Augeas[enable-ip-forwarding]/returns: executed successfully

notice: Finished catalog run in 3.53 seconds

4. Check that the setting has been correctly applied with the following command:

 # sysctl -p |grep forward

net.ipv4.ip_forward = 1

How it works...

This is what is going on in the preceding code:

1. We declare an augeas resource named enable-ip-forwarding:

```
        augeas { "enable-ip-forwarding":
```

2. We specify that we want to make changes in the context of the file /etc/sysctl.conf:

```
            context => "/files/etc/sysctl.conf",
```

3. The parameter changes is passed an array of settings that we want to make (in this case only one):

```
            changes => [
                "set net.ipv4.ip_forward 1",
            ],
```

In general Augeas changes take the following form:

```
set <parameter> <value>
```

Augeas uses a set of translation files called **lenses** to enable it to write these settings in the appropriate format for the given config file. In this case, the setting will be translated into a line such as the following in `/etc/sysctl.conf`:

```
net.ipv4.ip_forward=1
```

There's more...

The `/etc/sysctl.conf` file is used as the example because it can contain a wide variety of kernel settings, and you may want to change these settings for all sorts of different purposes and in different Puppet classes. You might want to enable IP forwarding for a router class as in the preceding example, but you might also want to tune the value of `net.core.somaxconn` for a load-balancer class.

This means that simply "Puppetizing" the `/etc/sysctl.conf` file and distributing it as a text file won't work, because you might have several different and conflicting versions, depending on the setting you want to modify. Augeas is the right solution here because you can define `augeas` resources in different places which modify the same file, such that they won't conflict.

Augeas is a powerful tool that ships with lenses for most of the standard Linux config files, and you can write your own for rare or proprietary config formats if you need to manage these. For more about using Puppet and Augeas, visit the page on the Puppet Labs wiki: `http://projects.puppetlabs.com/projects/1/wiki/Puppet_Augeas`.

Building config files using snippets

How do you eat an elephant? One bite at a time. Sometimes you have a situation where you want to build up a single config file from various snippets managed by different classes. For example, you might have two or three services that require `rsync` modules to be configured, so you can't distribute a single `rsyncd.conf`. Although you could use Augeas, there's a simple way to concatenate config snippets together into a single file using an `exec` resource.

How to do it...

1. Create the file `/etc/puppet/modules/admin/manifests/rsyncdconf.pp` with the following contents:

```
class admin::rsyncdconf {
    file { "/etc/rsyncd.d":
        ensure => directory,
    }

    exec { "update-rsyncd.conf":
        command    => "/bin/cat /etc/rsyncd.d/*.conf > /etc/
        rsyncd.conf",
```

```
        refreshonly => true,
    }
}
```

2. Add the following to your manifest:

```
class myapp::rsync {
    include admin::rsyncdconf

    file { "/etc/rsyncd.d/myapp.conf":
        ensure  => present,
        source  => "puppet:///modules/myapp/myapp.rsync",
        require => File["/etc/rsyncd.d"],
        notify  => Exec["update-rsyncd.conf"],
    }
}


include myapp::rsync
```

3. Create the file `/etc/puppet/modules/myapp/files/myapp.rsync` with the following contents:

```
[myapp]
    uid = myappuser
    gid = myappuser
    path = /opt/myapp/shared/data
    comment = Data for myapp
    list = no
    read only = no
    auth users = myappuser
```

4. Run Puppet:

```
# puppet agent --test

info: Retrieving plugin

info: Caching catalog for cookbook.bitfieldconsulting.com

info: Applying configuration version '1303731804'

notice: /Stage[main]/Admin::Rsyncdconf/File[/etc/rsyncd.d]/ensure:
created

notice: /Stage[main]/Myapp::Rsync/File[/etc/rsyncd.d/myapp.conf]/
ensure: defined content as '{md5}e1e57cf38bb88a7b4f2fd6eb1ea2823a'

info: /Stage[main]/Myapp::Rsync/File[/etc/rsyncd.d/myapp.conf]:
Scheduling refresh of Exec[update-rsyncd.conf]

notice: /Stage[main]/Admin::Rsyncdconf/Exec[update-rsyncd.conf]:
Triggered 'refresh' from 1 events

notice: Finished catalog run in 1.01 seconds
```

How it works...

The `admin::rsyncdconf` class creates a directory for `rsync` config snippets to be placed into as follows:

```
file { "/etc/rsyncd.d":
    ensure => directory,
}
```

When you create a config snippet (such as in `myapp::rsync`), all you need to do is `require` the directory— `require => File["/etc/rsyncd.d"]`, and `notify` the `exec` resource that updates the main config file as follows: `notify  => Exec["update-rsyncd.conf"],`.

This `exec` resource will then be run every time one of the following snippets is updated:

```
exec { "update-rsyncd.conf":
    command     => "/bin/cat /etc/rsyncd.d/*.conf > /etc/rsyncd.conf",
    refreshonly => true,
}
```

The preceding code snippet will concatenate all the snippets in `/etc/rsyncd.d` into `rsyncd.conf`.

The reason this is useful is that you can have many different snippet resources spread throughout different classes and modules, all of which will eventually be combined into a single `rsyncd.conf` file, but you can keep the code to combine this in one place.

There's more...

This is a useful pattern whenever you have a service like `rsync` that has a single config file which may contain distinct snippets. In effect, it gives you the functionality of Apache's `conf.d` or PHP's `php-ini.d` directories.

See also

▶ Using tags in *Chapter 5*

Using ERB templates

A **template** is a text file with a college degree. It can do calculations, execute Ruby code, or reference the values of variables from your Puppet manifests. Anywhere you might deploy a text file using Puppet, you can use a template instead. In the simplest case, a template can just be a static text file. More usefully, you can insert variables into it using **ERB (embedded Ruby)** syntax. For example:

```
<%= name %>, this is a very large drink.
```

If the template is used in a context where the variable $name contains Zaphod Beeblebrox, the template will evaluate as follows:

```
Zaphod Beeblebrox, this is a very large drink.
```

This simple technique is very useful for generating lots of files that only differ in the values of one or two variables such as virtual hosts— and for inserting values into a script such as database names and passwords. In this example, we'll use an ERB template to insert a password into a backup script.

How to do it...

1. Create the file /etc/puppet/modules/admin/templates/backup-mysql.sh with the following content:

   ```
   #!/bin/sh
   /usr/bin/mysqldump -uroot  p<%= mysql_password %> --all-databases
   | /bin/gzip > /backup/mysql/all-databases.sql.gz
   ```

2. Add the following to your manifest:

   ```
   $mysql_password = "secret"
   file { "/usr/local/bin/backup-mysql":
       content => template("admin/backup-mysql.sh"),
       mode    => "755",
   }
   ```

3. Run Puppet:

   ```
   # puppet agent --test

   info: Retrieving plugin

   info: Caching catalog for cookbook.bitfieldconsulting.com

   info: Applying configuration version '1308670971'

   notice: /Stage[main]//Node[cookbook]/File[/usr/local/bin/backup-
   mysql]/ensure: defined content as '{md5}5853b6d4dd72420e341fa7ecb8
   91ad43'

   notice: Finished catalog run in 0.96 seconds
   ```

4. Check that Puppet has correctly inserted the password into the template:

   ```
   # cat /usr/local/bin/backup-mysql
   ```

   ```
   #!/bin/sh
   ```

   ```
   /usr/bin/mysqldump -uroot -psecret --all-databases | /bin/gzip > /
   backup/mysql/all-databases.sql.gz
   ```

How it works...

Wherever a variable is referenced in the template, such as `<%= mysql_password %>`
Puppet will replace it with the corresponding value: `secret`.

There's more...

In the example, we only used one variable in the template, but you can have as many as you
like. These can also be facts, such as the following:

```
ServerName <%= fqdn %>
```

or Ruby expressions such as:

```
MAILTO=<%= emails.join(',') %>
```
or any Ruby code you want such as:

```
ServerAdmin <%= sitedomain == 'coldcomfort.com' ? 'seth@coldcomfort.
com' : 'flora@poste.com' %>
```

See also

▶ Using *array iteration in templates* in this chapter

Using array iteration in templates

In the preceding example we saw that you can use Ruby to interpolate different values in
templates depending on the result of an expression. You can also use a loop to generate
content based on; the elements of an array:

How to do it...

1. Add the following to your manifest:

```
$ipaddresses = [ '192.168.0.1',
                 '158.43.128.1',
                 '10.0.75.207' ]

file { "/tmp/addresslist.txt":
    content => template("admin/addresslist.erb")
}
```

2. Create the file `/etc/puppet/modules/admin/templates/addresslist.erb` with the following contents:

```
<% ipaddresses.each do |ip| -%>
IP address <%= ip %> is present.
<% end -%>
```

3. Run Puppet:

```
# puppet agent --test
info: Retrieving plugin
info: Caching catalog for cookbook.bitfieldconsulting.com
info: Applying configuration version '1304766335'
notice: /Stage[main]//Node[cookbook]/File[/tmp/addresslist.txt]/
ensure: defined content as '{md5}7ad1264ebdae101bb5ea0afef474b3ed'
notice: Finished catalog run in 0.64 seconds
```

4. Check the contents of the generated file as follows:

```
# cat /tmp/addresslist.txt
IP address 192.168.0.1 is present.
IP address 158.43.128.1 is present.
IP address 10.0.75.207 is present.
```

How it works...

1. In the first line of the template, we reference the array `ipaddresses`, and call the corresponding `each` method as follows:

```
<% ipaddresses.each do |ip| -%>
```

2. In Ruby, this creates a loop that will execute once for each element of the array. Each time round the loop, the variable `ip` will be set to the value of the current element.

3. In our example, the `ipaddresses` array contains three elements, so the following line will be executed three times, once for each element:

```
IP address <%= ip %> is present.
```

4. This will result in three output lines:

```
IP address 192.168.0.1 is present.
IP address 158.43.128.1 is present.
IP address 10.0.75.207 is present.
```

5. The final line ends the loop as follows:

```
<% end -%>
```

6. Note that the first and last lines end with `-%>`, instead of just `%>` as we saw before. The effect of the `-` is to suppress the newline that would otherwise be generated, giving us an unwanted blank line in the file.

There's more...

Templates can also iterate over hashes, or arrays of hashes as follows:

```
$interfaces = [ { name => 'eth0',
                  ip   => '192.168.0.1' },
                { name => 'eth1',
                  ip   => '158.43.128.1' },
                { name => 'eth2',
                  ip   => '10.0.75.207' } ]

<% interfaces.each do |interface| -%>
Interface <%= interface['name'] %> has the address <%= interface['ip']
%>.
<% end -%>

Interface eth0 has the address 192.168.0.1.
Interface eth1 has the address 158.43.128.1.
Interface eth2 has the address 10.0.75.207.
```

See also

▶ *Using ERB templates* in this chapter

Installing packages from a third-party repository

Most often, you will want to install packages from the main distribution repository, so a simple `package` resource will do:

```
package { "exim4": ensure => installed }
```

Sometimes, though, you need a package which is only found in a third-party repository (an **Ubuntu PPA**, for example). Or it might be that you need a more recent version of a package than that provided by the distribution, which is available from a third party.

On a manually administered machine, you would normally do this by adding the repository source configuration to `/etc/apt/sources.list.d` (and, if necessary, a GPG key for the repository) before installing the package. We can automate this process easily with Puppet.

How to do it...

1. Add the following to your manifest:

```
package { "python-software-properties": ensure => installed }

exec { "/usr/bin/add-apt-repository ppa:mathiaz/puppet-backports":
    creates => "/etc/apt/sources.list.d/mathiaz-puppet-backports-
    lucid.list",
    require => Package["python-software-properties"],
}
```

2. Run Puppet:

```
# puppet agent --test

info: Retrieving plugin

info: Caching catalog for cookbook.bitfieldconsulting.com

info: Applying configuration version '1304773240'

notice: /Stage[main]//Node[cookbook]/Exec[/usr/bin/add-apt-
repository ppa:mathiaz/puppet-backports]/returns: executed
successfully

notice: Finished catalog run in 5.97 seconds
```

How it works...

1. The `python-software-properties` package provides the command `add-apt-repository`, which simplifies the process of adding extra repositories as follows:

   ```
   package { "python-software-properties": ensure => installed }
   ```

2. We then call this command in the `exec` resource to add the required configuration:

   ```
   exec { "/usr/bin/add-apt-repository ppa:mathiaz/puppet-backports":
   ```

3. To ensure that the `exec` resource is not run every time Puppet runs, we specify a file that the command creates, so that Puppet will skip `exec` if this file already exists:

   ```
   creates => "/etc/apt/sources.list.d/mathiaz-puppet-backports-
   lucid.list",
   ```

   You might want to combine this with purging unwanted repository definitions in `/etc/apt/sources.list.d`, as described in the section on recursive file resources.

There's more...

This method of repository handling is specific to Debian and Ubuntu systems, which as we've said is our reference platform for the book. If you're on a RedHat-based system, you can use `yumrepo` resources to manage RPM repositories directly.

See also

► *Distributing directory trees* in *Chapter 6*

Setting up an APT package repository

Running your own package repository has several advantages. You can distribute your own packages with it. You can control the versions of upstream or third-party packages that you put into it. And you can locate it close to where your servers are, to avoid the problem of slow or unreliable mirror sites.

Even if you don't need to create your own packages, you may want to download the required versions of your critical dependency packages and store them in your own repo, thus preventing any surprises when things change upstream (for example, your distro version could reach end-of-life and the repos could be turned off).

It also makes it easier to auto-update packages within Puppet. You may occasionally need to update a package (for example, when a security update is available), so it's convenient to specify `ensure => latest` in the package definition. But when you don't control the repo, this puts you at risk of an unexpected upgrade which breaks something in your system.

Your own repository gives you the best of both worlds: you can auto-update the package in Puppet, but since it comes from your repository, a new version will only be available when you put one there. You can test the version from upstream before making it available in your production repository.

Getting ready...

You will need the `apache` module from the section, *Using ERB templates,* in this chapter. So create this if you don't already have it.

In the example, I've called the repository `packages.bitfieldconsulting.com`, because that's what mine is called. You'll probably want to use a different name, so replace it throughout the example with the name of your repo.

How to do it...

1. Create a new `repo` module:

   # **mkdir /etc/puppet/modules/repo**

   # **mkdir /etc/puppet/modules/repo/manifests**

   # **mkdir /etc/puppet/modules/repo/files**

2. Create the file /etc/puppet/modules/repo/manifests/bitfield-server.
   pp with the following contents:

```
class repo::bitfield-server {
    include apache

    package { "reprepro": ensure => installed }

    file { [ "/var/apt",
            "/var/apt/conf" ]:
        ensure => directory,
    }

    file { "/var/apt/conf/distributions":
        source  => "puppet:///modules/repo/distributions",
        require => File["/var/apt/conf"],
    }

    file { "/etc/apache2/sites-available/apt-repo":
        source  => "puppet:///modules/repo/apt-repo.conf",
        require => Package["apache2-mpm-worker"],
    }

    file { "/etc/apache2/sites-enabled/apt-repo":
        ensure  => symlink,
        target  => "/etc/apache2/sites-available/apt-repo",
        require => File["/etc/apache2/sites-available/apt-repo"],
        notify  => Service["apache2"],
    }
}
```

3. Create the file /etc/puppet/modules/repo/files/distributions with the
   following contents:

```
Origin: Bitfield Consulting
Label: bitfield
Suite: stable
Codename: lucid
Architectures: amd64 i386
Components: main non-free contrib
Description: Custom and cached packages for Bitfield Consulting
```

4. Create the file `/etc/puppet/modules/repo/files/apt-repo.conf` with the following contents:

```
<VirtualHost *:80>
    DocumentRoot /var/apt
    ServerName packages.bitfieldconsulting.com
    ErrorLog /var/log/apache2/packages.bitfieldconsulting.com.
    error.log

    LogLevel warn

    CustomLog /var/log/apache2/packages.bitfieldconsulting.com.
    access.log combined
    ServerSignature On

    # Allow directory listings so that people can browse the
    repository from their browser too
    <Directory "/var/apt">
        Options Indexes FollowSymLinks MultiViews
        DirectoryIndex index.html
        AllowOverride Options
        Order allow,deny
        allow from all
    </Directory>

    # Hide the conf/ directory for all repositories
    <Directory "/var/apt/conf">
        Order allow,deny
        Deny from all
        Satisfy all
    </Directory>

    # Hide the db/ directory for all repositories
    <Directory "/var/apt/db">
        Order allow,deny
        Deny from all
        Satisfy all
    </Directory>
</VirtualHost>
```

5. Add the following to the manifest for a node:

```
include repo::bitfield-server
```

6. Run Puppet:

```
# puppet agent --test
info: Retrieving plugin
info: Caching catalog for cookbook.bitfieldconsulting.com
```

```
info: Applying configuration version '1304775601'

notice: /Stage[main]/Repo::Bitfield-server/File[/var/apt]/ensure:
created

notice: /Stage[main]/Repo::Bitfield-server/File[/var/apt/conf]/
ensure: created

notice: /Stage[main]/Repo::Bitfield-server/File[/var/apt/conf/
distributions]/ensure: defined content as '{md5}65dc791b876f53318a
35fcc42c770283'

notice: /Stage[main]/Repo::Bitfield-server/Package[reprepro]/
ensure: created

notice: /Stage[main]/Repo::Bitfield-server/File[/etc/apache2/
sites-enabled/apt-repo]/ensure: created

notice: /Stage[main]/Repo::Bitfield-server/File[/etc/apache2/
sites-available/apt-repo]/ensure: defined content as '{md5}2da4686
957e5acf49220047fe6f6e6e1'

info: /Stage[main]/Repo::Bitfield-server/File[/etc/apache2/sites-
enabled/apt-repo]: Scheduling refresh of Service[apache2]

notice: /Stage[main]/Apache/Service[apache2]: Triggered 'refresh'
from 1 events

notice: Finished catalog run in 16.32 seconds
```

How it works...

Actually, you don't need very much to create an APT repository. It works over HTTP, so you just need an Apache virtual host. You can put the actual package files anywhere you like, as long as there is a `conf/distributions` file which will give APT information about the repository.

1. The first part of the `bitfield-server` class ensures we have Apache set up:

   ```
   class repo::bitfield-server {
       include apache
   ```

2. The `reprepro` tool is useful for managing the repository itself (for example, adding new packages):

   ```
   package { "reprepro": ensure => installed }
   ```

3. We create the root directory of the repository in `/var/apt`, along with the `conf/distributions` file:

   ```
   file { [ "/var/apt",
            "/var/apt/conf" ] :
       ensure => directory,
   }
   ```

```
file { "/var/apt/conf/distributions":
    source  => "puppet:///modules/repo/distributions",
    require => File["/var/apt/conf"],
}
```

4. The remainder of the class deploys the Apache virtual host file to enable it to serve requests on `packages.bitfieldconsulting.com` as follows:

```
file { "/etc/apache2/sites-available/apt-repo":
    source  => "puppet:///modules/repo/apt-repo.conf",
    require => Package["apache2-mpm-worker"],
}

file { "/etc/apache2/sites-enabled/apt-repo":
    ensure  => symlink,
    target  => "/etc/apache2/sites-available/apt-repo",
    require => File["/etc/apache2/sites-available/apt-repo"],
    notify  => Service["apache2"],
}
```

There's more...

Of course, a repository isn't much good without any packages in it. In this section we'll see how to add packages, and also how to configure machines to download packages from your repository.

Adding packages

To add a package to your repository, download it and then use `reprepro` to add it:

```
# cd /tmp
# wget http://archive.ubuntu.com/ubuntu/pool/main/n/ntp/ntp_4.2.4p8+dfsg-1ubuntu2.1_i386.deb
# cd /var/apt
# reprepro includedeb lucid /tmp/ntp_4.2.4p8+dfsg-1ubuntu2.1_i386.deb
Exporting indices...
```

Configuring nodes to use the repository

1. Create the file `/etc/puppet/modules/repo/manifests/bitfield.pp` with the following contents (replacing the IP address with that of your repository server):

```
class repo::bitfield {
    host { "packages.bitfieldconsulting.com":
        ip      => "10.0.2.15",
        ensure  => present,
        target  => "/etc/hosts",
    }
```

```
file { "/etc/apt/sources.list.d/bitfield.list":
    content => "deb http://packages.bitfieldconsulting.com/
    lucid main\n",
    require => Host["packages.bitfieldconsulting.com"],
    notify  => Exec["bitfield-update"],
}

exec { "bitfield-update":
    command     => "/usr/bin/apt-get update",
    require     => File["/etc/apt/sources.list.d/bitfield.
    list"],
    refreshonly => true,
}
}
```

If you have a DNS server or control of your DNS zone, you can skip the host entry.

2. Apply this class to a node as follows:

```
node cookbook {
    include repo::bitfield
}
```

3. Test whether the `ntp` package shows up as available from your repository:

```
# apt-cache madison ntp
```

```
    ntp | 1:4.2.4p8+dfsg-1ubuntu2.1 | http://us.archive.ubuntu.
    com/ubuntu/ lucid-updates/main Packages

    ntp | 1:4.2.4p8+dfsg-1ubuntu2.1 | http://packages.
    bitfieldconsulting.com/ lucid/main Packages

    ntp | 1:4.2.4p8+dfsg-1ubuntu2 | http://us.archive.ubuntu.
    com/ubuntu/ lucid/main Packages

    ntp | 1:4.2.4p8+dfsg-1ubuntu2 | http://us.archive.ubuntu.
    com/ubuntu/ lucid/main Sources

    ntp | 1:4.2.4p8+dfsg-1ubuntu2.1 | http://us.archive.ubuntu.
    com/ubuntu/ lucid-updates/main Sources
```

Signing your packages

For production use, you should sign your packages and repository with a GPG key; for information about how to set this up, see Sander Marechal's useful article on setting up and managing APT repositories at `http://www.jejik.com/articles/2006/09/setting_up_and_managing_an_apt_repository_with_reprepro/`.

Setting up a gem repository

It's every system administrator's dream: yet another incompatible packaging system. If you manage Ruby or Rails applications, you'll need to deal with Rubygems. Maintaining your own **gem repository** has many of the same advantages as having an APT repository. You can control availability and package versions, and you can also use it to distribute your own gems if you need to.

How to do it...

1. Create the file /etc/puppet/modules/repo/manifests/gem-server.pp with the following contents:

```
class repo::gem-server {
    include apache

    file { "/etc/apache2/sites-available/gemrepo":
        source  => "puppet:///modules/repo/gemrepo.conf",
        require => Package["apache2-mpm-worker"],
        notify  => Service["apache2"],
    }

    file { "/etc/apache2/sites-enabled/gemrepo":
        ensure  => symlink,
        target  => "/etc/apache2/sites-available/gemrepo",
        require => File["/etc/apache2/sites-available/gemrepo"],
        notify  => Service["apache2"],
    }

    file { "/var/gemrepo":
        ensure => directory,
    }
}
```

2. Create the file /etc/puppet/modules/repo/files/gemrepo.conf with the following contents:

```
<VirtualHost *:80>
    ServerAdmin john@bitfieldconsulting.com
    ServerName gems.bitfieldconsulting.com
    ErrorLog logs/gems.bitfieldconsulting.com-error_log
    CustomLog logs/gems.bitfieldconsulting.com-access_log common

    Alias / /var/gemrepo/
    <Location />
        Options Indexes
    </Location>
</VirtualHost>
```

3. Add the following to your manifest:

```
node cookbook {
    include repo::gem-server
}
```

4. Run Puppet:

```
# puppet agent --test
info: Retrieving plugin
info: Caching catalog for cookbook.bitfieldconsulting.com
info: Applying configuration version '1304949279'
notice: /Stage[main]/Repo::Gem-server/File[/etc/apache2/
sites-available/gemrepo]/ensure: defined content as '{md5}
ae1fd948098f14503de02441d02a825d'
info: /Stage[main]/Repo::Gem-server/File[/etc/apache2/sites-
available/gemrepo]: Scheduling refresh of Service[apache2]
notice: /Stage[main]/Repo::Gem-server/File[/etc/apache2/sites-
enabled/gemrepo]/ensure: created
info: /Stage[main]/Repo::Gem-server/File[/etc/apache2/sites-
enabled/gemrepo]: Scheduling refresh of Service[apache2]
notice: /Stage[main]/Apache/Service[apache2]: Triggered 'refresh'
from 2 events
notice: /Stage[main]/Repo::Gem-server/File[/var/gemrepo]/ensure:
created
notice: Finished catalog run in 6.52 seconds
```

How it works...

The principle is exactly the same as in the APT repository example. We define a directory where the gem repository will live, and a virtual host definition in Apache to enable it to serve requests for `gems.bitfieldconsulting.com`.

There's more...

Again, your gem repository will be more useful if you put something in it. We'll find out how to do that in the following text. We will also show you how to configure your nodes to access the gem repository.

Adding gems

Adding new gems to your repository is simple. Put the gem file in `/var/gemrepo/gems` and run this command in the `/var/gemrepo` directory:

```
# gem generate_index
```

Using the gem repo

As with the APT repository, make sure that your nodes know about the hostname `gems.bitfieldconsulting.com`, either by deploying a host entry with Puppet, or configuring it in DNS.

Then you can specify a package in Puppet as follows:

```
package { "json":
    provider => "gem",
    source => "http://gems.bitfieldconsulting.com ",
}
```

Building packages automatically from source

Tarballs can seriously damage your health. While using a **distro** or third-party package, or rolling your own package is always preferable to building software from source, sometimes it has to be done. Creating Debian packages (or any other flavor of packages) can be a lengthy and error-prone process, and there may not always be the time or budget available to do this.

If you have to build a program from source, Puppet can at least help with this process. The general procedure is to automate what you would otherwise do manually:

► Download the source **tarball**

► Unpack the tarball

► Configure and build the program

► Install the program

In this example we'll build **OpenSSL** from source (though for production you should use the distro package, but it makes a useful demonstration).

How to do it...

1. Add the following to your manifest:

```
exec { "build-openssl":
    cwd        => "/root",
    command    => "/usr/bin/wget ftp://ftp.openssl.org/source/
    openssl-0.9.8p.tar.gz && /bin/tar xvzf openssl-0.9.8p.tar.
    gz && cd openssl-0.9.8p && ./Configure linux-generic32 &&
    make install",
    creates    => "/usr/local/ssl/bin/openssl",
    logoutput => on_failure,
    timeout    => 0,
}
```

2. Run Puppet (it may take a while!):

```
# puppet agent --test
info: Retrieving plugin
info: Caching catalog for cookbook.bitfieldconsulting.com
info: Applying configuration version '1304954159'
notice: /Stage[main]//Node[cookbook]/Exec[build-openssl]/returns:
executed successfully
notice: Finished catalog run in 554.00 seconds
```

How it works...

The `exec` command is in five separate stages, delimited by `&&` operators. This means that should any sub-command fail, the whole command will stop and fail. It's a useful construct where you want to make sure each sub-command has succeeded before going on to the next.

1. The first stage downloads the source tarball:

   ```
   /usr/bin/wget ftp://ftp.openssl.org/source/openssl-0.9.8p.tar.gz
   ```

2. The second stage unpacks it:

   ```
   /bin/tar xvzf openssl-0.9.8p.tar.gz
   ```

3. The third stage changes working directory to the source tree:

   ```
   cd openssl-0.9.8p
   ```

4. The fourth stage runs the configure script (this is usually where you will need to specify any options or customizations):

   ```
   ./Configure linux-generic32
   ```

5. The final stage builds and installs the software:

   ```
   make install
   ```

6. So that this lengthy process isn't run every time Puppet runs, we specify a file that the build creates:

   ```
   creates   => "/usr/local/ssl/bin/openssl",
   ```

   If you need to force a rebuild for whatever reason, remove this file.

7. Things don't always compile first time. In case of problems, we specify the `logoutput` parameter which will show us what the build process is complaining about:

   ```
   logoutput => on_failure,
   ```

8. Finally, because the compilation may take a while, we set a zero `timeout` parameter (Puppet times out `exec` commands after 5 minutes by default):

   ```
   timeout   => 0,
   ```

There's more...

If you have to build quite a few packages from source, it may be worth converting the preceding recipe into a `define` function, so that you can use more or less the same code to build each package.

Comparing package versions

Package version numbers are odd things. They look like decimal numbers, but they're not —a version number is often in the form `2.6.4`, for example. If you need to compare one version number with another, you can't do a straightforward string comparison: `2.6.4` would be interpreted as greater than `2.6.12`. A numeric comparison won't work because they're not valid numbers.

Puppet's `versioncmp` function comes to the rescue. If you pass it two things that look like version numbers, it will compare them and return a value indicating which is the greater:

```
versioncmp( A, B )
```
returns the following:

- ▶ 0 if A and B are equal
- ▶ Greater than 1 if A is higher than B
- ▶ Less than 0 if A is less than B

How to do it...

1. Add the following to your manifest:

```
$app_version = "1.2.2"
$min_version = "1.2.10"

if versioncmp( $app_version, $min_version ) >= 0 {
    notify { "Version OK": }
} else {
    notify { "Upgrade needed": }
}
```

2. Run Puppet:

   notice: Upgrade needed

3. Now change the value of `$app_version`:

```
$app_version = "1.2.14"
```

4. Run Puppet again:

   notice: Version OK

How it works...

We've specified that the minimum acceptable version ($min_version) is 1.2.10. So in the preceding example, we want to compare it with an $app_version of 1.2.2. A simple alphabetic comparison of these two strings (in Ruby, for example) would give the wrong result, but versioncmp correctly determines that 1.2.2 is less than 1.2.10 and alerts us that we need to upgrade.

In the second example, $app_version is now 1.2.14 which versioncmp correctly recognizes as greater than $min_version and so we get the message Version OK.

6
Users and Virtual Resources

"How good the design is doesn't matter near as much as whether the design is getting better or worse. If it is getting better, day by day, I can live with it forever. If it is getting worse, I will die." — Kent Beck

In this chapter, we will cover the following topics:

- ▶ Using virtual resources
- ▶ Managing users with virtual resources
- ▶ Managing users' SSH access
- ▶ Managing users' customization files
- ▶ Efficiently distributing cron jobs
- ▶ Running a command when a file is updated
- ▶ Using host resources
- ▶ Using multiple file sources
- ▶ Distributing directory trees
- ▶ Cleaning up old files
- ▶ Using schedules with resources
- ▶ Auditing resources
- ▶ Temporarily disabling resources
- ▶ Managing timezones

Users can be a real pain. I don't mean the people, though doubtless that's sometimes true. But keeping UNIX user accounts and file permissions in sync across a network of machines, some of them running different operating systems, can be very challenging without some kind of centralized configuration management.

Consider a situation where a new developer has joined the organization. He needs an account on every machine along with `sudo` privileges and group memberships, and also needs his SSH key authorized for a bunch of different accounts. The sysadmin who has to take care of this manually, will be at the job all day. A sysadmin who uses Puppet will be done in minutes, heading out for an early lunch.

In this chapter, we'll look at some handy patterns and techniques for managing users and their associated resources. We'll also see how to schedule resources in Puppet, how to spread cron jobs around the clock for efficiency, how to handle time zones and `/etc/hosts` entries, and how to have Puppet collect audit data, so you know when someone's messing with your machines.

Using virtual resources

What are virtual resources and why do we need them? Let's look at a typical situation, where virtual resources might come in useful.

You are responsible for two applications, `facesquare` and `twitstagram`. Both are web apps running on Apache. The definition for `facesquare` might look something like the following:

```
class app::facesquare
{
    package { "apache2-mpm-worker": ensure => installed }

}
```

The definition for `twitstagram` might look like the following:

```
class app::twitstagram
{
    package { "apache2-mpm-worker": ensure => installed }

}
```

All is well until you need to consolidate both apps onto a single server as follows:

```
node micawber
{
    include app::facesquare
    include app::twitstagram
}
```

Now Puppet will complain, because you tried to define two resources with the same name: `apache2-mpm-worker`. The following error will be shown:

```
err: Could not retrieve catalog from remote server: Error 400 on SERVER:
Duplicate definition: Package[apache2-mpm-worker] is already defined in
file /etc/puppet/modules/app/manifests/facesquare.pp at line 2; cannot
redefine at /etc/puppet/modules/app/manifests/twitstagram.pp:2 on node
cookbook.bitfieldconsulting.com
```

You could remove the duplicate package definition from one of the classes, but then it would fail if you tried to include the app class on another server that didn't already have Apache.

You can get round this problem by putting the Apache package in its own class and then using `include apache`; Puppet doesn't mind you including the same class multiple times. But this has the disadvantage that every potentially conflicting resource must have its own class.

Virtual resources to the rescue. A virtual resource is just like a normal resource, except that it starts with an @ character, shown as follows:

```
@package { "apache2-mpm-worker": ensure => installed }
```

You can think of it as being like an 'FYI' resource: I'm just telling you about this resource, and I don't actually want you to do anything with it yet. Puppet will read and remember virtual resource definitions, but won't actually create the resource until you say so.

To create the resource, use the `realize` function as follows:

```
realize( Package["apache2-mpm-worker"] )
```

You can call `realize` as many times as you want on the resource and it won't result in a conflict. So, virtual resources are the way to go when several different classes all require the same resource and they may need to co-exist on the same node.

How to do it...

1. Create a new module app:

    ```
    # mkdir -p /etc/puppet/modules/app/manifests
    ```

2. Create the file `/etc/puppet/modules/app/manifests/facesquare.pp` with the following contents:

```
class app::facesquare
{
    realize( Package["apache2-mpm-worker"] )
}
```

3. Create the file `/etc/puppet/modules/app/manifests/twitstagram.pp` with the following contents:

```
class app::twitstagram
{
    realize( Package["apache2-mpm-worker"] )
}
```

4. Create the file `/etc/puppet/modules/admin/manifests/virtual-packages.pp` with the following contents:

```
class admin::virtual-packages
{
    @package { "apache2-mpm-worker": ensure => installed }
}
```

5. Include the following on the node:

```
node cookbook
{
    include admin::virtual-packages
    include app::facesquare
    include app::twitstagram
}
```

6. Run Puppet.

How it works...

You define the package as a virtual resource in one place, the `admin::virtual-packages` class. All nodes can include this class and you can put all your virtual packages in it. None of them will actually be installed on a node, until you call `realize`:

```
class admin::virtual-packages
{
    @package { "apache2-mpm-worker": ensure => installed }
}
```

Every class that needs the Apache package can call `realize` on the following virtual resource:

```
class app::twitstagram
{
    realize( Package["apache2-mpm-worker"] )
}
```

Puppet knows that because you made the resource virtual, you intended multiple references to the same package, and didn't just accidentally create two resources with the same name. So, it does the right thing.

There's more...

To realize virtual resources, you can also use the **collection** syntax:

```
Package <| title = "apache2-mpm-worker" |>
```

The advantage of this syntax is that you're not restricted to the resource name; you could also use a tag, for example:

```
Package <| tag = "security" |>
```

Or, you can just specify all instances of the resource type, by leaving the query section blank as follows:

```
Package <| |>
```

See also

Managing users with virtual resources in this chapter.

Managing users with virtual resources

Users are an excellent example of where virtual resources can come in handy. Consider the following setup. You have three users: John, Graham, and Steven. To simplify administration of a large number of machines, you have defined classes for two kinds of users: developers and sysadmins. All machines need to include sysadmins, but only some machines need developer access:

```
node server
{
    include user::sysadmins
}
```

```
node webserver inherits server
{
    include user::developers
}
```

John is a sysadmin, and Steven is a developer, but Graham is both, so Graham needs to be in both groups. This will cause a conflict on a web server as we end up with two definitions of the user Graham.

To avoid this situation, it's common practice to make all users virtual, defined in a single class `user::virtual`, which every machine includes, and then realizing the users where they are needed.

How to do it...

1. Create a user module as follows:

   ```
   # mkdir -p /etc/puppet/modules/user/manifests
   ```

2. Create the file `/etc/puppet/modules/user/manifests/virtual.pp` with the following contents:

   ```
   class user::virtual
   {
       @user { "john": }
       @user { "graham": }
       @user { "steven": }
   }
   ```

3. Create the file `/etc/puppet/modules/user/manifests/developers.pp` with the following contents:

   ```
   class user::developers
   {
       realize( User["graham"],
                User["steven"] )
   }
   ```

4. Create the file `/etc/puppet/modules/user/manifests/sysadmins.pp` with the following contents:

   ```
   class user::sysadmins
   {
       realize( User["john"],
                User["graham"] )
   }
   ```

5. Add the following to a node:

```
include user::virtual
include user::sysadmins
include user::developers
```

6. Run Puppet:

```
# puppet agent --test
info: Retrieving plugin
info: Caching catalog for cookbook.bitfieldconsulting.com
info: Applying configuration version '1305554239'
notice: /Stage[main]/User::Virtual/User[john]/ensure: created
notice: /Stage[main]/User::Virtual/User[steven]/ensure: created
notice: /Stage[main]/User::Virtual/User[graham]/ensure: created
notice: Finished catalog run in 2.36 seconds
```

How it works...

Every node should include the `user::virtual` class, as part of your basic housekeeping configuration, which is inherited by all servers. This class will define all users in your organization or site. This should also include any users who exist only to run applications or services (such as, `apache` or `git`, for example).

You can then organise your users into groups (not in the sense of UNIX groups, but perhaps as different teams or job roles) such as `developers` and `sysadmins`. The class for a group will `realize` whichever users are included in it, shown as follows:

```
class user::sysadmins
{
    realize( User["john"],
             User["graham"] )
}
```

You can then include these groups wherever they are needed, without worrying about conflicts caused by multiple definitions of the same user.

See also

▶ *Using virtual resources* in this chapter.
▶ *Managing users' customization files* in this chapter.

Managing users' SSH access

The only secure server is one that's turned off. Nonetheless, a good approach to access control for servers is to use named user accounts with passphrase-protected SSH keys, rather than having users share an account with a widely-known password. Puppet makes this easy to manage, thanks to the built-in `ssh_authorized_key` type.

To combine this with virtual users, as described in the previous section, you can create a `define`, which includes both the `user` and the `ssh_authorized_key`. This will also be useful for adding customization files and other per-user resources.

How to do it...

1. Change the `user::virtual` class that you created in the section on managing users with virtual resources, to the following:

```
class user::virtual
{
    define ssh_user( $key )
    {
        user { $name:
            ensure     => present,
            managehome => true,
            }

        ssh_authorized_key { "${name}_key":
            key  => $key,
            type => "ssh-rsa",
            user => $name,
                        }
    }

    @ssh_user { "phil":
        key => "AAAAB3NzaC1yc2EAAAABIwAAAIEA3ATqENg+GW
        ACa2BzeqTdGnJhNoBer8x6pfWkzNzeM8Zx7/2Tf2pl7kHdbsiT
        XEUawqzXZQtZzt/j3Oya+PZjcRpWNRzprSmd2UxEEPTqDw9LqY5S2B8og/
        NyzWaIYPsKoatcgC7VgYHplcTbzEhGu8BsoEVBGYu3IRy5RkAcZik=",
                    }
    }
}
```

2. Include the following on a node:

```
realize( User::Virtual::Ssh_user["phil"] )
```

3. Run Puppet:

```
# puppet agent --test
info: Retrieving plugin
info: Caching catalog for cookbook.bitfieldconsulting.com
info: Applying configuration version '1305561740'
notice: /Stage[main]/User::Virtual/User::Virtual::Ssh_user[phil]/
User[phil]/ensure: created
notice: /Stage[main]/User::Virtual/User::Virtual::Ssh_user[phil]/
Ssh_authorized_key[phil_key]/ensure: created
notice: Finished catalog run in 1.04 seconds
```

How it works...

We've created a new define called ssh_user, which includes both the user resource itself, and the associated ssh_authorized_key, shown as follows:

```
define ssh_user( $key )
{
    user { $name:
        ensure      => present,
        managehome => true,
        }

    ssh_authorized_key { "${name}_key":
        key  => $key,
        type => "ssh-rsa",
        user => $name,
                }
}
```

Then we create a virtual instance of ssh_user for the user phil:

```
@ssh_user { "phil":
    key => "AAAAB3NzaC1yc2EAAAABIwAAAIEA3ATqENg+GWACa
    2BzeqTdGnJhNoBer8x6pfWkzNzeM8Zx7/2Tf2pl7kHdbsiTXEUawq
    zXZQtZzt/j3Oya+PZjcRpWNRzprSmd2UxEEPTqDw9LqY5S2B8og/
    NyzWaIYPsKoatcgC7VgYHplcTbzEhGu8BsoEVBGYu3IRy5RkAcZik=",
}
```

Recall that because the resource is virtual, Puppet will take note of it but won't actually create anything until realize is called.

Finally, we added the following to the node:

```
realize( User::Virtual::Ssh_user["phil"] )
```

This actually creates the user and the authorized_keys file containing the user's public key.

There's more...

To use this idea with the organization of users into group classes that we saw in the previous section, modify the classes like the following:

```
class user::sysadmins
{
    search User::Virtual

    realize( Ssh_user["john"],
             Ssh_user["graham"] )
}
```

The `search, User::Virtual` is just to save on clutter; it allows you to refer to `Ssh_user` directly without prefixing it with `User::Virtual::` every time.

You may get an error like the following:

```
err: /Stage[main]/User::Virtual/User::Virtual::Ssh_user[graham]/Ssh_
authorized_key[graham_key]: Could not evaluate: No such file or directory
- /home/graham/.ssh
```

It may be because you previously created the `graham` user without having Puppet manage the home directory. In this situation, Puppet will not automatically create the `.ssh` directory for the `authorized_keys` file. Run the following command:

```
# userdel graham
```

To fix the problem, run Puppet again.

Managing users' customization files

Users, like cats, often feel the need to mark their territory. Unlike cats, users tend to customize their shell environments, terminal colors, aliases, and so on. This is usually achieved by a number of dotfiles in their home directory: for example, `.bash_profile`.

You can add this to your Puppet-based user management by modifying the `user::virtual::ssh_user` class, so that it can optionally include any dotfiles that are present in the Puppet repository.

How to do it...

1. Modify the `user::virtual` class as follows:

```
class user::virtual
{
    define user_dotfile( $username )
```

```
        {
            file { "/home/${username}/.${name}":
                source => "puppet:///modules/user/${username}-
                ${name}",
                owner  => $username,
                group => $username,
            }
    }

    define ssh_user( $key, $dotfile = false )
    {
        user { $name:
            ensure     => present,
            managehome => true,
            }

        ssh_authorized_key { "${name}_key":
            key  => $key,
            type => "ssh-rsa",
            user => $name,
                    }

        if $dotfile {
            user_dotfile { $dotfile:
                username => $name,
                    }
                }
    }

    @ssh_user { "john":
        key     => "AAAAB3NzaC1yc2EAAAABIwAAAIEA3ATqENg
        +GWACa2BzeqTdGnJhNoBer8x6pfWkzNzeM8Zx7/2Tf2pl7kHdbsi
        TXEUawqzXZQtZzt/j3Oya+PZjcRpWNRzprSmd2UxEEPTqDw9LqY5S2B8
        og/NyzWaIYPsKoatcgC7VgYHplcTbzEhGu8BsoEVBGYu3IRy5RkAcZik=",
        dotfile => [ "bashrc", "bash_profile" ],
                }
    }
```

2. Create the file `/etc/puppet/modules/user/files/john-bashrc` with the following contents:

   ```
   export PATH=$PATH:/var/lib/gems/1.8/bin
   ```

3. Create the file `/etc/puppet/modules/user/files/john-bash_profile` with the following contents:

   ```
   . ~/.bashrc
   ```

4. Run Puppet.

How it works...

We've added a new define, user_dotfile. This will be called once for each dotfile that the user wants to have. In the example, john has two dotfiles: .bashrc and .bash_profile. These are declared as follows:

```
@ssh_user { "john":
    key     => ...
    dotfile => [ "bashrc", "bash_profile" ],
}
```

You can supply either a single dotfile, or a list of them in array form, as shown previously.

For each dotfile, user_dotfile will look for a corresponding source file in the modules/user/files directory. For example, with the bashrc dotfile, Puppet will look for the following:

```
modules/user/files/john-bashrc
```

This will be copied to the node as the following:

```
/home/john/.bashrc
```

See also

Managing users with virtual resources in this chapter.

Efficiently distributing cron jobs

When you have many servers executing the same cron job, it's usually a good idea not to run them all at the same time. If all the jobs access a common server, it may put too much load on that server, and even if they don't, all the servers will be busy at the same time, which may affect their capacity to provide other services.

Puppet's inline_template function allows us to use some Ruby logic to set different runtimes for the job, depending on the hostname.

How to do it...

1. Add the following to a node:

```
define cron_random( $command, $hour )
{
    cron { $name:
        command => $command,
```

```
            minute  => inline_template("<%= (hostname+name).hash.abs %
            60 %>"),
            hour    => $hour,
            ensure  => "present",
            }
    }

    cron_random { "hello-world":
        command => "/bin/echo 'Hello world'",
        hour => 2,
    }

    cron_random { "hello-world-2":
        command => "/bin/echo 'Hello world'",
        hour => 1,
    }
```

2. Run Puppet:

    ```
    # puppet agent --test

    info: Retrieving plugin

    info: Caching catalog for cookbook.bitfieldconsulting.com

    info: Applying configuration version '1305713506'

    notice: /Stage[main]//Node[cookbook]/Cron_random[hello-world]/
    Cron[hello-world]/ensure: created

    notice: /Stage[main]//Node[cookbook]/Cron_random[hello-world-2]/
    Cron[hello-world-2]/ensure: created

    notice: Finished catalog run in 1.07 seconds
    ```

3. Check the crontab to see how the jobs have been configured:

    ```
    # crontab -l

    # HEADER: This file was autogenerated at Fri Jul 29 10:58:45 +0000
    2011 by puppet.

    # HEADER: While it can still be managed manually, it is definitely
    not recommended.

    # HEADER: Note particularly that the comments starting with
    'Puppet Name' should

    # HEADER: not be deleted, as doing so could cause duplicate cron
    jobs.

    # Puppet Name: hello-world

    25 2 * * * /bin/echo 'Hello world'

    # Puppet Name: hello-world-2

    49 1 * * * /bin/echo 'Hello world'
    ```

How it works...

We want to choose a 'random' minute for each cron job; that is, not genuinely random (or it would change every time Puppet runs), but more or less guaranteed to be different for each cron job on each host.

We can do this by using Ruby's `hash` method, which computes a numerical value from any object, in this case a `string`. The value will be the same each time, so although the value looks random, it will not change when Puppet runs again.

`hash` will generate a large integer, and we want values between 0 and 59, so we use the Ruby `%` (modulo) operator to restrict the result to this range. Although there are only 60 possible values, the `hash` function is designed to produce as uniform an output as possible, so there should be very few collisions and the `minute` values should be well-distributed.

We want the value to be different on different machines, so we use the hostname in computing the `hash` value. However, we also want the value to be different for different jobs on the same machine, so we combine the hostname with the `name` variable, which will be the name of the cron job (`hello-world`, for example).

There's more...

In this example, we only randomized the `minute` of the cron job, and supplied the `hour` as part of the definition. If you sometimes need to specify the day of the week as well, you could add it as an optional parameter for `cron_random` with a default value, shown as follows:

```
define cron_random( $command, $hour, $weekday = "*" ) {
```

If you also wanted to randomize the hour (for example, for jobs that could run at any time of the day and need to be distributed across all 24 hours evenly) you could modify `cron_random` as follows:

```
hour    => inline_template("<%= (hostname+name).hash.abs % 24 %>"),
```

See also

Running Puppet from cron in *Chapter 1*.

Running a command when a file is updated

It's a very common pattern to have Puppet take some action whenever a particular file is updated. For example, in the `rsync` config snippet example, each snippet file called an `exec` to update the main `rsyncd.conf` file when it changed.

An `exec` resource will normally be run every time Puppet runs, unless you specify one of the following parameters:

- `creates`
- `onlyif`
- `unless`
- `refreshonly => true`

The `refreshonly` parameter means that the `exec` should only be run if it receives a `notify` from another resource (such as a file, for example).

Getting ready...

Install the `nginx` package (actually, we just want the stock config file, but this is the easiest way to get it):

```
# apt-get install nginx
```

How to do it...

1. Create a new module `nginx` with the usual directory structure as follows:

   ```
   # mkdir /etc/puppet/modules/nginx
   # mkdir /etc/puppet/modules/nginx/files
   # mkdir /etc/puppet/modules/nginx/manifests
   ```

2. Create the file `/etc/puppet/modules/nginx/manifests/nginx.pp` with the following contents:

   ```
   class nginx {
       package { "nginx": ensure => installed }

       service { "nginx":
           enable => true,
           ensure => running,
       }

       exec { "reload nginx":
           command      => "/usr/sbin/service nginx reload",
           require      => Package["nginx"],
           refreshonly => true,
       }

       file { "/etc/nginx/nginx.conf":
           source  => "puppet:///modules/nginx/nginx.conf",
           notify  => Exec["reload nginx"],
           require => Package["nginx"],
       }
   }
   ```

3. Copy the `nginx.conf` file into the new module:

   cp /etc/nginx/nginx.conf /etc/puppet/modules/nginx/files

4. Add the following to your manifest:

   ```
   include nginx
   ```

5. Make a test change to Puppet's copy of the `nginx.conf` file:

   # echo \# >>/etc/puppet/modules/nginx/files/nginx.conf

6. Run Puppet:

   ```
   # puppet agent --test
   info: Retrieving plugin
   info: Caching catalog for cookbook.bitfieldconsulting.com
   info: Applying configuration version '1303745502'
   --- /etc/nginx/nginx.conf    2010-02-15 00:16:47.000000000 -0700
   +++ /tmp/puppet-file20110425-31239-158xcst-0      2011-04-25
   09:39:49.586322042 -0600
   @@ -48,3 +48,4 @@
    #          proxy      on;
    #      }
    # }
   +#
   info: FileBucket adding /etc/nginx/nginx.conf as {md5}7bf139588b5e
   cd5956f986c9c1442d44
   info: /Stage[main]/Nginx/File[/etc/nginx/nginx.conf]:
   Filebucketed /etc/nginx/nginx.conf to puppet with sum
   7bf139588b5ecd5956f986c9c1442d44
   notice: /Stage[main]/Nginx/File[/etc/nginx/nginx.conf]/content:
   content changed '{md5}7bf139588b5ecd5956f986c9c1442d44' to '{md5}
   d28d08925174c3f6917a78797c4cd3cc'
   info: /Stage[main]/Nginx/File[/etc/nginx/nginx.conf]: Scheduling
   refresh of Exec[reload nginx]
   notice: /Stage[main]/Nginx/Exec[reload nginx]: Triggered 'refresh'
   from 1 events
   notice: Finished catalog run in 1.69 seconds
   ```

How it works...

With most services, you'd simply define a service resource, which gets a `notify` from the `config` file. This causes Puppet to restart the service, so that it can pick up the changes.

However, nginx sometimes doesn't restart properly, especially when restarted by Puppet, and so I cooked up this remedy for one site to have Puppet run /etc/init.d/nginx reload instead of restarting it. Here's how it works.

The exec resource has the refreshonly parameter set to true as follows:

```
exec { "reload nginx":
    command      => "/usr/sbin/service nginx reload",
    require      => Package["nginx"],
    refreshonly => true,
    }
```

So, it will only run if it receives a notify.

The config file resource supplies the necessary notify if it's changed:

```
file { "/etc/nginx/nginx.conf":
    source  => "puppet:///modules/nginx/nginx.conf",
    notify  => Exec["reload nginx"],
    }
```

Whenever Puppet needs to update this file, it will also run the exec, which will call the following command to pick up the changes.:

/usr/sbin/service nginx reload

If a service supports the reload command, this will send the daemon a signal to re-read its config files without interrupting service.

In fact, in this example, it would be better to define a new restart command for the nginx service, such as the following:

```
service { "nginx":
    restart => "/etc/init.d/nginx reload",
}
```

But I wanted to share with you some real code that I wrote which demonstrates the notify -> Exec technique, and at the time either I didn't know about restart or it didn't exist yet. As a general pattern, though, you'll find it useful for any situation, where an action needs to be taken when a file is updated.

There's more...

You can use a similar pattern anywhere some action needs to be taken every time a resource is updated. Possible uses might include the following:

▶ Triggering service reloads

▶ Running a syntax check before restarting a service

 ▶ Concatenating `config` snippets
 ▶ Running tests
 ▶ Chaining execs

If you have several commands that all need to be run when a single file is updated, it might be easier to have all the commands `subscribe` to the file, rather than have the file `notify` the commands. The effect is the same.

Using host resources

"I am not a number." — Number Six, "The Prisoner"

It's a common practice to move machines around, especially on cloud infrastructure, so the IP of a particular machine may change quite often. Because of this, it's obviously a bad idea to hard-code IP addresses into your configuration. Where one machine needs to access another, for example, an app server accessing a database server: it's better to use a hostname than an IP address.

But how to map names to IP addresses? This is often done with DNS, but small organizations may not have a DNS server, and large organizations may make it so time-consuming and bureaucratic to implement DNS changes that no one bothers. Also, DNS information can propagate to machines at different times, so to ensure quick and consistent address updates, one approach is to use local `/etc/hosts` entries, controlled by Puppet.

How to do it...

1. Add the following to your manifest:

```
host { "www.bitfieldconsulting.com":
    ip      => "109.74.195.241",
    target => "/etc/hosts",
    ensure => present,
}
```

2. Run Puppet:

```
# puppet agent --test
info: Retrieving plugin
info: Caching catalog for cookbook.bitfieldconsulting.com
info: Applying configuration version '1305716418'
notice: /Stage[main]//Node[cookbook]/Host[www.bitfieldconsulting.
com]/ensure: created
info: FileBucket adding /etc/hosts as {md5}977bf5811de978b7f041301
9e77b4abe
notice: Finished catalog run in 0.21 seconds
```

How it works...

Puppet will check the target file to see if the host entry already exists, and if not, add it, or if it exists with a different address, Puppet will update it.

Although there are other possible targets than /etc/hosts, this is the default, and the only one you're likely to need. I think it's a good practice to specify it explicitly even so, as relying on default behavior has a tendency to make the code fragile.

There's more...

Organizing your host resources into classes can be helpful. For example, you could put the host resources for all your DB servers into one class called admin::dbhosts, which is included by all web servers.

When machines may need to be defined in multiple classes (for example, a database server might also be a repository server), virtual resources can solve this problem. For example, you could define all your hosts as virtual in a single class as follows:

```
class admin::allhosts
{
    @host { "db1.bitfieldconsulting.com":}
}
```

Then realize the hosts that you need in the various classes:

```
class admin::dbhosts
{
    realize( Host["db1.bitfieldconsulting.com"] )
}

class admin::repohosts
{
    realize( Host["db1.bitfieldconsulting.com"] )
}
```

Using multiple file sources

A neat feature of Puppet's file resource is that you can specify multiple sources for the file. Puppet will look for each of them in order. If the first isn't found, it moves on to the next, and so on. You can use this to specify a default substitute if the particular file isn't present, or even a series of increasingly generic substitutes.

How to do it...

1. Add the following class to your manifest:

```
class mysql::app-config( $app )
{
    file { "/etc/my.cnf":
        source  => [ "puppet:///modules/admin/${app}.my.cnf",
                     "puppet:///modules/admin/generic.my.cnf", ],
    }
}
```

2. Create the file /etc/puppet/modules/admin/files/minutespace.my.cnf with the following contents:

   # MinuteSpace config file

3. Create the file /etc/puppet/modules/admin/files/generic.my.cnf with the following contents:

   # Generic config file

4. Add the following to a node:

```
class { "mysql::app-config": app => "minutespace" }
```

5. Run Puppet:

   # puppet agent --test

   info: Retrieving plugin

   info: Caching catalog for cookbook.bitfieldconsulting.com

   info: Applying configuration version '1305897071'

   notice: /Stage[main]/Mysql::App-config/File[/etc/my.cnf]/ensure: defined content as '{md5}24f04b960f4d33c70449fbc4d9f708b6'

   notice: Finished catalog run in 0.35 seconds

6. Check that Puppet has deployed the app-specific config file:

   # cat /etc/my.cnf

   # MinuteSpace config file

7. Now change the node definition to:

```
class { "mysql::app-config": app => "shreddit" }
```

8. Run Puppet again:

   # puppet agent --test

   info: Retrieving plugin

   info: Caching catalog for cookbook.bitfieldconsulting.com

```
info: Applying configuration version '1305897864'

--- /etc/my.cnf 2011-05-20 13:17:56.006239489 +0000

+++ /tmp/puppet-file20110520-15575-1icobgs-0      2011-05-20
13:24:25.030296062 +0000

@@ -1 +1 @@

-# MinuteSpace config file

+# Generic config file

info: FileBucket adding /etc/my.cnf as {md5}24f04b960f4d33c70449fb
c4d9f708b6

info: /Stage[main]/Mysql::App-config/File[/etc/
my.cnf]: Filebucketed /etc/my.cnf to puppet with sum
24f04b960f4d33c70449fbc4d9f708b6

notice: /Stage[main]/Mysql::App-config/File[/etc/my.cnf]/content:
content changed '{md5}24f04b960f4d33c70449fbc4d9f708b6' to '{md5}
b3a6e744c3ab78dfb20e46ff55f6c33c'

notice: Finished catalog run in 0.93 seconds
```

How it works...

We've defined the /etc/my.cnf file as having two sources that are as follows:

```
file { "/etc/my.cnf":
    source  => [ "puppet:///modules/admin/${app}.my.cnf",
                 "puppet:///modules/admin/generic.my.cnf", ],
    }
```

The value of $app will be passed in by anyone using the class. In the first example, we passed in a value of minutespace:

```
class { "mysql::app-config": app => "minutespace" }
```

Puppet will look first of all for modules/admin/files/minutespace.my.cnf. This file exists, so it will be used. So far, so normal.

Then we change the value of app to shreddit. Puppet now looks for modules/admin/files/shreddit.my.cnf. This doesn't exist, so Puppet tries the next listed source: modules/admin/files/generic.my.cnf. This does exist, so it will be deployed.

There's more...

You can use this trick anywhere you have a `file` resource. For example, some nodes might need machine-specific `config`, but not others, so you could do something like the following:

```
file { "/etc/stuff.cfg":
    source => [ "puppet:///modules/stuff/${hostname}.cfg",
                "puppet:///modules/stuff/generic.cfg" ],
    }
```

Then you put the normal configuration in `generic.cfg`. If machine `cartman` needs a special `config`, just put it in the file `cartman.cfg`. This will be used in preference to the `generic` file, because it is listed first in the array of sources.

See also

Passing parameters to classes in *Chapter 4*.

Distributing directory trees

"To understand recursion, you must first understand recursion." — Saying

When you find yourself deploying several files with Puppet, all to the same directory, it might be worth considering a recursive file resource instead. If you set the `recurse` parameter on a directory, Puppet will copy the directory to the node along with its contents and all its subdirectories, shown as follows:

```
file { "/usr/lib/nagios/plugins/custom":
    source => "puppet:///modules/nagios/plugins",
    require => Package["nagios-plugins"],
    recurse => true,
    }
```

How to do it...

1. Create a suitable directory tree in the Puppet repository as follows:

    ```
    # mkdir /etc/puppet/modules/admin/files/tree
    # mkdir /etc/puppet/modules/admin/files/tree/a
    # mkdir /etc/puppet/modules/admin/files/tree/b
    # mkdir /etc/puppet/modules/admin/files/tree/c
    # mkdir /etc/puppet/modules/admin/files/tree/a/1
    ```

2. Add the following to your manifest:

```
file { "/tmp/tree":
    source  => "puppet:///modules/admin/tree",
    recurse => true,
    }
```

3. Run Puppet:

```
# puppet agent --test
info: Retrieving plugin
info: Caching catalog for cookbook.bitfieldconsulting.com
info: Applying configuration version '1304768523'
notice: /Stage[main]//Node[cookbook]/File[/tmp/tree]/ensure:
created
notice: /File[/tmp/tree/a]/ensure: created
notice: /File[/tmp/tree/a/1]/ensure: created
notice: /File[/tmp/tree/b]/ensure: created
notice: /File[/tmp/tree/c]/ensure: created
notice: Finished catalog run in 1.25 seconds
```

How it works...

If a `file` resource has the `recurse` parameter set on it, and if it is a directory, then Puppet will deploy not only the directory itself, but all its contents (including subdirectories and their contents). This is a great way to put a whole tree of files onto a node, or to quickly create a large number of paths using a single resource.

There's more...

Sometimes, you want to deploy files to an existing directory, but remove any files that aren't managed by Puppet. For example, in Ubuntu's `/etc/apt/sources.list.d` directory, you might want to make sure that there are no files present that don't come from Puppet.

The `purge` parameter will do this for you. Define the directory as a resource in Puppet:

```
file { "/etc/apt/sources.list.d":
    ensure  => directory,
    recurse => true,
    purge   => true,
    }
```

The combination of `recurse` and `purge` will remove all files and subdirectories in `/etc/apt/sources.list.d` that are not deployed by Puppet. You can then deploy your own files to that location using a separate resource as follows:

```
file { "/etc/apt/sources.list.d/bitfield.list":
    content => "deb http://packages.bitfieldconsulting.com/ lucid
    main\n",
    }
```

If there are subdirectories, which contain files you don't want to `purge`, just define the subdirectory as a Puppet resource, and it will be left alone:

```
file { "/etc/exim4/conf.d/acl":
    ensure => directory,
    }
```

 Be aware that, at least in current implementations of Puppet, recursive file copies can be quite slow and place a heavy memory load on the server. If the data doesn't change very often, it might be better to deploy a tarball instead.

Cleaning up old files

We all have to clean house once in a while. Puppet's `tidy` resource will help you clean up old or out-of-date files, reducing disk usage. For example, if you have Puppet reporting enabled as described in the section on generating reports, you might want to regularly delete old report files.

How to do it...

1. Add the following to your manifest:

```
tidy { "/var/lib/puppet/reports":
    age     => "1w",
    recurse => true,
    }
```

2. Run Puppet:

```
# puppet agent --test

info: Retrieving plugin info: Caching catalog for cookbook.
bitfieldconsulting.com

notice: /Stage[main]//Node[cookbook]/Tidy[/var/lib/puppet/
reports]: Tidying File[/var/lib/puppet/reports/cookbook.
bitfieldconsulting.com/201102241546.yaml]
```

```
notice: /Stage[main]//Node[cookbook]/Tidy[/var/lib/puppet/
reports]: Tidying File[/var/lib/puppet/reports/cookbook.
bitfieldconsulting.com/20110214727.yaml]

...

info: Applying configuration version '1306149187'

notice: /File[/var/lib/puppet/reports/cookbook.bitfieldconsulting.
com/201102241546.yaml]/ensure: removed

notice: /File[/var/lib/puppet/reports/cookbook.bitfieldconsulting.
com/201102141727.yaml]/ensure: removed ...

notice: Finished catalog run in 1.48 seconds
```

How it works...

Puppet searches the specified path for any files matching the `age` parameter: in this case, `1w` (one week). It also searches subdirectories (`recurse => true`).

Any files matching your criteria will be deleted.

There's more...

You can specify file ages in seconds, minutes, hours, days, or weeks, by using a single character to specify the time unit, like the following:

```
60s
180m
24h
30d
4w
```

You can specify that files greater than a given size should be removed, such as the following:

```
size => "100m",
```

This removes files of 100 megabytes and over. For kilobytes, use `k`, and for bytes, use `b`.

> Please note that if you specify both `age` and `size` parameters, they are treated as independent criteria. For example, if you specify the following files, then Puppet will remove all files older than one day, or over 512KB in size.
> ```
> age  => "1d",
> size => "512k",
> ```

Using schedules with resources

Using a `schedule` resource, you can control when other resources get applied. For example, the built-in `daily` schedule does what you'd expect: if you specify a resource, such as the following, then it'll be applied once a day:

```
exec { "/usr/bin/apt-get update":
    schedule => daily,
    }
```

The slightly tricky thing about `schedule` is that it doesn't guarantee that the resource will be applied once a day. It's just a limit: the resource won't be applied more than once a day. When and whether the resource is applied at all will depend on when and whether Puppet runs.

That being so, `schedule` is best used to restrict other resources, for example, you might want to make sure that `apt-get update` hasn't run more than once an hour, or that a maintenance job doesn't run during daytime production hours.

For this, you will need to create your own `schedule` resources.

How to do it...

1. Add the following to your manifest:

```
schedule { "not-in-office-hours":
    period => daily,
    range  => [ "17:00-23:59", "00:00-09:00" ],
    repeat => 1,
        }

exec { "/bin/echo Doing maintenance!":
    schedule => "not-in-office-hours",
    }
```

2. Run Puppet.

How it works...

We've created a `schedule` called `not-in-office-hours`, which specifies the repetition period as `daily`, and the allowable time range as after 5 p.m., or before 9 a.m. as follows:

```
period => daily,
range  => [ "17:00-23:59", "00:00-09:00" ],
```

We've also said that the maximum number of times a resource can be applied in one period is once:

```
repeat => 1,
```

Now, we apply that schedule to an `exec` resource as follows:

```
exec { "/bin/echo Doing maintenance!":
    schedule => "not-in-office-hours",
    }
```

Without the `schedule` parameter, this resource would run every time Puppet runs. Now, Puppet will check the `not-in-office-hours` schedule to see the following:

▶ Whether the time is in the permitted range

▶ Whether the resource has been run the maximum permitted number of times in this period

For example, let's consider what happens if Puppet runs every hour, on the following hours:

▶ 4 p.m.: It's outside the permitted time range, so Puppet will do nothing.

▶ 5 p.m.: It's inside the permitted time range, and the resource hasn't been run yet in this period, so Puppet will apply the resource.

▶ 6 p.m.: It's inside the permitted time range, but the resource has already been run once, so it has reached its maximum `repeat` count. Puppet will do nothing.

And so on until the next day.

There's more...

You can increase the `repeat` parameter if you want to, for example, run a job no more than 6 times an hour:

```
period => hourly,
repeat => 6,
```

Remember that this won't guarantee that the job will run 6 times an hour. It just sets an upper limit. No matter how often Puppet runs or anything else happens, the job won't run if it has already run 6 times this hour. If Puppet only runs once a day, the job will just be run once. So, `schedule` is best used for making sure that things **don't** happen at certain times (or don't exceed a given frequency).

Auditing resources

Not every problem has a technical answer. I once had to diagnose a server that was failing to respond to `ping`, SSH, or console connections. I wasn't sure whether it was a hardware or a network failure.

The mystery was solved when I called the site where the machine was located. They informed me that two unidentified men had arrived earlier, gone straight to the server room, unplugged the machine, and simply walked out of the building with it. We later found that there had been a spate of computer thefts in the area with the same M.O.

The message here is that it's good to know who's doing what to your servers.

Dry-run mode, using the `--noop` switch, is a simple way to audit any changes to a machine under Puppet's control. However, Puppet also has a dedicated audit feature, which can report changes to resources or specific attributes.

How to do it...

Define a resource with the `audit` metaparameter as follows:

```
file { "/etc/passwd":
    audit => [ owner, mode ],
      }
```

How it works...

The `audit` metaparameter (a **metaparameter** is a parameter which can be applied to any resource, not just to specific types) tells Puppet that you want to record and monitor certain things about the resource. The value can be a list of the parameters you want to audit.

In this case, when Puppet runs, it will now record the owner and mode of the `/etc/passwd` file. If either of these change, for example, if you run:

`# chmod 666 /etc/passwd`

Puppet will pick up this change and log it on the next run:

```
notice: /Stage[main]//Node[cookbook]/File[/etc/passwd]/mode: audit
change: previously recorded value 644 has been changed to 666
```

There's more...

This feature is very useful for auditing large networks for any changes to the machines, either malicious or accidental. You can use the `tagmail` reports feature to automatically send audit change notices by e-mail. It's also very handy for keeping an eye on things that aren't managed by Puppet, for example application code on production servers. You can read more about Puppet's auditing capability here: `http://www.puppetlabs.com/blog/all-about-auditing-with-puppet/`.

If you just want to audit everything about a resource, use the following:

```
file { "/etc/passwd":
    audit => all,
    }
```

See also

▶ *Dry-running your Puppet manifests* in *Chapter 2*
▶ *E-mailing log messages containing specific tags* in *Chapter 2*

Temporarily disabling resources

Sometimes, you want to disable a resource for the time being, so that it doesn't interfere with other work. For example, you might want to tweak a configuration file on the server, until you have the exact settings you want, before checking it into Puppet. You don't want Puppet to overwrite it with an old version in the meantime, so you can set the `noop` metaparameter on the resource as follows:

```
noop => true,
```

How to do it...

1. Add the following to your manifest:

   ```
   file { "/tmp/test.cfg":
       content => "Hello, world!\n",
       noop => true,
       }
   ```

2. Run Puppet:

   ```
   # puppet agent --test
   info: Retrieving plugin
   info: Caching catalog for cookbook.bitfieldconsulting.com
   ```

```
info: Applying configuration version '1306159566'

notice: /Stage[main]//Node[cookbook]/File[/tmp/test.cfg]/ensure:
is absent, should be file (noop)

notice: Finished catalog run in 0.53 seconds
```

3. Now, remove the `noop` parameter:

```
file { "/tmp/test.cfg":
    content => "Hello, world!\n",
    }
```

4. Run Puppet again:

```
# puppet agent --test

info: Retrieving plugin

info: Caching catalog for cookbook.bitfieldconsulting.com

info: Applying configuration version '1306159705'

notice: /Stage[main]//Node[cookbook]/File[/tmp/test.cfg]/ensure:
defined content as '{md5}746308829575e17c3331bbcb00c0898b'

notice: Finished catalog run in 0.52 seconds
```

How it works...

The first time we ran Puppet, the `noop` metaparameter was set to `true`, so for this particular resource, it's as if you had run Puppet with the `--noop` flag. Puppet noted that the resource would have been applied, but otherwise did nothing.

In the second case, with `noop` removed, the resource is applied as normal.

Managing timezones

"I try to take one day at a time, but sometimes several days attack at once."
— Ashleigh Brilliant

Sooner or later, you'll encounter a weird problem, which you'll eventually track down to servers having different time zones. It's wise to avoid this kind of issue by making sure that all your servers use the same time zone, whatever their geographical location (GMT is the logical choice).

Unless a server is solar powered, I can't think of any reason for it to care about the time zone it's in.

How to do it...

1. Create the file /etc/puppet/modules/admin/manifests/gmt.pp with the following contents:

```
class admin::gmt
{
    file { "/etc/localtime":
        ensure => link,
        target => "/usr/share/zoneinfo/GMT",
        }
}
```

2. Add the following to all nodes:

```
include admin::gmt
```

3. Run Puppet:

```
# puppet agent --test
info: Retrieving plugin
info: Caching catalog for cookbook.bitfieldconsulting.com
info: Applying configuration version '1304955158'
info: FileBucket adding /etc/localtime as {md5}02b73b0cf0d96e2f75c
ae56b178bf58e
info: /Stage[main]/Admin::Gmt/File[/etc/localtime]: Filebucketed /
etc/localtime to puppet with sum 02b73b0cf0d96e2f75cae56b178bf58e
notice: /Stage[main]/Admin::Gmt/File[/etc/localtime]/ensure:
ensure changed 'file' to 'link'
notice: Finished catalog run in 1.94 seconds
```

There's more...

If you want to use a different timezone, choose the appropriate file in /usr/share/zoneinfo: for example, US/Eastern.

7
Applications

"The best software in the world only sucks. The worst software is significantly worse than that."—Luke Kanies

In this chapter we will cover the following topics:

- ▶ Managing Apache servers
- ▶ Creating Apache virtual hosts
- ▶ Creating Nginx virtual hosts
- ▶ Creating MySQL databases and users
- ▶ Managing Drupal sites
- ▶ Managing Rails applications

Without applications, a server is just a very expensive space heater. This chapter will present some recipes for managing some specific applications with Puppet: MySQL, Apache, Nginx, Rails, and Drupal. These are very popular applications, so they should be useful to you in themselves. However, the patterns and techniques they use are applicable to almost any software, so you can adapt them to your own purposes without much difficulty.

Managing Apache servers

Apache is a popular web server, except with those who have to configure it. Puppet can ease the pain of managing Apache servers to a certain extent.

How to do it...

1. Create an Apache module, if you don't have one:

```
# mkdir /etc/puppet/modules/apache
# mkdir /etc/puppet/modules/apache/templates
# mkdir /etc/puppet/modules/apache/manifests
```

2. Create the file /etc/puppet/modules/apache/manifests/init.pp with the following contents:

```
class apache {
    package { "apache2-mpm-prefork": ensure => installed }

    service { "apache2":
        enable  => true,
        ensure  => running,
        require => Package["apache2-mpm-prefork"],
    }

    file { "/etc/apache2/logs":
        ensure  => directory,
        require => Package["apache2-mpm-prefork"],
    }

    file { "/etc/apache2/conf.d/name-based-vhosts.conf":
        content => "NameVirtualHost *:80",
        require => Package["apache2-mpm-prefork"],
        notify  => Service["apache2"],
    }
}
```

3. Add the following code to a node:

```
include apache
```

4. Run Puppet:

```
# puppet agent --test
info: Retrieving plugin
info: Caching catalog for cookbook.bitfieldconsulting.com
info: Applying configuration version '1309189590'
notice: /Stage[main]/Apache/Package[apache2-mpm-prefork]/ensure:
ensure changed 'purged' to 'present'
notice: /Stage[main]/Apache/File[/etc/apache2/logs]/ensure:
created
```

```
notice: /Stage[main]/Apache/File[/etc/apache2/conf.d/name-based-
vhosts.conf]/ensure: defined content as '{md5}78465aacbd01eb537b94
1b21ae0af8b8'
info: /Stage[main]/Apache/File[/etc/apache2/conf.d/name-based-
vhosts.conf]: Scheduling refresh of Service[apache2]
notice: Finished catalog run in 39.45 seconds
```

There's more...

In the next section, we'll look at how to create virtual host definitions for Apache. However, you may find that you need special configuration options for the Apache server as a whole. You could set these by deploying `apache2.conf` with Puppet, but it's neater to put a config snippet into `/etc/apache2/conf.d`. For example, you could add the following to `init.pp`:

```
define snippet() {
    file { "/etc/apache2/conf.d/${name}":
        source => "puppet:///modules/apache/${name}",
        notify => Service["apache2"],
    }
}
```

and include the following code snippet on a node:

```
apache::snippet { "site-specific.conf": }
```

Creating Apache virtual hosts

Virtual hosts are a great application for ERB templates, because they generally use similar boilerplate code for every instance, with just one or two variables. Obviously, for certain sites or applications you will need specific options in the virtual host definition, and this template won't apply - but it should save you some trouble for simple sites.

How to do it...

1. Add this to `/etc/puppet/modules/apache/manifests/init.pp`:

```
define site( $sitedomain = "", $documentroot = "" ) {
    include apache

    if $sitedomain == "" {
        $vhost_domain = $name
    } else {
        $vhost_domain = $sitedomain
    }
```

```
        if $documentroot == "" {
            $vhost_root = "/var/www/${name}"
        } else {
            $vhost_root = $documentroot
        }

        file { "/etc/apache2/sites-available/${vhost_domain}.
        conf":
            content => template("apache/vhost.erb"),
            require => File["/etc/apache2/conf.d/name-based-
            vhosts.conf"],
            notify  => Exec["enable-${vhost_domain}-vhost"],
        }

        exec { "enable-${vhost_domain}-vhost":
            command     => "/usr/sbin/a2ensite ${vhost_domain}.
            conf",
            require     => [ File["/etc/apache2/sites-
            available/${vhost_domain}.conf"], Package["apache2-
mpm-prefork"] ],
            refreshonly => true,
            notify      => Service["apache2"],
        }
    }
```

2. Create the file `/etc/puppet/modules/apache/templates/vhost.erb` with the following contents:

```
<VirtualHost *:80>
    ServerName <%= vhost_domain %>
    ServerAdmin admin@<%= vhost_domain %>
    DocumentRoot <%= vhost_root %>
    ErrorLog logs/<%= vhost_domain %>-error_log
    CustomLog logs/<%= vhost_domain %>-access_log common

    <Directory /var/www/<%= vhost_domain %>>
        Allow from all
        Options +Includes +Indexes +FollowSymLinks
        AllowOverride all
    </Directory>
</VirtualHost>

<VirtualHost *:80>
    ServerName www.<%= vhost_domain %>
    Redirect 301 / http://<%= vhost_domain %>/
</VirtualHost>
```

3. Add this to a node:

```
        apache::site { "keithlard.com": }
```

4. Run Puppet:

```
# puppet agent --test
info: Retrieving plugin
info: Caching catalog for cookbook.bitfieldconsulting.com
info: Applying configuration version '1309190720'
notice: /Stage[main]//Node[cookbook]/Apache::Site[keithlard.com]/
File[/etc/apache2/sites-available/keithlard.com.conf]/ensure:
defined content as '{md5}f2a558c02beeaed4beb7da250821b663'
info: /Stage[main]//Node[cookbook]/Apache::Site[keithlard.com]/
File[/etc/apache2/sites-available/keithlard.com.conf]: Scheduling
refresh of Exec[enable-keithlard.com-vhost]
notice: /Stage[main]//Node[cookbook]/Apache::Site[keithlard.com]/
Exec[enable-keithlard.com-vhost]: Triggered 'refresh' from 1
events
info: /Stage[main]//Node[cookbook]/Apache::Site[keithlard.
com]/Exec[enable-keithlard.com-vhost]: Scheduling refresh of
Service[apache2]
notice: /Stage[main]/Apache/Service[apache2]: Triggered 'refresh'
from 2 events
notice: Finished catalog run in 3.79 seconds
```

How it works...

The `define` function `apache::site` uses the `vhost.erb` template to generate an Apache virtual host definition. By default, the domain of the site is assumed to be the same as the name of the site instance, in this case, `keithlard.com`. So when Puppet sees the following:

```
apache::site { "keithlard.com": }
```

it will use `keithlard.com` as the site domain. If you want to specify a domain, add the `sitedomain` parameter:

```
apache::site { "networkr_production":
    sitedomain => "networkr.com",
}

apache::site { "networkr_staging":
    sitedomain => "staging.networkr.com",
}
```

The beauty of the template system is that if you want to make a slight change to the configuration for all sites (for example, changing the admin e-mail address) you can do it once in the template and Puppet will update all virtual hosts accordingly.

Similarly, if you need to specify a different `DocumentRoot` for the virtual host than the default (`/var/www/${name}`), just add a `documentroot` parameter as follows:

```
apache::site { "communitysafety.org":
    documentroot => "/var/apps/commsafe",
}
```

There's more...

In the preceding example, we only used one variable in the template, but you can have as many as you like. These can also be **facts** such as:

```
ServerName <%= fqdn %>
```

or Ruby expressions:

```
ServerAdmin<%= emails["admin"] %>
```

or any Ruby code you want such as:

```
ServerAdmin <%= vhost_domain == 'coldcomfort.com' ? 'seth@coldcomfort.
com' : 'flora@poste.com' %>
```

See also

> ▶ *Using array iteration in templates* in *Chapter 5*

Creating Nginx virtual hosts

Nginx is a fast, lightweight web server that has replaced Apache in many contexts, especially for running web applications. However, the configuration language is not a great improvement in clarity over Apache's. Also, much of the documentation is only available in Russian, which explains why you see so many copies around of "Understanding Russian for Nginx Administrators".

Getting ready...

You'll need the Nginx module we used in the section, *Running a command when a file is updated*. You'll also need to turn off the Apache server if you created one in the section on *Managing Apache servers* in this chapter using the following command:

```
# service apache2 stop
```

How to do it...

1. Add this to `/etc/puppet/modules/nginx/manifests/init.pp`:

```
define site( $sitedomain = "" ) {
    include nginx

    if $sitedomain == "" {
        $vhost_domain = $name
    } else {
        $vhost_domain = $sitedomain
    }

    file { "/etc/nginx/sites-available/${vhost_domain}.conf":
        content => template("nginx/vhost.erb"),
        require => Package["nginx"],
    }

    file { "/etc/nginx/sites-enabled/${vhost_domain}.conf":
        ensure  => link,
        target  => "/etc/nginx/sites-available/${vhost_domain}.
        conf",
        require => File["/etc/nginx/sites-available/${vhost_
        domain}.conf"],
        notify  => Exec["reload nginx"],
    }
}
```

2. Create the file `/etc/puppet/modules/nginx/templates/vhost.erb` with the following contents:

```
server {
    listen 80;
    server_name <%= vhost_domain %>;

    access_log /var/log/nginx/<%= vhost_domain %>-access_log;
    root /var/www/<%= vhost_domain %>;
}
```

3. Create the directory `/var/www/bbqrecipes.com` and place an `index.html` file in it with a suitable message such as:

```
Welcome to the BBQ Recipes site!
```

4. Add the following to a node:

```
nginx::site { "bbqrecipes.com": }
```

5. Run Puppet:

```
# puppet agent -test

info: Retrieving plugin info: Caching catalog for cookbook.
bitfieldconsulting.com info: Applying configuration version
'1309198476'

notice: /Stage[main]/Nginx/Package[nginx]/ensure: ensure changed
'purged' to 'present'

notice: /Stage[main]//Node[cookbook]/Nginx::Site[bbqrecipes.com]/
File[/etc/nginx/sites-available/bbqrecipes.com.conf]/ensure:
defined content as '{md5}fa92d2e7543b378e26827a063be34a31'

notice: /Stage[main]//Node[cookbook]/Nginx::Site[bbqrecipes.com]/
File[/etc/nginx/sites-enabled/bbqrecipes.com.conf]/ensure: created

info: /Stage[main]//Node[cookbook]/Nginx::Site[bbqrecipes.com]/
File[/etc/nginx/sites-enabled/bbqrecipes.com]: Scheduling refresh
of Exec[reload nginx]

notice: /Stage[main]/Nginx/Service[nginx]/ensure: ensure changed
'stopped' to 'running'

notice: /Stage[main]/Nginx/Exec[reload nginx]: Triggered 'refresh'
from 1 event

notice: Finished catalog run in 21.45 seconds
```

How it works...

Puppet inserts the site domain into the boilerplate code in the template file via the variable vhost_domain. This is all Nginx needs to know in order to respond to requests on the domain and serve files from the appropriate root directory in the file system.

There's more...

Unlike Apache, Nginx doesn't support dynamic modules (yet). This means if you want to add support for some special feature that isn't included by default, you need to recompile Nginx yourself. The right thing would be to build Nginx with the options that you want, and then create a package from this that you can serve from your own repository (as described in the section, *Setting up an APT package repository*).

However, some Puppet administrators skip this step and simply pull down and build the Nginx source on the target server. To do this, use an exec with a similar pattern to that in the section on 'Building packages automatically from source'. In an Agile development environment, which often means one where the management changes its mind about the product every few days, this kind of approach can be quicker and cheaper than continually repackaging.

▶ *Managing Rails applications* in this chapter

Creating MySQL databases and users

MySQL is a very widely used database server, and it's fairly certain you'll need to install and configure a MySQL server at some point. This recipe will show you how to do that, as well as how to automatically create databases and users for applications.

Getting ready...

1. If you don't already have a MySQL module, let's create one:

   ```
   # mkdir /etc/puppet/modules/mysql
   # mkdir /etc/puppet/modules/manifests
   # mkdir /etc/puppet/modules/files
   ```

2. Create the file `/etc/puppet/modules/mysql/manifests/server.pp` with the following contents:

   ```
   class mysql::server {
       package { "mysql-server": ensure => installed }

       service { "mysql":
           enable => true,
           ensure => running,
           require => Package["mysql-server"],
       }

       file { "/etc/mysql/my.cnf":
           owner   => "mysql", group => "mysql",
           source  => "puppet:///mysql/my.cnf",
           notify  => Service["mysql"],
           require => Package["mysql-server"],
       }

       exec { "set-mysql-password":
           unless => "/usr/bin/mysqladmin -uroot -p${mysql_password}
           status",
           command => "/usr/bin/mysqladmin -uroot password ${mysql_
           password}",
           require => Service["mysql"],
       }
   }
   ```

3. Create the file `/etc/puppet/modules/mysql/files/my.cnf` with the following contents:

```
[client]
port        = 3306
socket      = /var/run/mysqld/mysqld.sock

[mysqld_safe]
socket      = /var/run/mysqld/mysqld.sock
nice        = 0

[mysqld]
user        = mysql
socket      = /var/run/mysqld/mysqld.sock
port        = 3306
datadir     = /var/lib/mysql

!includedir /etc/mysql/conf.d/
```

4. Add this to `/etc/puppet/manifests/site.pp`:

```
$mysql_password = "secret"
```

5. Run Puppet:

```
# puppet agent --test
info: Retrieving plugin
info: Caching catalog for cookbook.bitfieldconsulting.com
info: Applying configuration version '1309448283'
notice: /Stage[main]/Mysql::Server/Package[mysql-server]/ensure:
ensure changed 'purged' to 'present'
notice: /Stage[main]/Mysql::Server/File[/etc/mysql/my.cnf]/owner:
owner changed 'root' to 'mysql'
notice: /Stage[main]/Mysql::Server/File[/etc/mysql/my.cnf]/group:
group changed 'root' to 'mysql'
info: /Stage[main]/Mysql::Server/File[/etc/mysql/my.cnf]:
Scheduling refresh of Service[mysql]
info: /Stage[main]/Mysql::Server/File[/etc/mysql/my.cnf]:
Scheduling refresh of Service[mysql]
notice: /Stage[main]/Mysql::Server/Service[mysql]/enable: enable
changed 'false' to 'true'
notice: /Stage[main]/Mysql::Server/Service[mysql]: Triggered
'refresh' from 2 events
notice: Finished catalog run in 61.78 seconds
```

How to do it...

1. Add the following to `/etc/puppet/modules/mysql/manifests/server.pp`:

```
define db( $user, $password ) {
    include mysql::server

    exec { "create-${name}-db":
        unless  => "/usr/bin/mysql -u${user} -p${password}
        ${name}",
        command => "/usr/bin/mysql -uroot -p${mysql_password} -e
        \"create database ${name}; grant all on ${name}.* to
        ${user}@localhost identified by '$password'; flush
        privileges;\"",
        require => Service["mysql"],
    }
}
```

2. Add this to a node as follows:

```
mysql::server::db { "johnstest":
    user => "john",
    password => "johnstest",
}
```

3. Run Puppet:

```
# puppet agent --test
info: Retrieving plugin
info: Caching catalog for cookbook.bitfieldconsulting.com
info: Applying configuration version '1309449259'
notice: /Stage[main]//Node[cookbook]/Mysql::Server::Db[johnstest]/
Exec[create-johnstest-db]/returns: executed successfully
notice: Finished catalog run in 1.61 seconds
```

4. Check that the database has been created with the correct user and permissions:

```
# mysql -ujohn -pjohnstest johnstest
Reading table information for completion of table and column names
You can turn off this feature to get a quicker startup with -A

Welcome to the MySQL monitor.  Commands end with ; or \g.
Your MySQL connection id is 36
Server version: 5.1.41-3ubuntu12.10 (Ubuntu)

Type 'help;' or '\h' for help. Type '\c' to clear the current
input statement.

mysql>
```

How it works...

The `mysql::server` class installs and configures MySQL with a root password that you can set in your `site.pp` file. The `define` function, `mysql::server::db` allows us to create a database with a given name, and an associated MySQL user that can access the database. For example, a typical web application might have a database named after the application, and a special username the application will use to log in to the database.

There's more...

To create more databases, just add more `mysql::server::db` instances:

```
mysql::server::db { [ "test1", "test2", "test3" ] :
    user => "john",
    password => "johnstest",
}
```

Managing Drupal sites

Drupal is a content management system that lets you build websites quickly by plugging together canned modules, and makes it relatively easy for users to create and edit their own content. It's particularly suited to management with Puppet because there is a powerful command-line tool, `drush`, which you can use to install and manage Drupal sites.

If we combine the automation power of `drush` with the recipes that we already created for MySQL databases and Apache virtual hosts, we can build a recipe that installs everything necessary for a Drupal site with a single resource.

Getting ready...

1. Create a new `drupal` module as follows:

   ```
   # mkdir /etc/puppet/modules/drupal
   # mkdir /etc/puppet/modules/drupal/manifests
   ```

2. Create the file `/etc/puppet/modules/drupal/manifests/init.pp` with the following contents:

   ```
   class drupal {
       $drupalversion = "7.2"

       exec { "download-drush":
           cwd     => "/root",
           command => "/usr/bin/wget http://ftp.drupal.org/files/
           projects/drush-7.x-4.4.tar.gz  ",
           creates => "/root/drush-7.x-4.4.tar.gz",
   ```

```
        require => Package["php5-mysql"],
    }

    exec { "install-drush":
        cwd     => "/usr/local",
        command => "/bin/tar xvzf /root/drush-7.x-4.4.tar.gz",
        creates => "/usr/local/drush",
        require => Exec["download-drush"],
    }

    file { "/usr/local/bin/drush":
        ensure  => link,
        target  => "/usr/local/drush/drush",
        require => Exec["install-drush"],
    }

    exec { "install-drupal":
        cwd     => "/var/www",
        command => "/usr/local/drush/drush dl drupal-
        ${drupalversion}",
        creates => "/var/www/drupal-${drupalversion}",
        require => Exec["install-drush"],
    }

    file { "/var/www/drupal":
        ensure  => link,
        target  => "/var/www/drupal-${drupalversion}",
        require => Exec["install-drupal"],
    }

    package { [ "libapache2-mod-php5",
                "php5-mysql" ]: ensure => installed }

    exec { "enable-mod-php5":
        command => "/usr/bin/a2enmod php5",
        creates => "/etc/apache2/mods-enabled/php5.conf",
        require => Package["libapache2-mod-php5"],
    }
}
```

How to do it...

1. Add the following to `init.pp` within the `drupal` class:

```
define site( $password, $sitedomain = "" ) {
    include drupal

    if $sitedomain == "" {
        $drupal_domain = $name
```

```
    } else {
        $drupal_domain = $sitedomain
    }

    $dbname = regsubst( $drupal_domain, "\.", "" )
    mysql::server::db { $dbname:
        user     => $dbname,
        password => $password,
    }

    exec { "site-install-${name}":
        cwd       => "/var/www/drupal",
        command   => "/usr/local/bin/drush site-install -y --site-
        name=${name} --sites-subdir=${drupal_domain} --db-url=mysq
        l://${dbname}:${password}@localhost/${dbname}",
        creates   => "/var/www/drupal/sites/${drupal_domain}",
        require   => [ File["/var/www/drupal"], Exec["install-
        drupal"], Mysql::Server::Db[$dbname] ],
        logoutput => on_failure,
    }

    apache::site { $drupal_domain:
        documentroot => "/var/www/drupal",
    }
}
```

2. Add the following to a node:

```
drupal::site { "crispinfo.com":
    password    => "crunch",
}
```

3. Run Puppet:

```
# puppet agent --test

info: Retrieving plugin

info: Caching catalog for cookbook.bitfieldconsulting.com

info: Applying configuration version '1309783783'

notice: /Stage[main]//Node[cookbook]/Drupal::Site[crispinfo.com]/
Mysql::Server::Db[crispinfocom]/Exec[create-crispinfocom-db]/
returns: executed successfully

notice: /Stage[main]//Node[cookbook]/Drupal::Site[crispinfo.com]/
Apache::Site[crispinfo.com]/File[/etc/apache2/sites-available/
crispinfo.com.conf]/ensure: defined content as '{md5}15c5bbffa6128
fce0b8a3996914af549'
```

```
info: /Stage[main]//Node[cookbook]/Drupal::Site[crispinfo.com]/
Apache::Site[crispinfo.com]/File[/etc/apache2/sites-available/
crispinfo.com.conf]: Scheduling refresh of Exec[enable-crispinfo.
com-vhost]
```

```
notice: /Stage[main]//Node[cookbook]/Drupal::Site[crispinfo.com]/
Apache::Site[crispinfo.com]/Exec[enable-crispinfo.com-vhost]:
Triggered 'refresh' from 1 events
```

```
info: /Stage[main]//Node[cookbook]/Drupal::Site[crispinfo.com]/
Apache::Site[crispinfo.com]/Exec[enable-crispinfo.com-vhost]:
Scheduling refresh of Service[apache2]
```

```
notice: /Stage[main]/Apache/Service[apache2]: Triggered 'refresh'
from 1 events
```

```
notice: /Stage[main]//Node[cookbook]/Drupal::Site[crispinfo.com]/
Exec[site-install-crispinfo.com]/returns: executed successfully
```

```
notice: Finished catalog run in 22.51 seconds
```

4. Create an `/etc/hosts` entry pointing `crispinfo.com` to the node you're using (if it's not already set in DNS) as follows:

```
10.0.2.15    crispinfo.com
```

5. Check the site in a web browser to make sure everything has been properly created. You should see the Drupal login prompt as shown in the following screenshot:

The default administrator login created by `drush site-install` is username `admin` and password `admin`. Obviously you should set a stronger password for production sites (see the `drush` documentation for how to do this on the command line).

How it works...

Magic! Specifically—the `drupal` class first installs `drush`, and then uses it to install the Drupal core code (you can change the version used by altering the value of `$drupalversion`).

The `drupal::sitedefine` runs `drush site-install` for each site you want to create. In our example, we created a site called `crispinfo.com` and passed in the database password; `drush` does the rest.

`drupal::site` also creates the necessary **Apache vhost** for our site (using the recipe *Creating Apache virtual hosts* in this chapter) and a MySQL database (using the recipe *Creating MySQL databases and users* in this chapter).

There's more...

`drush` can do a great deal to help you manage Drupal sites, including updating Drupal core code, installing modules and themes, managing users, and backing up your databases. You can find out more about `drush` at `http://drush.ws/`.

Managing Rails applications

Rails is an enormously popular web app framework (in the sense that it's widely used, rather than that people like it). So it's probable that you'll be called upon to manage it at some point. The recipe presented here contains most of what you'll need to prepare a server to have a Rails application installed on it. This recipe assumes that you'll be using Nginx and **Passenger** as the web server, though you can easily modify the recipe to use Apache instead.

How to do it...

1. Create the directory structure for a `rails` module:

   ```
   # mkdir /etc/puppet/modules/rails
   # mkdir /etc/puppet/modules/rails/manifests
   # mkdir /etc/puppet/modules/rails/templates
   # mkdir /etc/puppet/modules/rails/files
   ```

2. Create the file `/etc/puppet/modules/rails/manifests/init.pp` with the following contents:

```
class rails {
    include rails::passenger

    package { "bundler":
        provider => gem,
        ensure   => installed,
    }

    define app( $sitedomain ) {
        include rails

        file { "/opt/nginx/sites-available/${name}.conf":
          content => template("rails/app.conf.erb"),
          require => File["/opt/nginx/sites-available"],
        }

        file { "/opt/nginx/sites-enabled/${name}.conf":
          ensure   => link,
          target   => "/opt/nginx/sites-available/${name}.conf",
          require  => File["/opt/nginx/sites-enabled"],
          notify   => Exec["reload-nginx"],
        }

        file { "/opt/nginx/conf/includes/${name}.conf":
          source   => [ "puppet:///modules/rails/${name}.conf",
                        "puppet:///modules/rails/empty.conf" ],
          notify   => Exec["reload-nginx"],
        }

        file { [ "/var/www",
                 "/var/www/${name}",
                 "/var/www/${name}/releases",
                 "/var/www/${name}/shared",
                 "/var/www/${name}/shared/config",
                 "/var/www/${name}/shared/log",
                 "/var/www/${name}/shared/system" ]:
          ensure => directory,
          mode   => 775,
          owner  => "www-data",
          group  => "www-data",
        }
    }
}
```

3. Create the file `/etc/puppet/modules/rails/manifests/passenger.pp` with the following contents:

```
class rails::passenger {
    $passenger_version = "3.0.7"
    $passenger_dependencies = [ "build-essential",
                                "libcurl4-openssl-dev",
                                "libssl-dev",
                                "ruby",
                                "rubygems" ]

    package { $passenger_dependencies: ensure => installed }

    exec { "install-passenger":
        command => "/usr/bin/gem install passenger
        --version=${passenger_version}",
        unless  => "/usr/bin/gem list | /bin/grep passenger |/bin/
        grep ${passenger_version}",
        require => [ Package["rubygems"], Package[$passenger_
        dependencies] ],
        timeout => "-1",
    }

    exec { "install-passenger-nginx-module":
        command => "/usr/lib/ruby/gems/1.8/gems/passenger-
        ${passenger_version}/bin/passenger-install-nginx-module
        --auto --auto-download --prefix=/opt/nginx",
        creates => "/opt/nginx/sbin/nginx",
        require => Exec["install-passenger"],
        timeout => "-1",
    }

    file { [ "/opt/nginx",
             "/opt/nginx/conf",
             "/opt/nginx/conf/includes",
             "/opt/nginx/sites-enabled",
             "/opt/nginx/sites-available",
             "/var/log/nginx" ]:
        ensure  => directory,
        owner   => "www-data",
        group   => "www-data",
    }

    file { "/opt/nginx/sites-enabled/default":
        ensure  => absent,
        require => Exec["install-passenger-nginx-module"],
    }
```

```
        file { "/opt/nginx/conf/nginx.conf":
            content  => template("rails/nginx.conf.erb"),
            notify   => Exec["reload-nginx"],
            require  => Exec["install-passenger-nginx-module"],
        }

        file { "/etc/init.d/nginx":
            source  => "puppet:///modules/rails/nginx.init",
            mode    => "700",
            require => Exec["install-passenger-nginx-module"],
        }

        service { "nginx":
            enable  => true,
            ensure  => running,
            require => File["/etc/init.d/nginx"],
        }

        exec { "reload-nginx":
            command     => "/opt/nginx/sbin/nginx -t && /etc/init.d/
            nginx reload",
            refreshonly => true,
            require     => Exec["install-passenger-nginx-module"],
        }
    }
```

4. Create the file /etc/puppet/modules/rails/templates/app.conf.erb
    with the following contents:

```
server {
    listen 80;
    root /var/www/<%= name %>/current/public;
    server_name <%= sitedomain %>;
    access_log /var/log/nginx/<%= name %>.access.log;
    error_log /var/log/nginx/<%= name %>.error.log;

    passenger_enabled on;
    passenger_min_instances 1;
}

passenger_pre_start http://<%= sitedomain %>;
```

5. Create the file /etc/puppet/modules/rails/templates/nginx.conf.erb
    with the following contents:

```
events {
  worker_connections 1024;
  use epoll;
}
```

```
http {
  passenger_root /usr/lib/ruby/gems/1.8/gems/passenger-<%=
  passenger_version %>;

  server_names_hash_bucket_size 64;

  sendfile on;
  tcp_nopush   on;
  tcp_nodelay off;

  client_body_temp_path /var/spool/nginx-client-body 1 2;

  client_max_body_size 100m;

  include /opt/nginx/conf/mime.types;
  default_type application/octet-stream;

  log_format main '$remote_addr - $remote_user [$time_local] '
                  '"$request" $status $body_bytes_sent "$http_
                  referer" '
                  '"$http_user_agent" "$http_x_forwarded_for"' ;

  access_log /var/log/nginx/access.log main;

  gzip on;
  gzip_http_version 1.0;
  gzip_comp_level 2;
  gzip_proxied any;
  gzip_min_length  1100;
  gzip_buffers 16 8k;
  gzip_types text/plain text/html text/css application/x-
  javascript text/xml application/xml application/xml+rss text/
  javascript;
  gzip_disable "MSIE [1-6].(?!.*SV1)";
  gzip_vary on;

  include /opt/nginx/sites-enabled/*;
}
```

6. Create the file `/etc/puppet/modules/rails/files/nginx.init` with the following contents:

```
#!/bin/sh

### BEGIN INIT INFO
# Provides:          nginx
# Required-Start:    $all
# Required-Stop:     $all
```

```
# Default-Start:     2 3 4 5
# Default-Stop:      0 1 6
# Short-Description: starts the nginx web server
# Description:       starts nginx using start-stop-daemon
### END INIT INFO

PATH=/usr/local/sbin:/usr/local/bin:/sbin:/bin:/usr/sbin:/usr/bin
DAEMON=/opt/nginx/sbin/nginx
NAME=nginx
DESC=nginx

test -x $DAEMON || exit 0

# Include nginx defaults if available
if [ -f /etc/default/nginx ] ; then
    . /etc/default/nginx
fi

set -e

# Return LSB status, grabbed from a newer lsb-base
status_of_proc () {
    local pidfile daemon name status

    pidfile=
    OPTIND=1
    while getopts p: opt ; do
        case "$opt" in
            p)  pidfile="$OPTARG";;
        esac
    done
    shift $(($OPTIND - 1))

    if [ -n "$pidfile" ]; then
        pidfile="-p $pidfile"
    fi
    daemon="$1"
    name="$2"

    status="0"
    pidofproc $pidfile $daemon >/dev/null || status="$?"
    if [ "$status" = 0 ]; then
        log_success_msg "$name is running"
        return 0
    else
        log_failure_msg "$name is not running"
        return $status
    fi
}
```

```
. /lib/lsb/init-functions

case "$1" in
  start)
    echo -n "Starting $DESC: "
    start-stop-daemon --start --quiet --pidfile /var/run/$NAME.pid \
    --exec $DAEMON -- $DAEMON_OPTS || true
    echo "$NAME."
    ;;
  stop)
    echo -n "Stopping $DESC: "
    start-stop-daemon --stop --quiet --pidfile /var/run/$NAME.pid \
    --exec $DAEMON || true
    echo "$NAME."
    ;;
  restart|force-reload)
    echo -n "Restarting $DESC: "
    start-stop-daemon --stop --quiet --pidfile \
        /var/run/$NAME.pid --exec $DAEMON || true
    sleep 1
    start-stop-daemon --start --quiet --pidfile \
        /var/run/$NAME.pid --exec $DAEMON -- $DAEMON_OPTS || true
    echo "$NAME."
    ;;
  reload)
      echo -n "Reloading $DESC configuration: "
      start-stop-daemon --stop --signal HUP --quiet --pidfile /
      var/run/$NAME.pid \
          --exec $DAEMON || true
      echo "$NAME."
      ;;
  status)
      status_of_proc -p /var/run/$NAME.pid "$DAEMON" nginx && exit
      0 || exit $?
      ;;
  *)
    N=/etc/init.d/$NAME
    echo "Usage: $N {start|stop|restart|reload|force-
    reload|status}" >&2
    exit 1
    ;;
esac

exit 0
```

7. Add the following to a node:

```
rails::app { "furiouspigs":
    sitedomain => "furiouspigs.com",
}
```

8. Run Puppet:

```
# puppet agent --test

info: Retrieving plugin

info: Caching catalog for cookbook.bitfieldconsulting.com

info: Applying configuration version '1309960678'

notice: /Stage[main]/Rails::Passenger/File[/opt/nginx]/ensure:
created

notice: /Stage[main]/Rails::Passenger/File[/opt/nginx/sites-
enabled]/ensure: created

notice: /Stage[main]//Node[cookbook]/Rails::App[furiouspigs]/
File[/opt/nginx/sites-enabled/furiouspigs.conf]/ensure: created

notice: /Stage[main]/Rails::Passenger/File[/opt/nginx/conf]/
ensure: created

notice: /Stage[main]/Rails::Passenger/File[/opt/nginx/conf/
includes]/ensure: created

notice: /Stage[main]//Node[cookbook]/Rails::App[furiouspigs]/
File[/opt/nginx/conf/includes/furiouspigs.conf]/ensure: defined
content as '{md5}d41d8cd98f00b204e9800998ecf8427e'

notice: /Stage[main]/Rails::Passenger/File[/opt/nginx/sites-
available]/ensure: created

notice: /Stage[main]//Node[cookbook]/Rails::App[furiouspigs]/
File[/opt/nginx/sites-available/furiouspigs.conf]/ensure: defined
content as '{md5}c1a4c2bc4e7381b1c2f88dfee004a594'

notice: /Stage[main]/Rails::Passenger/Exec[install-passenger]/
returns: executed successfully

notice: /Stage[main]/Rails::Passenger/Exec[install-passenger-
nginx-module]/returns: executed successfully

--- /opt/nginx/conf/nginx.conf   2011-07-06 14:04:33.231999538
+0000

+++ /tmp/puppet-file20110706-5343-k8ouds-0   2011-07-06
14:04:34.246867124 +0000

...

info: /Stage[main]/Rails::Passenger/File[/opt/nginx/conf/nginx.
conf]: Filebucketed /opt/nginx/conf/nginx.conf to puppet with sum
34d60856b6570e9d59cd6eecde5da000
```

```
notice: /Stage[main]/Rails::Passenger/File[/opt/nginx/conf/nginx.
conf]/content: content changed '{md5}34d60856b6570e9d59cd6eecde5
da000' to '{md5}72132deeb45e6ee5b83cd246dffefc5f'

info: /Stage[main]/Rails::Passenger/File[/opt/nginx/conf/nginx.
conf]: Scheduling refresh of Exec[reload-nginx]

notice: /Stage[main]/Rails::Passenger/Exec[reload-nginx]:
Triggered 'refresh' from 1 events

notice: Finished catalog run in 398.73 seconds
```

How it works...

This is a longer and more complicated recipe than many in this book and hence is explained in greater detail. If you find this tiresome, just go ahead and use the recipe without worrying about how it works. You can come back to the explanation later when you want to learn more.

The aim of all the preceding code is to enable you to write this:

```
rails::app { "furiouspigs":
    sitedomain => "furiouspigs.com",
}
```

That requires quite a bit of work behind the scenes. We have to install Nginx with the Passenger module, configure it, add a virtual host for the application, include any application-specific configuration such as redirects and asset servers, install Ruby and Rubygems, Bundler, and create all the directories required for the application to be deployed.

Nginx and Passenger

Here's a breakdown of the `passenger.pp` file, that takes care of installing everything relating to Nginx and Passenger. It's worth recalling that Nginx doesn't have the concept of dynamic modules like Apache does, so you can't just install the distribution Nginx and some package that adds Passenger capability. Nginx has to be compiled together with any modules that you want to include in it.

Fortunately, the nice people at **Phusion** have provided a script to do that for us (`passenger-install-nginx-module`). Once you've installed the Passenger gem, this script will take care of the rest. So the first thing we need to do is install the Passenger **gem** as follows:

```
class rails::passenger {
    $passenger_version = "3.0.7"
    $passenger_dependencies = [ "build-essential",
                                "libcurl4-openssl-dev",
                                "libssl-dev",
                                "ruby",
                                "rubygems" ]
```

```
package { $passenger_dependencies: ensure => installed }

exec { "install-passenger":
    command => "/usr/bin/gem install passenger
    --version=${passenger_version}",
    unless  => "/usr/bin/gem list | /bin/grep passenger |/bin/grep
${passenger_version}",
    require => [ Package["rubygems"], Package[$passenger_
    dependencies] ],
    timeout => "-1",
}
```

We set the Passenger version to be installed in $passenger_version because Nginx needs to know the path where Passenger is installed, and that varies with the version number. So we will refer back to the $passenger_version variable in the template for nginx.conf.

The next step is to run the passenger-install-nginx-module script:

```
exec { "install-passenger-nginx-module":
    command => "/usr/lib/ruby/gems/1.8/gems/passenger-${passenger_
    version}/bin/passenger-install-nginx-module --auto --auto-
    download --prefix=/opt/nginx",
    creates => "/opt/nginx/sbin/nginx",
    require => Exec["install-passenger"],
    timeout => "-1",
}
```

> You'll notice that the path to the **gem** is hard-wired here to /usr/lib/
> ruby/gems/1.8/gems. That's a bit fragile—in most of my production
> infrastructures I use **RVM** for managing Ruby versions and **gemsets**, and
> that takes care of things like this. However, adding RVM makes this recipe
> even more complicated, so I've supplied it as a side dish, in the *There's
> more...* section. Once you're familiar with this recipe, you can start adapting it
> to your own purposes, including RVM integration.

It also means that this recipe won't work if you're using Ruby 1.9, which by the time you read this you may well be. If so, or if you run into other problems with this part of the recipe, just run gem contents passenger by hand and see where the passenger-install-nginx-module script ends up.

Next, we create some of the directory structure for the Nginx configuration files:

```
file { [ "/opt/nginx",
         "/opt/nginx/conf",
         "/opt/nginx/conf/includes",
```

```
        "/opt/nginx/sites-enabled",
        "/opt/nginx/sites-available",
        "/var/log/nginx" ]:
    ensure  => directory,
    owner   => "www-data",
    group   => "www-data",
}
```

We want to remove the default Nginx virtual host, which otherwise might interfere with the virtual hosts we're going to create. This is done as follows

```
file { "/opt/nginx/sites-enabled/default":
    ensure  => absent,
    require => Exec["install-passenger-nginx-module"],
}
```

In fact, this isn't necessary when you build Nginx from source, or via Passenger as we do here, but if you want to adapt this recipe to use the distribution Nginx package, this will come in useful.

Next is the main Nginx configuration file:

```
file { "/opt/nginx/conf/nginx.conf":
    content  => template("rails/nginx.conf.erb"),
    notify   => Exec["reload-nginx"],
    require  => Exec["install-passenger-nginx-module"],
}
```

This is made into a template in `nginx.conf.erb` because we need to insert the Passenger version we defined earlier on as follows:

```
passenger_root /usr/lib/ruby/gems/1.8/gems/passenger-<%= passenger_
version %>;
```

Otherwise, it's a reasonably standard Nginx configuration, and you can add in any special parameters that you might need for your server.

Because we're not using the distro package, we need to supply an `init` script (minimally adapted from the Ubuntu version):

```
file { "/etc/init.d/nginx":
    source  => "puppet:///modules/rails/nginx.init",
    mode    => "700",
    require => Exec["install-passenger-nginx-module"],
}
```

We want the Nginx service to run as follows:

```
service { "nginx":
    enable    => true,
    ensure    => running,
    require   => File["/etc/init.d/nginx"],
}
```

And to make sure broken configuration changes won't bring the server down, there's a configuration-check-and-reload resource that is notified by the configuration files:

```
exec { "reload-nginx":
    command     => "/opt/nginx/sbin/nginx -t && /etc/init.d/nginx
    reload",
    refreshonly => true,
    require     => Exec["install-passenger-nginx-module"],
}
```

Rails

Having set up Passenger and Nginx, we can go on to the requirements for **Rails**:

```
class rails {
    include rails::passenger

    package { "bundler":
        provider => gem,
        ensure   => installed,
    }
}
```

Bundler is a tool for managing an application or gem's dependencies. Instead of having to specify and install all the dependent gems manually or via Puppet, a better way is to have Bundler do this as part of your Rails deployment. For example, note that we don't install the `rails` gem; it will usually either be supplied ready-frozen in the applications `vendor` directory, or installed by Bundler. If you're not using Bundler, or you have some extra dependencies for your Rails setup, install them here.

The main part of the `rails` class is the `define` function `app`, which will be instantiated once for each application that you want to manage:

```
define app( $sitedomain ) {
    include rails
```

The first thing that's installed is the Nginx virtual host file for the app, which is generated from the `app.conf.erb` template:

```
file { "/opt/nginx/sites-available/${name}.conf":
    content => template("rails/app.conf.erb"),
```

```
            require => File["/opt/nginx/sites-available"],
        }

        file { "/opt/nginx/sites-enabled/${name}.conf":
            ensure   => link,
            target   => "/opt/nginx/sites-available/${name}.conf",
            require  => File["/opt/nginx/sites-enabled"],
            notify   => Exec["reload-nginx"],
        }
```

The virtual host template is pretty minimal:

```
server {
    listen 80;
    root /var/www/<%= name %>/current/public;
    server_name <%= sitedomain %>;
    access_log /var/log/nginx/<%= name %>.access.log;
    error_log /var/log/nginx/<%= name %>.error.log;

    passenger_enabled on;
    passenger_min_instances 1;
}

passenger_pre_start http://<%= sitedomain %>;
```

Often an app will need specific Nginx directives, such as redirects. You can include these by adding a file called `files/furiouspigs.conf` in the Rails module. This bit of code will find such a file and include it:

```
        file { "/opt/nginx/conf/includes/${name}.conf":
            source   => [ "puppet:///modules/rails/${name}.conf",
                          "puppet:///modules/rails/empty.conf" ],
            notify   => Exec["reload-nginx"],
        }
```

Note the use of multiple sources for this file, with the second source being `empty.conf`. This makes sure that if there isn't an app-specific config file present, Puppet won't complain.

Finally we make sure that the standard Rails directory structure is in place ready for deployment with the appropriate permissions for the `www-data` user. If you deploy the application and run Nginx as a different user, replace `www-data` with your username throughout.

```
        file { [ "/var/www",
                 "/var/www/${name}",
                 "/var/www/${name}/releases",
                 "/var/www/${name}/shared",
                 "/var/www/${name}/shared/config",
                 "/var/www/${name}/shared/log",
```

```
                    "/var/www/${name}/shared/system" ] :
            ensure => directory,
            mode   => 775,
            owner  => "www-data",
            group  => "www-data",
        }
    }
}
```

There's more...

Here are a few other things you might like to consider when managing Rails applications with Puppet.

RVM

As I mentioned, RVM can be a great solution to the problem of managing multiple Rubies, multiple gemsets, smoothly upgrading Ruby, and so on. Of course, it brings its own interesting problems with it - among them that RVM is under active development and subject to change. However, on balance it cures more pain than it causes. It is recommended that you use RVM for production Rails sites, perhaps with something similar to this:

```
class rails::rvm {
  package { [ "autoconf",
              "bison",
              "curl",
              "libreadline-dev",
              "subversion",
              "zlib1g-dev" ]: ensure => installed }

  file { "/usr/local/bin/rvm-install-system-wide":
    source  => "puppet:///modules/rails/rvm-install-system-wide",
    mode    => "700",
  }

  exec { "install-rvm":
    command => "/usr/local/bin/rvm-install-system-wide",
    creates => "/usr/local/bin/rvm",
    require => [ Package["curl"], Package["subversion"], File["/usr/
    local/bin/rvm-install-system-wide"] ],
    logoutput => on_failure,
  }

  append_if_no_such_line { "setup-rvm-shell-environment":
    file    => "/etc/bash.bashrc",
    line    => "[[ -s /usr/local/rvm/scripts/rvm ]] && . /usr/local/
    rvm/scripts/rvm",
  }
}
```

The `rvm-install-system-wide` script comes from the RVM website: `https://rvm.beginrescueend.com/install/rvm`.

Log rotation

In production you'll probably want to add `logrotate` snippets to take care of the logs generated by Nginx and Rails, to make sure they don't gradually fill up your disks. They have been omitted in this recipe, again for reasons of simplicity and space.

Databases

This recipe doesn't create any databases or users for the Rails application; depending on whether your developers are using MySQL, Postgres, MongoDB, or something else, you'll need to add that yourself. If it's MySQL, you can adapt the recipe *Creating MySQL databases and users*.

SSL certificates

Some applications will require an SSL certificate and **vhost** for secure URLs, for example, to handle payments. These are outside the scope of this recipe, but you shouldn't find it too difficult to add the necessary code. You could add an optional parameter to the define function `rails::app`, for instance:

```
define app( $sitedomain, $ssl = false ) {
```

and then handle it as follows:

```
if $ssl {
  file { "/etc/ssl/certs/${name}.crt":
    source => "puppet:///modules/rails/${name}.crt",
  }
}
```

Then, just instantiate your application with the following:

```
rails::app { "irritatedbadgers":
    sitedomain => "irritatedbadgers.com",
    ssl        => true,
}
```

8
Servers and Cloud Infrastructure

"Rest is not idleness, and to lie sometimes on the grass under trees on a summer's day, listening to the murmur of the water, or watching the clouds float across the sky, is by no means a waste of time."—J. Lubbock

In this chapter we will cover the following topics:

- ▶ Deploying a Nagios monitoring server
- ▶ Building high-availability services using Heartbeat
- ▶ Managing NFS servers and file shares
- ▶ Using HAProxy to load-balance multiple web servers
- ▶ Managing firewalls with iptables
- ▶ Managing EC2 instances
- ▶ Managing virtual machines with Vagrant

As powerful as Puppet is for managing the configuration of a single server, its true benefits become apparent only when controlling networks of many machines. In this chapter we'll explore ways of using Puppet to help you monitor your infrastructure, create high-availability clusters, share files across your network, set up automated firewalls, use load-balancing to get more out of the machines you have, and create new virtual machines in the cloud and on the desktop.

Deploying a Nagios monitoring server

"My roommate lost his pet elephant. It's in the apartment somewhere."
—Steven Wright

We can't keep an eye on everything. Question: How do you know when one of your servers goes down? The wrong answer is, "My client calls me and tells me the server is down." But you'd be surprised how many organizations don't have any kind of automated monitoring of their systems. It's very simple to set up. There are several excellent free and open-source monitoring tools available, including Nagios, Icinga, Zabbix, and Zenoss. Nagios has been around the longest and is among the most sophisticated, although it has a (partly deserved) reputation for being difficult to configure.

This recipe will show you how to build a Nagios-based monitoring server using Puppet and also how to have Puppet configure each of your boxes to be monitored by Nagios.

Getting ready...

You'll need the `apache` module that we created in the section *Managing Apache servers* in *Chapter 7*.

How to do it...

1. Create a `nagios` module:

   ```
   # mkdir /etc/puppet/modules/nagios

   # mkdir /etc/puppet/modules/nagios/files

   # mkdir /etc/puppet/modules/nagios/manifests
   ```

2. Create the file `/etc/puppet/modules/nagios/manifests/server.pp` with the following contents:

   ```
   class nagios::server {
       include apache

       package { [ "nagios3",
                   "nagios-images",
                   "nagios-nrpe-plugin" ]:
           ensure => installed,
       }

       service { "nagios3":
           ensure  => running,
           enable  => true,
   ```

```
            require => Package["nagios3"],
}

exec { "nagios-config-check":
    command     => "/usr/sbin/nagios3 -v /etc/nagios3/nagios.
    cfg && /usr/sbin/service nagios3 restart",
    refreshonly => true,
}

file { "/etc/apache2/sites-available/nagios.conf":
    source  => "puppet:///modules/nagios/nagios.conf",
    notify  => Service["apache2"],
    require => Package["apache2-mpm-prefork"],
}

file { "/etc/apache2/sites-enabled/nagios.conf":
    ensure  => symlink,
    target  => "/etc/apache2/sites-available/nagios.conf",
    require => Package["apache2-mpm-prefork"],
}

file { [ "/etc/nagios3/generic-service_nagios2.cfg",
         "/etc/nagios3/services_nagios2.cfg",
         "/etc/nagios3/hostgroups_nagios2.cfg",
         "/etc/nagios3/extinfo_nagios2.cfg",
         "/etc/nagios3/localhost_nagios2.cfg",
         "/etc/nagios3/contacts_nagios2.cfg",
         "/etc/nagios3/conf.d"
         ]:
    ensure => absent,
    force  => true,
}

define nagios-config() {
    file { "/etc/nagios3/${name}":
        source  => "puppet:///modules/nagios/${name}",
        require => Package["nagios3"],
        notify  => Exec["nagios-config-check"],
    }
}

nagios-config { [ "htpasswd.nagios",
                  "nagios.cfg",
                  "cgi.cfg",
                  "hostgroups.cfg",
                  "hosts.cfg",
```

```
                                  "host_templates.cfg",
                                  "service_templates.cfg",
                                  "services.cfg",
                                  "timeperiods.cfg",
                                  "contacts.cfg",
                                  "commands.cfg" ]: }

        file { "/var/lib/nagios3": # see http://bugs.debian.org/cgi-
        bin/bugreport.cgi?bug=478889
            mode    => 751,
            require => Package["nagios3"],
            notify  => Service["nagios3"],
        }

        file { "/var/lib/nagios3/rw": # see http://bugs.debian.org/
        cgi-bin/bugreport.cgi?bug=478889
            mode    => 2710,
            require => Package["nagios3"],
            notify  => Service["nagios3"],
        }
    }
```

3. Create the file `/etc/puppet/modules/nagios/files/nagios.cfg` with the following contents:

```
# Config files to read
cfg_file=/etc/nagios3/commands.cfg
cfg_file=/etc/nagios3/service_templates.cfg
cfg_file=/etc/nagios3/host_templates.cfg
cfg_file=/etc/nagios3/timeperiods.cfg
cfg_file=/etc/nagios3/contacts.cfg
cfg_file=/etc/nagios3/hostgroups.cfg
cfg_file=/etc/nagios3/hosts.cfg
cfg_file=/etc/nagios3/services.cfg

# Nagios settings
log_file=/var/log/nagios3/nagios.log
illegal_macro_output_chars=`~$&|'"<>
check_result_path=/var/lib/nagios3/spool/checkresults
nagios_user=nagios
nagios_group=nagios
command_file=/var/lib/nagios3/rw/nagios.cmd
lock_file=/var/run/nagios3/nagios3.pid
p1_file=/usr/lib/nagios3/p1.pl
check_external_commands=1
resource_file=/etc/nagios3/resource.cfg
```

4. Create the file `/etc/puppet/modules/nagios/files/service_templates.cfg` with the following contents:

```
define service{
    name                            generic_service ; The 'name'
    of this service template
    active_checks_enabled           1       ; Active service
    checks are enabled
    passive_checks_enabled          1       ; Passive service
    checks are enabled/accepted
    parallelize_check               1       ; Active service
    checks should be parallelized (disabling this can lead to
    major performance problems)
    obsess_over_service             1       ; We should obsess
    over this service (if necessary)
    check_freshness                 0       ; Default is to NOT
    check service 'freshness'
    notifications_enabled           1       ; Service
    notifications are enabled
    event_handler_enabled           1       ; Service event
    handler is enabled
    flap_detection_enabled          1       ; Flap detection is
    enabled
    failure_prediction_enabled      1       ; Failure prediction
    is enabled
    process_perf_data               1       ; Process performance
    data
    retain_status_information       1       ; Retain status
    information across program restarts
    retain_nonstatus_information    1       ; Retain non-status
    information across program restarts
    notification_interval           0       ; Only send
    notifications on status change by default.
    is_volatile                     0
    check_period                    24x7
    normal_check_interval           5
    retry_check_interval            2
    max_check_attempts              3
    notification_period             24x7
    notification_options            c,r
    contact_groups                  sysadmin
    register                        0       ; DONT REGISTER THIS
    DEFINITION - ITS NOT A REAL SERVICE, JUST A TEMPLATE!
}

# Defaults
define service {
```

```
        name                    every_5_mins
        normal_check_interval 5
        use                     generic_service
        register                0
    }

    define service {
        name                    every_hour
        normal_check_interval 60
        use                     generic_service
        register                0
    }

    define service {
        name                    every_day
        normal_check_interval 1440
        use                     generic_service
        register                0
    }
```

5. Create the file `/etc/puppet/modules/nagios/files/services.cfg` with the following contents:

```
define service {
        hostgroup_name          all
        service_description     Disk
        check_command           check_nrpe!check_all_disks!20%!10%
        use                     every_day
}

define service {
        hostgroup_name          all
        service_description     Load
        check_command           check_nrpe!check_load!10,10,10!15,15,15
        use                     every_hour
}
```

6. Create the file `/etc/puppet/modules/nagios/files/cgi.cfg` with the following contents:

```
main_config_file=/etc/nagios3/nagios.cfg
physical_html_path=/usr/share/nagios3/htdocs
url_html_path=/nagios3
show_context_help=1
use_pending_states=1
nagios_check_command=/usr/lib/nagios/plugins/check_nagios /var/
cache/nagios3/status.dat 5 '/usr/sbin/nagios3'
```

```
use_authentication=1
use_ssl_authentication=0
authorized_for_system_information=nagios
authorized_for_configuration_information=nagios
authorized_for_system_commands=nagios
authorized_for_all_services=nagios
authorized_for_all_hosts=nagios
authorized_for_all_service_commands=nagios
authorized_for_all_host_commands=nagios
default_statusmap_layout=5
default_statuswrl_layout=4
ping_syntax=/bin/ping -n -U -c 5 $HOSTADDRESS$
refresh_rate=90
escape_html_tags=1
action_url_target=_blank
notes_url_target=_blank
lock_author_names=1
```

7. Create the file `/etc/puppet/modules/nagios/files/host_templates.cfg` with the following contents:

```
define host{
    name                           generic_host
    check_command                  check-host-alive
    max_check_attempts             3
    checks_enabled                 1
    failure_prediction_enabled     1
    retain_status_information      1
    retain_nonstatus_information   1
    notification_interval          0
    notification_options           d,u,r
    check_interval                 300
    contact_groups                 sysadmin
    register                       0
}
```

8. Create the file `/etc/puppet/modules/nagios/files/contacts.cfg` with the following contents (use your own e-mail address, or at least that of someone who won't mind getting a lot of e-mail from your monitoring server):

```
define contact {
    contact_name                   helen
    alias                          Helen Highwater
    service_notification_period    24x7
    host_notification_period       24x7
```

```
        service_notification_options       w,u,c,r
        host_notification_options          d,r
        service_notification_commands      notify-service-by-email
        host_notification_commands         notify-host-by-email
        email                              helen@example.com
}


define contactgroup {
        contactgroup_name   sysadmin
        alias               Sysadmins
        members             helen
}
```

9. Create the file `/etc/puppet/modules/nagios/files/hostgroups.cfg` with the following contents:

```
define hostgroup {
        hostgroup_name all
        alias          All Servers
        members        *
}
```

10. Create the file `/etc/puppet/modules/nagios/files/timeperiods.cfg` with the following contents:

```
define timeperiod {
        timeperiod_name 24x7
        alias       24 Hours A Day, 7 Days A Week
        sunday      00:00-24:00
        monday      00:00-24:00
        tuesday     00:00-24:00
        wednesday   00:00-24:00
        thursday    00:00-24:00
        friday      00:00-24:00
        saturday    00:00-24:00
}
```

11. Create the file `/etc/puppet/modules/nagios/files/hosts.cfg` with the following contents (replace with your own server details):

```
define host {
        host_name   cookbook
        address     cookbook.bitfieldconsulting.com
        use         generic_host
}
```

12. Create the file `/etc/puppet/modules/nagios/files/commands.cfg` with the following contents:

```
define command {
    command_name        check_nrpe
    command_line        $USER1$/check_nrpe -H $HOSTADDRESS$ -c $ARG1$
    -a $ARG2$ $ARG3$ $ARG4$ $ARG5$
                }

define command{
    command_name        check-host-alive
    command_line        $USER1$/check_ping -H '$HOSTADDRESS$' -w
    5000,100% -c 5000,100% -p 1
                }

define command{
    command_name        check_all_disks
    command_line        /usr/lib/nagios/plugins/check_disk -w '$ARG1$'
    -c '$ARG2$' -e
                }

define command{
    command_name        notify-host-by-email
    command_line        /usr/bin/printf "%b" "***** Nagios *****\n\
    nNotification Type: $NOTIFICATIONTYPE$\nHost: $HOSTNAME$\
    nState: $HOSTSTATE$\nAddress: $HOSTADDRESS$\nInfo:
    $HOSTOUTPUT$\n\nDate/Time: $LONGDATETIME$\n" | /usr/bin/mail
    -s "** $NOTIFICATIONTYPE$ Host Alert: $HOSTNAME$ is
    $HOSTSTATE$ **" $CONTACTEMAIL$
                }

define command{
    command_name        notify-service-by-email
    command_line        /usr/bin/printf "%b" "***** Nagios
    *****\n\nNotification Type: $NOTIFICATIONTYPE$\n\nService:
    $SERVICEDESC$\nHost: $HOSTALIAS$\nAddress: $HOSTADDRESS$\
    nState: $SERVICESTATE$\n\nDate/Time: $LONGDATETIME$\n\
    nAdditional Info:\n\n$SERVICEOUTPUT$" | /usr/bin/mail -s "**
    $NOTIFICATIONTYPE$ Service Alert: $HOSTALIAS$/$SERVICEDESC$ is
    $SERVICESTATE$ **" $CONTACTEMAIL$
                }
```

13. Create the file `/etc/puppet/modules/nagios/files/nagios.conf` with the following contents (replace the `ServerName` with your own server):

```
ScriptAlias /cgi-bin/nagios3 /usr/lib/cgi-bin/nagios3
ScriptAlias /nagios3/cgi-bin /usr/lib/cgi-bin/nagios3
Alias /nagios3/stylesheets /etc/nagios3/stylesheets
Alias /nagios3 /usr/share/nagios3/htdocs
```

```
Alias / /usr/share/nagios3/htdocs/

<DirectoryMatch (/usr/share/nagios3/htdocs|/usr/lib/cgi-bin/
nagios3|/etc/nagios3/stylesheets)>
        Options FollowSymLinks

        DirectoryIndex index.html

        AllowOverride AuthConfig
        Order Allow,Deny
        Allow From All

        AuthName "Nagios Access"
        AuthType Basic
        AuthUserFile /etc/nagios3/htpasswd.nagios
        require valid-user
</DirectoryMatch>

<VirtualHost *:80>
    ServerName nagios.bitfieldconsulting.com
    ErrorLog /var/log/apache2/nagios-error_log
    CustomLog /var/log/apache2/nagios-access_log common
    DocumentRoot /usr/share/nagios3
</VirtualHost>
```

14. Create the password file to control access to the Nagios web interface:

    ```
    # htpasswd -c /etc/puppet/modules/nagios/files/htpasswd.nagios
    nagios
    ```

    ```
    Password: (type password)
    ```

15. If the program htpasswd isn't on your system, run the following command:

    ```
    # apt-get install apache2-utils
    ```

16. Create an /etc/hosts entry or DNS record for the ServerName you specified in the preceding code; in this case:

    ```
    nagios.bitfieldconsulting.com
    ```

17. Include the following in the node definition for your Nagios server:

    ```
    include nagios::server
    ```

18. Create the file /etc/puppet/modules/nagios/files/nrpe.cfg with the following contents (replace the allowed_hosts setting with the name or IP address of your monitoring server):

    ```
    log_facility=daemon
    pid_file=/var/run/nagios/nrpe.pid
    server_port=5666
    ```

```
nrpe_user=nagios
nrpe_group=nagios
allowed_hosts=cookbook.bitfieldconsulting.com
dont_blame_nrpe=1
debug=0
command_timeout=60
connection_timeout=300
command[check_load]=/usr/lib/nagios/plugins/check_load -w $ARG1$
-c $ARG2$
command[check_all_disks]=/usr/lib/nagios/plugins/check_disk -w
$ARG1$ -c $ARG2$ -e -A -i '.gvfs'
```

19. Create the file `/etc/puppet/modules/nagios/manifests/target.pp` with the following contents:

```
class nagios::target {
    package { [ "nagios-nrpe-server",
                "nagios-plugins",
                "nagios-plugins-basic",
                "nagios-plugins-standard",
                "nagios-plugins-extra" ]:
        ensure => installed,
    }

    service { "nagios-nrpe-server":
        enable  => true,
        ensure  => running,
        pattern => "/usr/sbin/nrpe",
        require => Package["nagios-nrpe-server"],
    }

    file { "/etc/nagios/nrpe.cfg":
        source  => "puppet:///modules/nagios/nrpe.cfg",
        require => Package["nagios-nrpe-server"],
        notify  => Service["nagios-nrpe-server"],
    }
}
```

20. Include this class on the nodes you want to monitor (this should also include the Nagios server itself):

```
include nagios::target
```

21. Run Puppet on the Nagios server as follows:

```
# puppet agent --test
```

22. Go to the web interface in your browser (log in with the username `nagios` and the password you set in the preceding code) and check that you see the Nagios welcome screen as shown in the following screenshot:

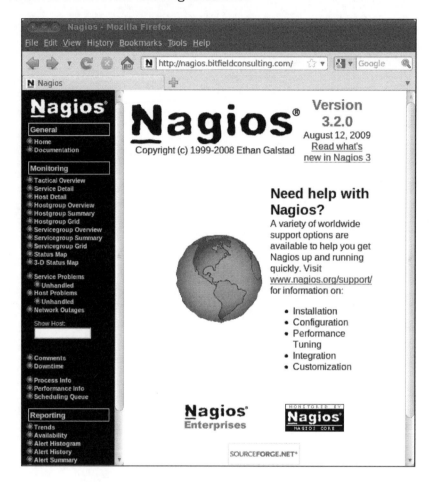

23. Go to the **Host detail** screen and you should see your target nodes listed.

24. Click on the name of a node and then select "Schedule a check of all services on this host" from the **Host commands** menu.

25. Tick the box that says "Force check" and click "Commit". It will take a few seconds for Nagios to run the checks. Go to the "Service detail" screen and you should see the services listed in green like this:

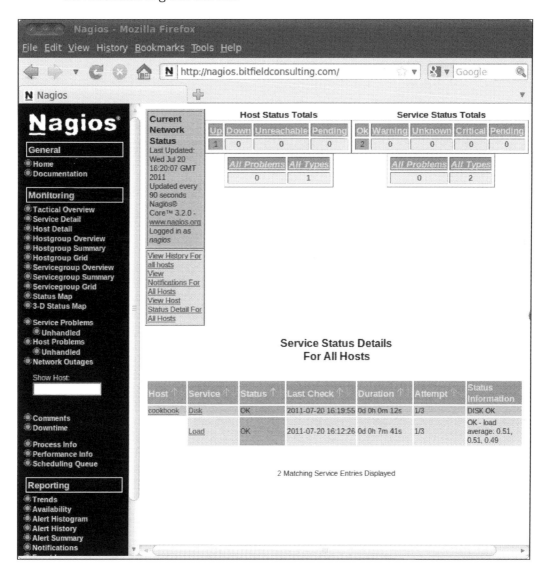

How it works...

Although this recipe is quite a lengthy one, the Puppet manifest itself is pretty simple; there's nothing here that we haven't used already in other recipes.

Essentially, what we're doing is installing the Nagios package itself, configuring a virtual host for Apache to serve it, and deploying a bunch of config files for Nagios that tell it what hosts to check, which services to check, and other assorted things.

On the client side, each node that's monitored by Nagios needs the `nagios-nrpe-server` package installed (**NRPE** is the protocol that Nagios uses to securely execute commands on remote servers) and a configuration file that tells the NRPE server which commands are allowed to be executed.

> You should be aware that the `dont_blame_nrpe` setting in `nrpe.cfg` is a potential security hole, as it allows remote execution of commands with user-supplied arguments. This is a very useful feature, as it means you can alter alert thresholds or other parameters without having to reconfigure every monitored machine. However, if you don't need this feature, it's safer to disable `dont_blame_nrpe`.

There's more...

The tricky thing with Nagios is getting it set up and running in the first place. Although the monitoring configuration presented here is very basic (just disk space and CPU load checking), you can use this working Nagios setup as a starting point to add more service checks and more hosts. Here are some things that you might like to add:

▶ Host groups (for example, web servers or database servers): You can configure a check to apply to all members of a host group automatically.

▶ Website checks: The `check_http` plugin that comes with Nagios is quite sophisticated, and can handle redirects, SSL, authentication, and matching text from a web page.

▶ Process checks: It's common to want to monitor a specific process on a box. Use the `check_procs` plugin for this.

▶ Different check frequencies: I've defined the service templates `every_hour`, `every_day`, and `every_5_mins` in `service_templates.cfg`; you may want to add some new ones.

▶ New time periods: Currently the only one defined in `timeperiods.cfg` is `24x7`, but you may want to create your own. For example, if your database maintenance jobs run from midnight to 1 a.m., you could define a time period that excludes those hours, so that you don't get false alarms on the database server.

To find out more about how to configure Nagios, have a look at the documentation at `http://nagios.sourceforge.net/docs/nagioscore/3/en/toc.html`.

There is also some built-in support for Nagios in Puppet; you can have Puppet generate host and service definitions automatically from your manifests, which is a powerful and useful feature. Although I use this on some production sites, I have had to regretfully exclude coverage of it from this book for space reasons. If you want to find out about this, check the official Puppet documentation and also Mike Gurski's excellent article on the subject: `http://blog.gurski.org/index.php/2010/01/28/automatic-monitoring-with-puppet-and-nagios/`.

Building high-availability services using Heartbeat

"Even in the future, nothing works!"—'Spaceballs'

Sooner or later, everything breaks. High-availability services are those that can survive the failure of an individual machine or network connection. The primary technique for high availability is redundancy, otherwise known as throwing hardware at the problem. Although the eventual failure of an individual server is certain, the simultaneous failure of two servers is unlikely enough that this provides a good level of redundancy for most applications.

One of the simplest ways to build a redundant pair of servers is to have them share an IP address using Heartbeat. **Heartbeat** is a daemon which runs on both machines and exchanges regular messages—heartbeats—between the two. One server is the primary, and normally has the resource: in this case, an IP address. If the secondary server fails to detect a heartbeat from the primary, it can take over the address, ensuring continuity of service.

In this recipe we'll set up two machines in this configuration using Puppet, and I'll explain how to use it to provide a high-availability service.

How to do it...

1. Create a `heartbeat` module as follows:

   ```
   # mkdir /etc/puppet/modules/heartbeat
   ```

   ```
   # mkdir /etc/puppet/modules/heartbeat/manifests
   ```

   ```
   # mkdir /etc/puppet/modules/heartbeat/files
   ```

2. Create the file `/etc/puppet/modules/heartbeat/manifests/init.pp` with the following contents:

   ```
   class heartbeat {
     package { "heartbeat":
       ensure => installed,
     }
   ```

```
service { "heartbeat":
  ensure  => running,
  require => Package["heartbeat"],
}

exec { "reload-heartbeat":
  command     => "/usr/sbin/service heartbeat reload",
  refreshonly => true,
}

file { "/etc/ha.d/authkeys":
  source  => "puppet:///modules/heartbeat/authkeys",
  mode    => "600",
  require => Package["heartbeat"],
  notify  => Exec["reload-heartbeat"],
}

file { "/etc/ha.d/haresources":
  source  => "puppet:///modules/heartbeat/haresources",
  notify  => Exec["reload-heartbeat"],
  require => Package["heartbeat"],
}

file { "/etc/ha.d/ha.cf":
  source  => "puppet:///modules/heartbeat/ha.cf",
  notify  => Exec["reload-heartbeat"],
  require => Package["heartbeat"],
}
}
```

3. Create the file /etc/puppet/modules/heartbeat/files/haresources with the following contents. Substitute for cookbook the name of your primary server. This should be whatever is returned by uname -n on the server. For 10.0.2.100 substitute the IP address you want to share between the two machines. This should be an address that is currently unused on your network. Heartbeat will assign it to the interface listed at the end (eth0:1 in this case).

```
cookbook IPaddr::10.0.2.100/24/eth0:1
```

4. Create the file /etc/puppet/modules/heartbeat/files/authkeys with the following contents (replace topsecretpassword with a password of your own choosing):

```
auth 1
1 sha1 topsecretpassword
```

5. Create the file `/etc/puppet/modules/heartbeat/files/ha.cf` with the following contents. Replace the two IP addresses with the main addresses of your two machines. Similarly, replace `cookbook` and `cookbook2` with the node names of your machines (whatever is returned by `uname -n`).

```
autojoin none
ucast eth0 10.0.2.15
ucast eth0 10.0.2.16
keepalive 1
deadtime 10
warntime 5
udpport 694
auto_failback on
node cookbook
node cookbook2
use_logd yes
```

6. Run Puppet on each of the two servers:

```
# puppet agent --test
info: Retrieving plugin
info: Caching catalog for cookbook.bitfieldconsulting.com
info: Applying configuration version '1311440876'
notice: /Stage[main]/Heartbeat/Package[heartbeat]/ensure: created
notice: /Stage[main]/Heartbeat/File[/etc/ha.d/authkeys]/ensure:
defined content as '{md5}e908c869aabe519aa69acc9e51da3399'
info: /Stage[main]/Heartbeat/File[/etc/ha.d/authkeys]: Scheduling
refresh of Exec[reload-heartbeat]
notice: /Stage[main]/Heartbeat/File[/etc/ha.d/ha.cf]/ensure:
defined content as '{md5}a8d3fdd62a1172cdff150fc1d86d8a6b'
info: /Stage[main]/Heartbeat/File[/etc/ha.d/ha.cf]: Scheduling
refresh of Exec[reload-heartbeat]
notice: /Stage[main]/Heartbeat/File[/etc/ha.d/haresources]/ensure:
defined content as '{md5}0f25aefe7f6c4c8e81b3bb6c86a42d60'
info: /Stage[main]/Heartbeat/File[/etc/ha.d/haresources]:
Scheduling refresh of Exec[reload-heartbeat]
notice: /Stage[main]/Heartbeat/Exec[reload-heartbeat]: Triggered
'refresh' from 3 events
notice: Finished catalog run in 27.01 seconds
```

7. On the primary node, check that it has the resource:

```
# cl_status rscstatus -m
This node is holding all resources.
```

8. On the secondary, you should see this:

    # cl_status rscstatus -m

    This node is holding none resources.

9. Stop the Heartbeat service on the primary node:

    # service heartbeat stop

10. The secondary node should now be holding the resource:

    ```
    # cl_status rscstatus -m
    This node is holding all resources.
    ```

How it works...

The Heartbeat daemon runs on each machine, listening for heartbeats from the other. If the primary detects that the secondary has gone down, nothing happens. On the other hand, if the secondary detects that the primary has gone down, it fails over (takes over) the IP address. When the primary comes back up, the secondary will relinquish the address again (if `auto_failback` is set to `on`). In some cases, for example if you're sharing the IP address between a master and slave database server, you may not want this behavior, in which case set `auto_failback` to `off`.

There's more...

Now that you have a shared IP address (really a misnomer, since the address is not 'shared', but swaps between one server and the other) you can use it to provide a high-availability service on this address. For example, if the servers are hosting a website, you can set the DNS record for the website to point to the shared address. When the primary server goes down, the secondary will take over and continue responding to HTTP requests on the address.

> If you're using an SSL site, you will need to configure the SSL virtual host with the shared IP address, or it won't be able to respond to requests on that IP. Also, if the website uses sessions, any sessions on the primary server will be lost following a failover, unless the sessions are stored in a separate shared database.

A shared IP address is a great way of pairing redundant load balancers (see the section on `haproxy`). You can also use it to provide redundant Puppetmaster machines. A suitable pattern is presented on the Puppet Labs site: `http://projects.puppetlabs.com/projects/1/wiki/High_Availability_Patterns`.

Managing NFS servers and file shares

"There are three kinds of death in this world. There's heart death, there's brain death, and there's being off the network."—Guy Almes

NFS (the **Network File System**) is a way of mounting a shared directory from a remote server. For example, a pool of web servers might all mount the same NFS share to serve static assets such as images and stylesheets. Although NFS is old technology, it's still widely used, so here's a recipe that will show you how to create an NFS server and share files from it.

How to do it...

1. Create an `nfs` module:

   ```
   # mkdir /etc/puppet/modules/nfs
   ```

   ```
   # mkdir /etc/puppet/modules/nfs/manifests
   ```

2. Create the file `/etc/puppet/modules/nfs/manifests/init.pp` with the following contents:

   ```
   class nfs {
       package { "nfs-kernel-server": ensure => installed }

       service { "nfs-kernel-server":
           ensure      => running,
           enable      => true,
           hasrestart => true,
           require     => Package["nfs-kernel-server"],
       }

       file { "/etc/exports.d":
           ensure => directory,
       }

       exec { "update-etc-exports":
           command     => "/bin/cat /etc/exports.d/* >/etc/exports",
           notify      => Service["nfs-kernel-server"],
           refreshonly => true,
       }

       define share( $path, $allowed, $options = "" ) {
           include nfs

           file { $path:
               ensure => directory,
           }
   ```

```
            file { "/etc/exports.d/${name}":
                content => "${path} ${allowed}(${options})\n",
                notify  => Exec["update-etc-exports"],
            }
        }
    }
```

3. Add the following to the node you want to export an NFS share from (change the IP address range to one suitable for your network):

```
nfs::share { "data":
    path    => "/data",
    allowed => "10.0.2.0/24",
    options => "rw,sync,no_root_squash",
}

nfs::share { "data2":
    path    => "/data2",
    allowed => "10.0.2.0/24",
    options => "rw,sync,no_root_squash",
}
```

4. Run Puppet:

```
# puppet agent --test
info: Retrieving plugin
info: Caching catalog for cookbook.bitfieldconsulting.com
info: Applying configuration version '1311526219'
notice: /Stage[main]/Nfs/Package[nfs-kernel-server]/ensure:
created
notice: /Stage[main]/Nfs/Service[nfs-kernel-server]/ensure: ensure
changed 'stopped' to 'running'
notice: /Stage[main]//Node[cookbook]/Nfs::Share[data2]/File[/
data2]/ensure: created
notice: /Stage[main]//Node[cookbook]/Nfs::Share[data2]/File[/etc/
exports.d/data]/ensure: defined content as '{md5}408f8b40815ff4b6e
ec2f324ca7eafc4'
info: /Stage[main]//Node[cookbook]/Nfs::Share[data]/File[/etc/
exports.d/data]: Scheduling refresh of Exec[update-etc-exports]
notice: /Stage[main]//Node[cookbook]/Nfs::Share[data2]/
File[/etc/exports.d/data2]/ensure: defined content as '{md5}
ec2f324ca7eafc4408f8b40815ff4b6e'
info: /Stage[main]//Node[cookbook]/Nfs::Share[data2]/File[/etc/
exports.d/data2]: Scheduling refresh of Exec[update-etc-exports]
```

```
notice: /Stage[main]/Nfs/Exec[update-etc-exports]: Triggered
'refresh' from 2 events

info: /Stage[main]/Nfs/Exec[update-etc-exports]: Scheduling
refresh of Service[nfs-kernel-server]

notice: /Stage[main]/Nfs/Service[nfs-kernel-server]/ensure: ensure
changed 'stopped' to 'running'

notice: /Stage[main]/Nfs/Service[nfs-kernel-server]: Triggered
'refresh' from 1 events

notice: Finished catalog run in 3.13 seconds
```

5. Test the export settings by mounting one of the shares from another server as follows:

```
# mkdir /mnt/data

# mount cookbook:/data /mnt/data

# ls /mnt/data
```

How it works...

The `nfs` class installs and starts the `nfs-kernel-server` service, which listens for network connections to the file share. It also defines the `nfs::share` resource, which you can use anywhere in your manifests to export a directory via NFS:

```
nfs::share { "data":
    path    => "/data",
    allowed => "10.0.2.0/24",
    options => "rw,sync,no_root_squash",
}
```

The `name` of the resource is whatever label you want to give it: `data`, in this case. The `path` specifies the directory to share. The `allowed` parameter can be a CIDR network address (as here), an IP address, a hostname, or a whitespace-separated list of addresses and hostnames. Only the specified hosts will be allowed to mount the resource.

The `options` parameter specifies the options to NFS (as they appear in the `/etc/exports` file; see `man exports` for precise details).

Note that we use the same snippet pattern as we did in the `rsyncd.conf` example. Any instance of `nfs::share` creates a file snippet in `/etc/exports.d`, which also triggers an `exec` to concatenate all the snippets into `/etc/exports` and bounce the NFS service to pick up the changes.

There's more...

NFS shares should only be used for data that's not critical to your application, because the NFS server creates a single point of failure. For a clustered file system, check out GlusterFS instead.

Using HAProxy to load-balance multiple web servers

"The inside of a computer is as dumb as hell but it goes like mad!"—Richard Feynman

Back in the day, the way to speed up slow web servers was to add more cores. I recall one employer buying a monster 24-core Sun box the size of a Hummer. We had to have the data center door widened to get it in.

Scaling websites nowadays is still a matter of adding cores, but they either come in their own little beige boxes, as commodity hardware, or you rent them as as a wholesale compute resource from a cloud provider. In order to group all these cores together to serve a single website, we use load balancers.

Once, a load balancer was a big box that sat in a rack and cost eighty thousand dollars. Although you can still buy those, for most organizations a software load balancer solution using commodity Linux servers is a better value proposition.

HAProxy is the software load balancer of choice for most people: fast, powerful, and highly configurable. In this recipe, I'll show you how to build an HAProxy server to load-balance web requests across two existing backend servers.

How to do it...

1. Create a `loadbalancer` module:

   ```
   # mkdir /etc/puppet/modules/loadbalancer
   # mkdir /etc/puppet/modules/loadbalancer/manifests
   # mkdir /etc/puppet/modules/loadbalancer/files
   ```

2. Create the file `/etc/puppet/modules/loadbalancer/manifests/init.pp` with the following contents:

   ```
   class loadbalancer {
       package { "haproxy": ensure => installed }

       file { "/etc/default/haproxy":
           source  => "puppet:///modules/loadbalancer/haproxy.
           defaults",
           require => Package["haproxy"],
       }

       service { "haproxy":
           ensure  => running,
   ```

```
        enable  => true,
        require => Package["haproxy"],
    }

    file { "/etc/haproxy/haproxy.cfg":
        source  => "puppet:///modules/loadbalancer/haproxy.cfg",
        require => Package["haproxy"],
        notify  => Service["haproxy"],
    }
}
```

3. Create the file `/etc/puppet/modules/loadbalancer/files/haproxy.`
   `defaults` with the following contents:

```
# Don't edit this file - it's managed by Puppet
# Set ENABLED to 1 if you want the init script to start haproxy.
ENABLED=1
# Add extra flags here.
#EXTRAOPTS="-de -m 16"
```

4. Create the file `/etc/puppet/modules/loadbalancer/files/haproxy.cfg`
   with the following contents. In the `myapp` section, replace the IP address in each
   `server` line with the IP address of your backend server, and the `:8000` port number
   with the port number where your server is listening.

```
global
        daemon
        user haproxy
        group haproxy
        pidfile /var/run/haproxy.pid

defaults
        log     global
        stats   enable
        mode    http
        option  httplog
        option  dontlognull
        option  dontlog-normal
        retries 3
        option  redispatch
        contimeout 4000
        clitimeout 60000
        srvtimeout 30000

listen  stats :8080
        mode http
```

```
            stats uri /
            stats auth haproxy:topsecret

listen  myapp 0.0.0.0:80
            balance leastconn
            server myapp1 10.0.2.30:8000    check maxconn 100
            server myapp2 10.0.2.40:8000    check maxconn 100
```

5. Include the following on your HAProxy node:

```
include loadbalancer
```

6. Run Puppet:

```
# puppet agent --test

info: Retrieving plugin

info: Caching catalog for cookbook.bitfieldconsulting.com

info: Applying configuration version '1311616315'

notice: /Stage[main]/Loadbalancer/Package[haproxy]/ensure: ensure
changed 'purged' to 'present'

--- /etc/haproxy/haproxy.cfg    2009-11-06 17:59:44.000000000
+0000

+++ /tmp/puppet-file20110725-16369-1b85cr8-0    2011-07-25
18:09:03.749146699 +0000

@@ -1,86 +1,28 @@

-# this config needs haproxy-1.1.28 or haproxy-1.2.1

...

info: /Stage[main]/Loadbalancer/File[/etc/haproxy/haproxy.
cfg]: Filebucketed /etc/haproxy/haproxy.cfg to puppet with sum
c3bfb0c86138552475dea458e8ab36f3

notice: /Stage[main]/Loadbalancer/File[/etc/haproxy/haproxy.cfg]/
content: content changed '{md5}c3bfb0c86138552475dea458e8ab36f3'
to '{md5}fa5fac3cf31f043f0120d0d45cef3f54'

info: /Stage[main]/Loadbalancer/File[/etc/haproxy/haproxy.cfg]:
Scheduling refresh of Service[haproxy]

notice: /Stage[main]/Loadbalancer/Service[haproxy]/ensure: ensure
changed 'stopped' to 'running'

notice: /Stage[main]/Loadbalancer/Service[haproxy]: Triggered
'refresh' from 1 events

--- /etc/default/haproxy    2009-11-06 17:59:21.000000000 +0000

+++ /tmp/puppet-file20110725-16369-1ndfrti-0    2011-07-25
18:09:05.749136866 +0000

@@ -1,4 +1,5 @@
```

```
# Set ENABLED to 1 if you want the init script to start haproxy.
-ENABLED=0
+ENABLED=1
# Add extra flags here.
#EXTRAOPTS="-de -m 16"
+
```

```
notice: /Stage[main]/Loadbalancer/File[/etc/default/haproxy]/
content: content changed '{md5}a1f2deb7c7a10e55dc7c971a2288f5d4'
to '{md5}2217d74d66bd72630268598b1f11f173'
```

```
notice: Finished catalog run in 22.21 seconds
```

7. Check the HAProxy **stats** interface in your web browser to make sure everything is OK (note that my **Backend** servers are shown as **DOWN** because those VMs aren't running: when I start them, HAProxy will detect this automatically and mark them up).

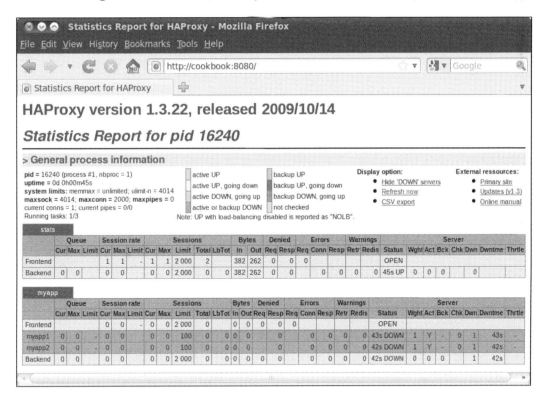

How it works...

The `haproxy` daemon listens for incoming requests and distributes them to the pool of backend servers (**myapp1** and **myapp2** in our example). If one backend server becomes overloaded, HAProxy will avoid sending it more traffic until it recovers. This helps prevent the drastic slowdown as a single web server becomes overloaded and queues up more and more requests that it can't serve. If a server fails altogether, HAProxy won't send it any more requests until it becomes available again.

The **stats** interface will show you how your backend servers are performing, how many sessions they are handling, whether HAProxy has marked them up or down, and so on.

There's more...

If you want to add more backends to handle increased demand, just add more `server` lines to `haproxy.cfg`. If you find that the existing servers are getting swamped, try decreasing the per-server `maxconn` setting a little. HAProxy has a vast range of configuration parameters that you can explore: see the HAProxy documentation at `http://haproxy.1wt.eu/#docs`.

If you need SSL capabilities, you can put Nginx in front of HAProxy to handle this.

Although it's most often used as a web server, HAProxy can proxy a lot more than just HTTP. It can handle any TCP traffic, so you can use it to load-balance MySQL servers, SMTP, video servers, or anything you like.

Managing firewalls with iptables

> *"Programming can be fun, so can cryptography; however they should not be combined."—Kreitzberg and Shneiderman*

The programming language C has been described as a 'write-only' language; it's so terse and efficient that it can be difficult to understand even code that you've written yourself. The same might be said of `iptables`, the Linux kernel's built-in packet filtering firewall. Raw `iptables` rules look something like this:

```
iptables -A INPUT -d 10.0.2.15/32 -p tcp -m tcp --dport 80 -j ACCEPT
```

Unless you derive a sense of machismo from mastering apparently meaningless strings of line noise, which admittedly is an occupational disease of UNIX sysadmins, it would be nice to be able to express firewall rules in a more symbolic and readable way. Puppet can help, because we can use it to abstract away some of the implementation detail of `iptables` and define firewall rules by reference to the services they control:

```
iptables::role { "web-server": }
```

Getting ready...

You will need the `append_if_no_such_line` utility function we created in the section, *Making quick edits to config files* in *Chapter 5*.

How to do it...

1. Create an `iptables` module:

   ```
   # mkdir /etc/puppet/modules/iptables
   # mkdir /etc/puppet/modules/iptables/manifests
   # mkdir /etc/puppet/modules/iptables/files
   ```

2. Create the file `/etc/puppet/modules/iptables/manifests/init.pp` with the following contents:

   ```
   class iptables {
       file { [ "/root/iptables",
                "/root/iptables/hosts",
                "/root/iptables/roles" ]:
           ensure => directory,
       }

       file { "/root/iptables/roles/common":
           source => "puppet:///modules/iptables/common.role",
           notify => Exec["run-iptables"],
       }

       file { "/root/iptables/names":
           source => "puppet:///modules/iptables/names",
           notify => Exec["run-iptables"],
       }

       file { "/root/iptables/iptables.sh":
           source => "puppet:///modules/iptables/iptables.sh",
           mode   => "755",
           notify => Exec["run-iptables"],
       }

       file { "/root/iptables/hosts/${hostname}":
           content => "export MAIN_IP=${ipaddress}\n",
           replace => false,
           require => File["/root/iptables/hosts"],
           notify  => Exec["run-iptables"],
       }
   ```

```
exec { "run-iptables":
    cwd          => "/root/iptables",
    command      => "/usr/bin/test -f hosts/${hostname} && /
    root/iptables/iptables.sh && /sbin/iptables-save >/etc/
    iptables.rules",
    refreshonly => true,
}

append_if_no_such_line { "restore iptables rules":
    file => "/etc/network/interfaces",
    line => "pre-up iptables-restore < /etc/iptables.rules",
}

define role() {
    include iptables

    file { "/root/iptables/roles/${name}":
        source  => "puppet:///modules/iptables/${name}.role",
        replace => false,
        require => File["/root/iptables/roles"],
        notify  => Exec["run-iptables"],
    }

    append_if_no_such_line { "${name} role":
        file    => "/root/iptables/hosts/${hostname}",
        line    => ". `dirname \$0`/roles/${name}",
        require => File["/root/iptables/hosts/${hostname}"],
        notify  => Exec["run-iptables"],
    }
  }
}
```

3. Create the file `/etc/puppet/modules/iptables/files/iptables.sh` with the following contents:

```
# Server names and ports
. `dirname $0`/names

# Interfaces (override in host-specific file if necessary)
export EXT_INTERFACE=eth0

# Flush and remove all chains
iptables -P INPUT  ACCEPT
iptables -P OUTPUT ACCEPT
iptables -F
iptables -X
```

```
# Allow all traffic on loopback interface
iptables -I INPUT 1 -i lo -j ACCEPT
iptables -I OUTPUT 1 -o lo -j ACCEPT

# Allow established and related connections
iptables -I INPUT 2 -m state --state ESTABLISHED,RELATED -j ACCEPT
iptables -I OUTPUT 2 -m state --state ESTABLISHED,RELATED -j
ACCEPT

# Include machine specific settings
HOST_RULES=`dirname $0`/hosts/`hostname -s`
[ -f ${HOST_RULES} ] && . ${HOST_RULES}
[ "${MAIN_IP}" == "" ] && ( echo No MAIN_IP was set, please set
the primary IP address in ${HOST_RULES}. ; exit 1 )

# Include common settings
. `dirname $0`/roles/common

# Drop all non-matching packets
iptables -A INPUT -j LOG --log-prefix "INPUT: "
iptables -A INPUT -j DROP
iptables -A OUTPUT -j LOG --log-prefix "OUTPUT: "
iptables -A OUTPUT -j DROP

echo -e "Test remote login and then:\n iptables-save >/etc/
iptables.rules"
```

4. Create the file /etc/puppet/modules/iptables/files/names with the following contents:

```
# Servers
export PUPPETMASTER=10.0.2.15

# Well-known ports
export DNS=53
export FTP=21
export GIT=9418
export HEARTBEAT=694
export IMAPS=993
export IRC=6667
export MONIT=2828
export MYSQL=3306
export MYSQL_MASTER=3307
export NRPE=5666
export NTP=123
export POSTGRES=5432
export PUPPET=8140
```

```
export RSYNCD=873
export SMTP=25
export SPHINX=3312
export SSH=22
export STARLING=3307
export SYSLOG=514
export WEB=80
export WEB_SSL=443
export ZABBIX=10051
```

5. Create the file `/etc/puppet/modules/iptables/files/common.role` with the following contents:

```
# Common rules for all hosts
iptables -A INPUT -p tcp -m tcp -d ${MAIN_IP} --dport ${SSH} -j
ACCEPT

iptables -A INPUT -p ICMP --icmp-type echo-request -j ACCEPT
iptables -A OUTPUT -p ICMP --icmp-type echo-request -j ACCEPT

iptables -A OUTPUT -p tcp --dport ${SSH} -j ACCEPT
iptables -A OUTPUT -p tcp --dport ${SMTP} -j ACCEPT
iptables -A OUTPUT -p udp --dport ${NTP} -j ACCEPT
iptables -A OUTPUT -p tcp --dport ${NTP} -j ACCEPT
iptables -A OUTPUT -p udp --dport ${DNS} -j ACCEPT
iptables -A OUTPUT -p tcp --dport ${WEB} -j ACCEPT
iptables -A OUTPUT -p tcp --dport ${WEB_SSL} -j ACCEPT
iptables -A OUTPUT -p tcp -d ${PUPPETMASTER} --dport ${PUPPET} -j
ACCEPT
iptables -A OUTPUT -p tcp --dport ${MYSQL} -j ACCEPT

# Drop some commonly probed ports
iptables -A INPUT -p tcp --dport 23 -j DROP # telnet
iptables -A INPUT -p tcp --dport 135 -j DROP # epmap
iptables -A INPUT -p tcp --dport 139 -j DROP # netbios
iptables -A INPUT -p tcp --dport 445 -j DROP # Microsoft DS
iptables -A INPUT -p udp --dport 1433 -j DROP # SQL server
iptables -A INPUT -p tcp --dport 1433 -j DROP # SQL server
iptables -A INPUT -p udp --dport 1434 -j DROP # SQL server
iptables -A INPUT -p tcp --dport 1434 -j DROP # SQL server
iptables -A INPUT -p tcp --dport 2967 -j DROP # SSC-agent
```

6. Create the file `/etc/puppet/modules/iptables/files/web-server.role` with the following contents:

```
# Access to web
iptables -A INPUT -p tcp -d ${MAIN_IP} --dport ${WEB} -j ACCEPT

# Send mail from web applications
iptables -A OUTPUT -p tcp --dport ${SMTP} -j ACCEPT
```

7. Create the file `/etc/puppet/modules/iptables/files/puppet-server.role` with the following contents:

```
# Access to puppet
iptables -A INPUT -p tcp -d ${MAIN_IP} --dport ${PUPPET} -j ACCEPT
```

8. Include the following on your Puppetmaster node:

```
iptables::role { "web-server": }
iptables::role { "puppet-server": }
```

9. Run Puppet:

```
# puppet agent --test
info: Retrieving plugin
info: Caching catalog for cookbook.bitfieldconsulting.com
info: Applying configuration version '1311682880'
notice: /Stage[main]/Iptables/File[/root/iptables]/ensure: created
notice: /Stage[main]/Iptables/File[/root/iptables/names]/ensure:
defined content as '{md5}9bb004a7d2c6d70616b149d044c22669'
info: /Stage[main]/Iptables/File[/root/iptables/names]: Scheduling
refresh of Exec[run-iptables]
notice: /Stage[main]/Iptables/File[/root/iptables/hosts]/ensure:
created
notice: /Stage[main]/Iptables/File[/root/iptables/hosts/cookbook]/
ensure: defined content as '{md5}d00bc730514bbb74cdef3dad70058a81'
info: /Stage[main]/Iptables/File[/root/iptables/hosts/cookbook]:
Scheduling refresh of Exec[run-iptables]
notice: /Stage[main]//Node[cookbook]/Iptables::Role[web-server]/
Append_if_no_such_line[web-server role]/Exec[/bin/echo '. `dirname
$0`/roles/web-server' >> '/root/iptables/hosts/cookbook']/returns:
executed successfully
info: /Stage[main]//Node[cookbook]/Iptables::Role[web-server]/
Append_if_no_such_line[web-server role]/Exec[/bin/echo '. `dirname
$0`/roles/web-server' >> '/root/iptables/hosts/cookbook']:
Scheduling refresh of Exec[run-iptables]
notice: /Stage[main]//Node[cookbook]/Iptables::Role[puppet-
server]/Append_if_no_such_line[puppet-server role]/Exec[/bin/echo
```

```
'. `dirname $0`/roles/puppet-server' >> '/root/iptables/hosts/
cookbook']/returns: executed successfully
```

info: /Stage[main]//Node[cookbook]/Iptables::Role[puppet-server]/
Append_if_no_such_line[puppet-server role]/Exec[/bin/echo '.
`dirname $0`/roles/puppet-server' >> '/root/iptables/hosts/
cookbook']: Scheduling refresh of Exec[run-iptables]

notice: /Stage[main]/Iptables/File[/root/iptables/roles]/ensure:
created

notice: /Stage[main]//Node[cookbook]/Iptables::Role[puppet-
server]/File[/root/iptables/roles/puppet-server]/ensure: defined
content as '{md5}c30a13f7792525c181e14e78c9a510cd'

info: /Stage[main]//Node[cookbook]/Iptables::Role[puppet-server]/
File[/root/iptables/roles/puppet-server]: Scheduling refresh of
Exec[run-iptables]

notice: /Stage[main]//Node[cookbook]/Iptables::Role[web-server]/
File[/root/iptables/roles/web-server]/ensure: defined content as
'{md5}11e5747cb2737903ffc34133f5fe2452'

info: /Stage[main]//Node[cookbook]/Iptables::Role[web-server]/
File[/root/iptables/roles/web-server]: Scheduling refresh of
Exec[run-iptables]

notice: /Stage[main]/Iptables/File[/root/iptables/roles/common]/
ensure: defined content as '{md5}116f57d4e31f3e0b351da6679dca15e3'

info: /Stage[main]/Iptables/File[/root/iptables/roles/common]:
Scheduling refresh of Exec[run-iptables]

notice: /Stage[main]/Iptables/File[/root/iptables/iptables.sh]/
ensure: defined content as '{md5}340ff9fb5945e9fc7dd78b21f45dd823'

info: /Stage[main]/Iptables/File[/root/iptables/iptables.sh]:
Scheduling refresh of Exec[run-iptables]

notice: /Stage[main]/Iptables/Exec[run-iptables]: Triggered
'refresh' from 8 events

notice: /Stage[main]/Iptables/Append_if_no_such_line[restore
iptables rules]/Exec[/bin/echo 'pre-up iptables-restore < /etc/
iptables.rules' >> '/etc/network/interfaces']/returns: executed
successfully

notice: Finished catalog run in 4.86 seconds

10. Check that the required rules have been installed as follows:

```
# iptables -nL
Chain INPUT (policy ACCEPT)
target     prot opt source              destination
ACCEPT     all  --  0.0.0.0/0           0.0.0.0/0
ACCEPT     all  --  0.0.0.0/0           0.0.0.0/0            state
RELATED,ESTABLISHED
```

ACCEPT	tcp	--	0.0.0.0/0	10.0.2.15	tcp	dpt:80
ACCEPT	tcp	--	0.0.0.0/0	10.0.2.15	tcp	dpt:8140
ACCEPT	tcp	--	0.0.0.0/0	10.0.2.15	tcp	dpt:22
ACCEPT	icmp	--	0.0.0.0/0	0.0.0.0/0	icmp	type 8
DROP	tcp	--	0.0.0.0/0	0.0.0.0/0	tcp	dpt:23
DROP	tcp	--	0.0.0.0/0	0.0.0.0/0	tcp	dpt:135
DROP	tcp	--	0.0.0.0/0	0.0.0.0/0	tcp	dpt:139
DROP	tcp	--	0.0.0.0/0	0.0.0.0/0	tcp	dpt:445
DROP	udp	--	0.0.0.0/0	0.0.0.0/0	udp	dpt:1433
DROP	tcp	--	0.0.0.0/0	0.0.0.0/0	tcp	dpt:1433
DROP	udp	--	0.0.0.0/0	0.0.0.0/0	udp	dpt:1434
DROP	tcp	--	0.0.0.0/0	0.0.0.0/0	tcp	dpt:1434
DROP	tcp	--	0.0.0.0/0	0.0.0.0/0	tcp	dpt:2967
LOG	all	--	0.0.0.0/0	0.0.0.0/0	LOG	flags 0 level 4 prefix `INPUT: '
DROP	all	--	0.0.0.0/0	0.0.0.0/0		

```
Chain FORWARD (policy ACCEPT)
target     prot opt source              destination

Chain OUTPUT (policy ACCEPT)
target     prot opt source              destination
```

ACCEPT	all	--	0.0.0.0/0	0.0.0.0/0		
ACCEPT	all	--	0.0.0.0/0	0.0.0.0/0	state	RELATED,ESTABLISHED
ACCEPT	tcp	--	0.0.0.0/0	0.0.0.0/0	tcp	dpt:25
ACCEPT	icmp	--	0.0.0.0/0	0.0.0.0/0	icmp	type 8
ACCEPT	tcp	--	0.0.0.0/0	0.0.0.0/0	tcp	dpt:22
ACCEPT	tcp	--	0.0.0.0/0	0.0.0.0/0	tcp	dpt:25

ACCEPT	udp	--	0.0.0.0/0	0.0.0.0/0	udp
dpt:123					
ACCEPT	tcp	--	0.0.0.0/0	0.0.0.0/0	tcp
dpt:123					
ACCEPT	udp	--	0.0.0.0/0	0.0.0.0/0	udp
dpt:53					
ACCEPT	tcp	--	0.0.0.0/0	0.0.0.0/0	tcp
dpt:80					
ACCEPT	tcp	--	0.0.0.0/0	0.0.0.0/0	tcp
dpt:443					
ACCEPT	tcp	--	0.0.0.0/0	10.0.2.15	tcp
dpt:8140					
ACCEPT	tcp	--	0.0.0.0/0	0.0.0.0/0	tcp
dpt:3306					
LOG	all	--	0.0.0.0/0	0.0.0.0/0	LOG
flags 0 level 4 prefix `OUTPUT: '					
DROP	all	--	0.0.0.0/0	0.0.0.0/0	

How it works...

In order to create a suitable set of firewall rules, we need to know the main IP address of the machine in question, and also what services it is running. We also want to add some common rules that all machines will have (allow SSH, for example), and to run a series of `iptables` commands that will activate the rules we've generated. Having done this, we want to save the rules so that they can be reactivated at boot time. So here's how it's all done.

First, we create a `names` file that defines shell variables for some commonly-used ports. This means when we define firewall rules we can refer to a named variable like `${MYSQL}` instead of the numeric value `3306` for the MySQL port.

The `common.role` file contains some useful rules for all machines. Modify these to suit your own installation (for example, you might allow SSH access only from specific IP ranges).

The `web-server.role` and `puppet-server.role` files contain rules for these specific roles. Add more files to define the roles you need on your network: for example, database servers, application workers, DNS servers, and so on. The rules are in the following format:

```
iptables -A INPUT -p tcp -d ${MAIN_IP} --dport ${WEB} -j ACCEPT
```

Usually, the only part you need to modify is the `${WEB}`: substitute another named port such as `${POSTGRES}`, defined in the `names` file. Add more definitions to the `names` file if you need them.

The `iptables.sh` script reads all of these other files and executes the required `iptables` commands. Puppet executes this script whenever any of the dependent files change, so all you need to do to refresh the firewall is to check in a change and run Puppet.

Puppet also saves the current ruleset to `/etc/iptables.rules`. In order to reload the ruleset when the machine boots, Puppet adds a line to the `/etc/network/interfaces` file to do this:

```
pre-up iptables-restore < /etc/iptables.rules
```

What all this means is that you can create a suitable firewall for a machine simply by including a line like this in the relevant module:

```
iptables::role { "web-server": }
```

Once the firewall is activated, any packets that don't match the rules will be blocked and logged in `/var/log/messages`. Check this file to help troubleshoot any problems with the firewall.

There's more...

If you have certain specific machines that will be referenced in your rules (for example, your monitoring server) you can add it to the `names` file like this:

```
MONITOR=10.0.2.15
```

Then in a suitable place (such as `common.role`) you can allow access from this machine to, for example, the NRPE port:

```
iptables -A INPUT -p tcp -m tcp -d ${MAIN_IP} -s ${MONITOR}  --dport
${NRPE} -j ACCEPT
```

You can also do this for database servers and anything else where you need to reference a specific address, network, or IP range in a `.role` file.

Dynamically generating the firewall ruleset like this can be very useful for cloud infrastructures where the list of servers is constantly changing as new ones are created and destroyed. All you need to do to have any resource trigger a firewall rebuild is to add:

```
notify => Exec["run-iptables"],
```

So you might have a "master server list" that you maintain in version control or update automatically from a cloud API such as Rackspace or Amazon EC2. This list might be a `file` resource in Puppet that can trigger a firewall rebuild, so every time you check in a change to the master list, every machine that runs Puppet will update its firewall accordingly.

Of course, such a high degree of automation means that you need to be quite careful about what you check in, or you can take your whole infrastructure offline by mistake.

A good way to test changes is to use a Git branch for your Puppet manifests, which is only applied on one or two servers. Once you have verified that the changes are good you can merge them into the master branch and roll them out.

Managing EC2 instances

"The most amazing achievement of the computer software industry is its continuing cancellation of the steady and staggering gains made by the computer hardware industry."—Henry Petroski

If you think your computer's gotten slower in recent years, you're probably right. For many applications, you can no longer squeeze all the computing power you need into a single beige box under your desk. To address this issue, computing power has become a commodity you can buy online.

Amazon doesn't just sell books anymore: they also sell jewelry, motorcycles, leaf blowers, and more usefully for our present purposes, computing power. You can sign up for Amazon Web Services with a credit card and proceed to create as many server instances as you like, for which you pay by the hour. If you just want to test the water, you can run a Micro instance for up to a year for free. If you're looking at moving some parts of your infrastructure into public cloud, this is a great way to experiment.

This recipe will show you a simple way to provision an **EC2** instance automatically and build it with Puppet. Although there are more powerful ways to do this, including using MCollective, for teaching purposes we're going to do the bare minimum necessary to get an instance running and apply a Puppet manifest to it. You can use this as a foundation for adding your own refinements and improvements once you've got the basic idea.

Getting ready...

You'll need an **Amazon Web Services** (**AWS**) account if you don't already have one. You can sign up here: `http://aws-portal.amazon.com/gp/aws/developer/subscription/index.html?productCode=AmazonEC2`.

You'll need the AWS access key ID and secret access key corresponding to your account. You can find these on this page: `http://aws-portal.amazon.com/gp/aws/developer/account/index.html?action=access-key`.

You'll also need your SSH Keypair for accessing EC2 instances. To find this, log in to the AWS Management Console at `https://console.aws.amazon.com/ec2/home`.

Select the **Amazon EC2 tab**, and click **Key Pairs** under the **Network & Security** heading in the navigation section.

Click **Create key pair** and then download the `keypair` file when prompted. Save this somewhere safe, and set the file permissions to `mode 0600` as follows:

```
# chmod 600 bitfield.pem
```

How to do it...

1. Create a `fog` module:

```
# mkdir /etc/puppet/modules/fog
# mkdir /etc/puppet/modules/fog/manifests
# mkdir /etc/puppet/modules/fog/files
```

2. Create the file `/etc/puppet/modules/fog/manifests/init.pp` with the following contents:

```
class fog {
    package { "fog":
        ensure   => installed,
        provider => gem,
    }

    file { "/usr/local/etc/fog_credentials":
        source => "puppet:///modules/fog/fog_credentials",
    }

    file { "/usr/local/bin/boot-ec2":
        source => "puppet:///modules/fog/boot-ec2.rb",
        mode   => "755",
    }

    file { "/usr/local/bin/bootstrap-ec2":
        source => "puppet:///modules/fog/bootstrap-ec2.sh",
        mode   => "755",
    }
}
```

3. Create the file `/etc/puppet/modules/fog/files/boot-ec2.rb` with the following contents (change the `:private_key_path` argument to point to your own AWS private key file):

```
#!/usr/bin/ruby
require 'rubygems'
require 'fog'

HOSTNAME = 'devbox'
@server = ''
Fog.credentials_path = '/usr/local/etc/fog_credentials'

def command( cmdline )
    puts "Running command: #{cmdline}"
    res = @server.ssh( "sudo #{cmdline}" )[0]
```

```
    puts res.stdout
    puts res.stderr
end

def create()
    puts "Bootstrapping instance..."
    connection = Fog::Compute.new( { :provider => 'AWS' } )
    @server = connection.servers.bootstrap( :key_name =>
                                            'bitfield',
                                            :private_key_path =>
                                            '~/bitfield.pem',
                                            :username => 'ubuntu')
    @server.wait_for { ready? }
    @server.reload
    puts "Instance name: #{@server.dns_name}"
    puts "Setting hostname..."
    @server.ssh( "sudo hostname #{HOSTNAME}" )
end

def copy_bootstrap_files()
    puts "Copying bootstrap files..."
    @server.scp( "puppet.tar.gz", "/tmp" )
    @server.scp( "/usr/local/bin/bootstrap-ec2", "/tmp" )
end

def bootstrap()
    puts "Bootstrapping..."
    command( "sudo sh /tmp/bootstrap-ec2" )
end

create()
copy_bootstrap_files()
bootstrap()
```

4. Create the file `/etc/puppet/modules/fog/files/bootstrap-ec2.sh` with the following contents:

```
#!/bin/bash
apt-get update
apt-get -y install puppet
apt-get -y install git-core
cd /root
tar xzf /tmp/puppet.tar.gz
puppet --modulepath=/root/puppet/modules /root/puppet/manifests/
site.pp
```

5. Create the file `/etc/puppet/modules/fog/files/fog_credentials` with the following contents (replace with your own AWS credentials):

```
:default:
    :aws_access_key_id: AKIAI5RGMC3QRPO3AJWR
    :aws_secret_access_key: iygf2+7SfKV/OlEyrh+otazeVin9G3XXrvJYKx8E
```

6. Add the following node definition, which will be applied to the EC2 instance:

```
node devbox {
    file { "/etc/motd":
        content => "Puppet power!\n",
    }
}
```

7. Add the following to a node:

```
include fog
```

8. Run Puppet:

```
# puppet agent --test

info: Retrieving plugin

info: Caching catalog for cookbook.bitfieldconsulting.com

info: Applying configuration version '1313160844'

notice: /Stage[main]/Fog/Package[fog]/ensure: ensure changed
'purged' to 'present'

notice: /Stage[main]/Fog/File[/usr/local/bin/bootstrap-ec2]/
ensure: defined content as '{md5}5bc2ffb3b5aa94b33b17d419625ecbab'

notice: /Stage[main]/Fog/File[/usr/local/bin/boot-ec2]/ensure:
defined content as '{md5}dadc835c6e52c89cb928d60db7677713'

notice: /Stage[main]/Fog/File[/usr/local/etc/fog_credentials]/
ensure: defined content as '{md5}3b140aedac170bbfcc2837077e03bb93'

notice: Finished catalog run in 1.67 seconds
```

9. Create a Puppet tarball in your working directory for distribution to the EC2 instance. The simplest way to do this is to `tar` up your existing Puppet repo or checkout:

```
# cd /etc

# tar czf /tmp/puppet.tar.gz --exclude .git puppet

# cd -

# mv /tmp/puppet.tar.gz .
```

10. Run the `boot-ec2` script:

```
# boot-ec2

Bootstrapping instance...

Instance name: ec2-107-20-59-174.compute-1.amazonaws.com
```

```
Setting hostname...

Copying bootstrap files...

Bootstrapping...

Running command: sudo sh /tmp/bootstrap.sh

sudo: unable to resolve host devbox

sudo: unable to resolve host devbox

...

notice: //Node[devbox]/File[/etc/motd]/content: defined content as
'unknown checksum'
```

11. Log in to the instance to check your manifest has been applied properly:

```
# ssh -i bitfield.pem ubuntu@ec2-107-20-59-174.compute-1.
amazonaws.com

Puppet power!

ubuntu@devbox:~$
```

12. You've got a Puppet-controlled cloud server! If you want ten more instances, run the script ten more times. Don't forget to shut your instances down after you're finished using them. You can do this from the AWS Management Console.

How it works...

Fog is a Ruby library for managing cloud resources, including EC2 and other providers such as Rackspace. Although you can use Amazon's own `ec2-tools` scripts to start and manage instances, using Fog makes it much easier to move your instances to another provider, and you don't need to install Java or other dependencies for `ec2-tools`. Having built EC2 infrastructure both ways, I can confidently say that I prefer using Fog, despite the fact that it has almost no documentation (Amazon actually has too much).

In the `boot-ec2` script, we've used Fog to create a new EC2 instance using our credentials, and to transfer a copy of the Puppet manifest onto it. We then copy the `bootstrap-ec2` script which installs Puppet and applies the manifest.

In this example, the manifest is pretty simple:

```
file { "/etc/motd":
    content => "Puppet power!\n",
}
```

You can easily change it to be, for example, the same as for your production app server. This would be a good way of quickly deploying a large pool of app servers behind a physical load balancer, for example, to handle a sudden spike in demand. Alternatively, you can use EC2 instances as test or staging servers—it's up to you.

There's more...

There's no limit to the number of instances you can deploy with EC2—except perhaps the limit imposed by your credit card. So you could try modifying the script shown here to start a number of instances, set by a command-line argument.

You might also want different types of instances—web servers and queue worker servers, for example. You could modify the boot script to take an argument specifying the instance type to start.

The script shown here has an important limitation in that it supplies the instance with a snapshot of your Puppet manifest, in the form of a tarball. Obviously, as you make changes to your Puppet manifest, that won't be reflected on the instance. For the purposes of simplicity, the example in this recipe just uses Puppet to build the server initially; and it doesn't run the Puppet daemon or connect to a Puppetmaster server.

This is often fine for EC2 instances that are short-lived and only spun up for specific purposes. If you need servers that run for a longer time or you need to be able to push changes out to them with Puppet, you'll need to modify the script to have the instance contact your Puppet server. To solve the problem of signing certificates, you might pre-generate the certificate and deploy it to the instance along with the bootstrap script, for example. Alternatively, you could have the script log in to your Puppet server and sign the instance's certificate request via SSH or MCollective. The mechanism can be as simple or as sophisticated as you like.

You might also want to be able to use other cloud providers, such as Rackspace or Linode. To do this, you will need to make small modifications to the script. Consult the Fog documentation for more information on this at `http://fog.io`.

 You can also use Puppet's new Cloud Provisioner extension to manage your EC2 instances; for more on this see the Puppet Labs page at `http://docs.puppetlabs.com/guides/cloud_pack_getting_started.html`.

See also

▶ *Managing virtual machines with Vagrant* in this chapter

Managing virtual machines with Vagrant

"In 1974 computers were oppressive devices in far-off air-conditioned places. Now you can be oppressed in your own living room."—Ted Nelson

While it's great to be able to deploy virtual machines in the cloud, running them on your own desktop is sometimes even more convenient, especially for testing. If every developer can have a clone of the production system in a VM on her own machine, she's less likely to run into problems when deploying for real. Similarly, if every sysadmin can test his configuration management changes on a private VM, it's a great way to catch issues before they affect customers.

For some years tools like VirtualBox and VMware have been available to do this. However, desktop cloud has really taken off with the arrival of **Vagrant**, a tool for managing and provisioning VM environments automatically. Vagrant drives VirtualBox to automate the process of creating a VM, provisioning it with Chef or Puppet, setting up networking, port forwarding, and packaging running VMs into images for others to use.

You can use Vagrant to manage your development VMs on your own desktop, or on a shared machine such as a continuous integration server. For example, you might use a CI tool such as Jenkins to boot a VM with Vagrant, deploy your app, and then run your tests against it as though it were in production.

How to do it...

1. Create a `vagrant` module:

   ```
   # mkdir /etc/puppet/modules/vagrant
   # mkdir /etc/puppet/modules/vagrant/manifests
   # mkdir /etc/puppet/modules/vagrant/files
   ```

2. Create the file `/etc/puppet/modules/vagrant/manifests/init.pp` with the following contents:

   ```
   class vagrant {
       $virtualbox_deps = [ "libgl1-mesa-glx",
                            "libqt4-network",
                            "libqt4-opengl",
                            "libqtcore4",
                            "libqtgui4",
                            "libsdl1.2debian",
                            "libxmu6",
                            "libxt6",
                            "gawk",
                            "linux-headers-${kernelrelease}" ]
   ```

```
package { $virtualbox_deps: ensure => installed }

exec { "download-virtualbox":
    cwd     => "/root",
    command => "/usr/bin/wget http://download.virtualbox.org/
    virtualbox/4.1.0/virtualbox-4.1_4.1.0-73009~Ubuntu~lucid_
    i386.deb",
    creates => "/root/virtualbox-4.1_4.1.0-73009~Ubuntu~lucid_
    i386.deb",
    timeout => "-1",
}

exec { "install-virtualbox":
    command => "/usr/bin/dpkg -i /root/virtualbox-4.1_4.1.0-
    73009~Ubuntu~lucid_i386.deb",
    unless  => "/usr/bin/dpkg -l |/bin/grep virtualbox-4.1",
    require => [ Exec["download-virtualbox"],
    Package[$virtualbox_deps] ],
}

$vagrant_deps = [ "build-essential",
                  "rubygems" ]

package { $vagrant_deps: ensure => installed }

exec { "install-rubygems-update":
    command => "/usr/bin/gem install -v 1.8.6 rubygems-
    update",
    unless  => "/usr/bin/gem -v |/bin/grep 1.8.6",
    require => Package["rubygems"],
}

exec { "run-rubygems-update":
    command => "/var/lib/gems/1.8/bin/update_rubygems",
    unless  => "/usr/bin/gem -v |/bin/grep 1.8.6",
    require => Exec["install-rubygems-update"],
}

package { "vagrant":
    provider => gem,
    ensure   => installed,
    require  => [ Package["build-essential"], Exec["run-
    rubygems-update"] ],
}

define devbox( $vm_user ) {
    include vagrant

    $vm_dir = "/home/${vm_user}/${name}"

    file { [ $vm_dir,
```

```
                    "${vm_dir}/data" ]:
            ensure => directory,
            owner   => $vm_user,
        }

        file { "${vm_dir}/Vagrantfile":
            source  => "puppet:///modules/vagrant/devbox.
            Vagrantfile",
            require => File[$vm_dir],
        }
    }
}
```

3. Create the file `/etc/puppet/modules/vagrant/files/devbox.Vagrantfile` with the following contents:

```
Vagrant::Config.run do |config|
  config.vm.box = "lucid32"
  config.vm.box_url = "http://files.vagrantup.com/lucid32.box"
  config.vm.forward_port "http", 80, 8080
  config.vm.share_folder "v-data", "/vagrant_data", "./data"

  config.vm.customize do |vm|
    vm.name = "devbox"
  end

  config.vm.provision :puppet,:module_path => "puppet/modules-0"
  do |puppet|
      puppet.manifests_path = "puppet/manifests"
      puppet.manifest_file  = "site.pp"
  end
end
```

4. Include the following on the node where you want to run the VM (replace `john` with your own username).

```
vagrant::devbox { "devbox":
    vm_user => "john",
}
```

5. Add a node definition for `devbox`:

```
node devbox {
    group { "puppet": ensure => present }

    file { "/etc/motd":
        content => "Puppet power!\n",
    }
}
```

6. Run Puppet:

   ```
   # puppet agent --test
   ```

7. You should find a directory `devbox` created in your home directory. In this directory, either check out your Puppet repository to a directory named `puppet`, or make a **symlink** to an existing Puppet checkout:

   ```
   # cd ~/devbox
   # git clone git@github.com:Example/Puppet.git puppet
   ```

   or

   ```
   # ln -s /etc/puppet ~/devbox/puppet
   ```

8. In the `devbox` directory, run the following command line:

   ```
   # vagrant up
   [default] Box lucid32 was not found. Fetching box from specified URL...
   [default] Downloading with Vagrant::Downloaders::HTTP...
   [default] Downloading box: http://files.vagrantup.com/lucid32.box
   [default] Extracting box...
   [default] Verifying box...
   [default] Cleaning up downloaded box...
   [default] Importing base box 'lucid32'...
   [default] Matching MAC address for NAT networking...
   [default] Clearing any previously set forwarded ports...
   [default] Forwarding ports...
   [default] -- http: 80 => 8080 (adapter 1)
   [default] -- ssh: 22 => 2222 (adapter 1)
   [default] Creating shared folders metadata...
   [default] Running any VM customizations...
   [default] Booting VM...
   [default] Waiting for VM to boot. This can take a few minutes.
   [default] VM booted and ready for use!
   [default] Mounting shared folders...
   [default] -- v-root: /vagrant
   [default] -- v-data: /vagrant_data
   [default] -- manifests: /tmp/vagrant-puppet/manifests
   [default] Running provisioner: Vagrant::Provisioners::Puppet...
   [default] Running Puppet with site.pp...
   ```

```
[default] stdin: is not a tty
[default] notice: /Stage[main]//Node[devbox]/File[/etc/motd]/
ensure: defined content as '{md5}0bdeca690dbb409d48391f3772d389b7'
[default]
[default] notice: /Group[puppet]/ensure: created
[default]
[default] notice: Finished catalog run in 0.36 seconds
[default]
```

Log into the `devbox` VM to test it:

```
# vagrant ssh
Puppet power!
Last login: Thu Jul 21 13:07:53 2011 from 10.0.2.2
vagrant@devbox:~$ logout
Connection to 127.0.0.1 closed.
```

How it works...

The `vagrant` class installs Vagrant and VirtualBox and all their dependencies. It also makes the `devbox` define available. You can then use it to create multiple `devbox` instances for multiple users on a machine. An instance of `devbox` such as:

```
vagrant::devbox { "app-foo-devbox":
    vm_user => "john",
}
```

will create a Vagrant project directory named `app-foo-devbox` (a directory containing a `Vagrantfile` that specifies a virtual machine definition) in the user's (in this case `john`) home directory.

When Vagrant boots the VM for the first time, it's configured to look in a subdirectory of the project directory named `puppet` for the Puppet manifest to provision the machine. This can be a symlink to your Puppet working copy, or a standalone Puppet manifest just for the devbox—whatever you like, so long as Vagrant can find it.

Once the VM has been provisioned, it's ready for use. Just run `vagrant up` to start the machine, `vagrant ssh` to log into it, and `vagrant halt` to stop it.

By the way, the `puppet` group resource in the node definition is there to work around a bug in Vagrant's Puppet provisioning that may be fixed by the time you read this. Vagrant is under active development so one or two things may not work exactly as they do here: if in doubt, check the documentation link at the end of this recipe.

You may find that the VM does not boot fully sometimes, and Vagrant just times out waiting for it. This seems to be due to a bug that may be fixed by the time you read this. If not, you can work around the problem by adding the following code snippet to the Vagrantfile:

```
config.vm.boot_mode = :gui
```

and restarting the VM. It will now boot in GUI mode, with a console window. Log in via this window as user `vagrant`, with password `vagrant`, and run the following command:

```
# sudo /etc/init.d/networking restart
```

You should find that Vagrant now completes the provisioning phase and that `vagrant ssh` will work.

There's more...

In this example we just configured `devbox` with a simple manifest that adds a message to the `/etc/motd` file. To make this more useful, have `devbox` pick up the same manifest as the real server you'll be deploying to. For example:

```
node production, devbox {
    include myapp::production
}
```

Thus, any changes you make to the production server config will be reflected in the machine you run your tests on, so that you can pick up problems before deploying. Similarly, if you need to make a config change to support a new feature, you can test it on the VM first to see if anything doesn't work.

If you want to suspend or shut down your VM while you're not using it, run:

```
# vagrant suspend
```

or

```
# vagrant halt
```

To wipe the VM completely, so that you can test re-provisioning it, for example, run:

```
# vagrant destroy
```

The Vagrant maintainers have done a great job of making it very straightforward to use, but you can read more about Vagrant if you need to at the documentation site: `http://vagrantup.com/docs/index.html`.

9
External Tools and the Puppet Ecosystem

"Unix is the answer, but only if you phrase the question very carefully."—Belinda Asbell

In this chapter we will cover the following topics:

- ▶ Creating custom Facter facts
- ▶ Executing commands before and after Puppet runs
- ▶ Generating manifests from shell sessions
- ▶ Generating manifests from a running system
- ▶ Using Puppet Dashboard
- ▶ Using Foreman
- ▶ Using MCollective
- ▶ Using public modules
- ▶ Using an external node classifier
- ▶ Creating your own resource types
- ▶ Creating your own providers

Puppet is a useful tool by itself, but you can get much greater benefits from using Puppet in combination with other tools and frameworks. We'll look at some of these in this chapter, from tools for getting data into Puppet - Facter, `cft`, and `puppet resource`—to tools for managing and reporting the data that comes out of Puppet—Foreman and Puppet Dashboard.

You'll also learn how to extend Puppet by creating your own custom resource types and implementing them on different platforms, how to use an external node classifier script to integrate Puppet with databases such as LDAP, how to use public modules from Puppet Forge, and how Puppet plays with the systems management framework MCollective.

Creating custom Facter facts

While Facter's built-in facts are useful, it's actually quite easy to add your own facts. For example, if you have machines in different data centers or hosting providers, you can add a **custom fact** for this so that Puppet can determine if any local settings need to be applied (for example, local DNS servers).

Getting ready...

1. Enable the `pluginsync` option in `puppet.conf`:

   ```
   [main]
   pluginsync = true
   ```

2. Create a directory for the fact. This should be called `lib/facter`, and placed in a suitable module directory. For example, you might use the directory `modules/admin/lib/facter`. Any custom facts you create can then be placed in this directory and Puppet will sync them to clients.

How to do it...

1. Create a text file named `hello.rb` with the following contents:

   ```
   Facter.add(:hello) do
       setcode do
           "Hello, world"
       end
   end
   ```

2. Run Puppet on a client. This should sync the fact to the client machine:

   ```
   # puppet agent --test
   info: Retrieving plugin
   notice: /File[/var/lib/puppet/lib/facter/hello.rb]/ensure: defined
   content as '{md5}7314e71d35db83b563a253e741121b1d'
   ```

```
info: Loading downloaded plugin /var/lib/puppet/lib/facter/hello.rb

info: Loading facts in hello

info: Loading facts in hello

info: Loading facts in hello

info: Loading facts in hello

info: Connecting to sqlite3 database: /var/lib/puppet/state/
clientconfigs.sqlite3

info: Caching catalog for cookbook.bitfieldconsulting.com

info: Applying configuration version '1297258039'

notice: Finished catalog run in 0.57 seconds
```

3. Test the fact by running Facter directly as follows:

   ```
   # facter hello
   Hello, world
   ```

4. Now you can reference the fact in a Puppet manifest:

   ```
   notify { $hello: }
   ```

5. When you run Puppet, the value returned by the fact will be inserted as follows:

   ```
   notice: Hello, world
   ```

How it works...

The built-in facts in Facter are defined in the same way as the custom fact that we just created. This architecture makes it very easy to add or modify facts, and provides a standard way for you to read information about the host into your Puppet manifests.

Facts can contain any Ruby code, and the last value evaluated inside the setcode do ... end block will be the value returned by the fact. For example, you could make a more useful fact that returns the number of users currently logged in:

```
Facter.add(:users) do
    setcode do
        %x{/usr/bin/who |wc -l}.chomp
    end
end
```

The output is:

```
notice:  2 users logged in
```

There's more...

You can extend the use of facts to build a completely 'nodeless' Puppet configuration: in other words, Puppet can decide what resources to apply to a machine based solely on the results of facts. Jordan Sissel has written about this approach at `http://www.semicomplete.com/blog/geekery/puppet-nodeless-configuration.html`.

There are many examples of custom facts available on the web, including Cosimo Streppone's article on deriving data-center location from IP addresses at `http://my.opera.com/cstrep/blog/puppet-custom-facts-and-master-less-puppet-deployment`.

Executing commands before and after Puppet runs

If you need to have a command executed before each Puppet run, you can do this using the `prerun_command` configuration setting. Similarly, you can use `postrun_command` to execute a command after the run has completed. This mechanism gives you a powerful hook to integrate Puppet with other software, or even trigger events on other machines.

The `prerun` and `postrun` commands must succeed (that is, return a zero exit status), or Puppet will report an error. This enables you to have any command failures reported using Puppet's reporting mechanism, for example.

How to do it...

Set `prerun_command` or `postrun_command` in `puppet.conf` to the commands you want to run:

```
prerun_command = /usr/local/bin/before-puppet-run.sh
postrun_command = /usr/local/bin/after-puppet-run.sh
```

There's more...

You can use prerun and postrun commands to integrate Puppet with Ubuntu's `etckeeper` system. **Etckeeper** is a version control system for tracking changes to files in the `/etc` directory. To do this, define these commands in `puppet.conf`:

```
prerun_command=/etc/puppet/etckeeper-commit-pre
postrun_command=/etc/puppet/etckeeper-commit-post
```

Generating manifests from shell sessions

"I object to being called a chess genius, because I consider myself to be an all around genius who just happens to play chess, which is rather different."—Bobby Fischer

We're not all geniuses. If you know exactly what needs to be done to install some application or service, you can create the Puppet manifest right away. Often, though, you need to experiment a little bit first, to find out what packages you need to install, what config files need to be edited, and so on. You can record your shell session using the `script` command and then work from the session file to develop the Puppet manifest, and this can be very helpful.

But wouldn't it be wonderful if there was a tool that could read your session file and generate the Puppet manifest for you? It so happens that **cft** (pronounced 'sift') does just this. Once you activate it, `cft` watches your shell session and remembers any packages you install, any services that you configure, any files that you create or edit, and so on. When you're done, it generates a complete Puppet manifest that will reproduce all the changes you just made.

Getting ready...

1. Currently full `cft` support is only available for Red Hat / CentOS distributions; a port to Debian / Ubuntu is in progress, though, and should soon be completed. If you're using Red Hat or CentOS, then, installation is easy:

   ```
   # yum install cft
   ```

2. For Debian / Ubuntu systems, follow the instructions here: `http://fmtyewtk.blogspot.com/2011/01/porting-cft-to-debian.html`.

How to do it...

1. In this example we'll use `cft` to monitor the installation of the NTP package, and then generate a manifest to do the same thing.

   ```
   # cft begin ntp
   # apt-get install ntp
   Reading package lists... Done
   Building dependency tree
   Reading state information... Done
   Suggested packages:
     ntp-doc
   The following NEW packages will be installed:
     ntp
   0 upgraded, 1 newly installed, 0 to remove and 385 not upgraded.
   ```

```
Need to get 517kB of archives.
After this operation, 1,323kB of additional disk space will be
used.
Get:1 http://us.archive.ubuntu.com/ubuntu/ lucid/main ntp
1:4.2.4p8+dfsg-1ubuntu2 [517kB]
Fetched 517kB in 5s (101kB/s)
Selecting previously deselected package ntp.
(Reading database ... 135278 files and directories currently
installed.)
Unpacking ntp (from .../ntp_1%3a4.2.4p8+dfsg-1ubuntu2_i386.deb)
...
Processing triggers for man-db ...
Processing triggers for ureadahead ...
ureadahead will be reprofiled on next reboot
Setting up ntp (1:4.2.4p8+dfsg-1ubuntu2) ...
 * Starting NTP server ntpd

# vi /etc/ntp.conf
# service ntp restart
 * Stopping NTP server ntpd
[ OK ]
 * Starting NTP server ntpd

# cft finish ntp
# cft manifest ntp

class ntp {
    package { 'ntp':
      ensure => '1:4.2.4p8+dfsg-1ubuntu2'
    }

    service { 'ntp':
        enable => 'true',
        ensure => 'running'
    }

    file { '/etc/ntp.conf':
        group => 'root',
        owner => 'root',
        mode => '0644',
        source => '/tmp/cft/ntp/after/etc/ntp.conf'
    }
}
```

How it works...

The first line tells `cft` to start recording changes to the system, and store them in a session named ntp—# `cft begin ntp`.

Then, when you install the `ntp` package, `cft` records this fact. The package install scripts start the service and configure it to start at boot, so `cft` records this too. Finally, it notices that you edited the file `/etc/ntp.conf`, and saves a copy of this for later.

When you run the command # `cft finish ntp` it stops recording changes. You can now generate the manifest, which is the Puppet equivalent of your console session with the command # `cft manifest ntp`.

As you can see, the generated manifest contains the package declaration (triggered by `apt-get install ntp`):

```
package { 'ntp':
ensure => '1:4.2.4p8+dfsg-1ubuntu2'
}
```

It also contains the service declaration that reproduces the effect of the package install scripts, starting the service and enabling it on boot:

```
service { 'ntp':
enable => 'true',
ensure => 'running'
}
```

This declaration would also have been generated if you configured the service manually, with the following command:

service ntp start

update-rc.d ntp defaults

The final part of the manifest encapsulates the changes to the `ntp.conf` file. `cft` doesn't know what changes you made, but only that the file was changed, so it takes a copy of the whole file and makes this available for you to distribute from Puppet:

```
file { '/etc/ntp.conf':
group => 'root',
owner => 'root',
mode => '0644',
source => '/tmp/cft/ntp/after/etc/ntp.conf'
}
```

When you add this manifest to Puppet, you will need to also copy the `ntp.conf` file from the path shown (`/tmp/cft/ntp/after/etc/ntp.conf`), place this somewhere appropriate in your module tree, and then update the `source` parameter accordingly.

There's more...

`cft` is a powerful tool for quickly prototyping Puppet manifests. You could take a newly built box, work on it all day under `cft` getting everything installed and working, and then generate the Puppet manifest that encodes your entire session. This will need some editing, of course, but it's much faster than writing the manifests from scratch.

Generating manifests from a running system

While `cft` generates Puppet manifests from a system administrator's console session, **puppet resource** generates Puppet manifests from the existing configuration of a system. For example, you can have `puppet resource` generate a manifest that creates all the users found on the system. This is very useful for taking a snapshot of a working system and getting its configuration quickly into Puppet.

How to do it...

1. To generate the manifest for a particular user, run:

```
# puppet resource user john
user { 'john':
    password_min_age => '0',
    password_max_age => '99999',
    uid => '1002',
    password => '!',
    gid => '1001',
    groups => ['git'],
    ensure => 'present',
    comment => 'John Arundel',
    home => '/home/john',
    shell => '/bin/bash'
}
```

2. For a particular service, run:

```
# puppet resource service ntp
service { 'ntp':
    ensure => 'running',
    enable => 'true'
}
```

3. For a package, run:

```
# puppet resource package exim4
package { 'exim4':
    ensure => '4.71-3ubuntu1'
}
```

There's more...

You can use `puppet resource` to examine each of the resource types available in Puppet. In the preceding examples, we generated a manifest for a specific instance of the resource type, but you can also use `puppet resource` to dump all instances of the resource:

```
# puppet resource user
user { 'Debian-exim':
    ensure => 'present',
    uid => '117',
    gid => '124',
    home => '/var/spool/exim4',
    password => '!',
    password_min_age => '0',
    password_max_age => '99999',
    shell => '/bin/false'
}
user { 'avahi':
    ensure => 'present',
    uid => '104',
    gid => '111',
    home => '/var/run/avahi-daemon',
    password => '*',
    password_min_age => '0',
    comment => 'Avahi mDNS daemon,,,',
    password_max_age => '99999',
    shell => '/bin/false'
}
...
```

This will generate a lot of output!

Using Puppet Dashboard

Puppet Dashboard is a useful tool for managing Puppet installations, especially large ones, and being able to see node information and reports through a web interface. It can show you which of your nodes have run Puppet recently, how long the runs took, whether any nodes are reporting errors, and whether any nodes have not run Puppet in a while.

Getting ready...

1. Download the Puppet Dashboard package from the Puppet Labs site at
   `http://www.puppetlabs.com/misc/download-options/` and unpack it.
   The installation instructions are contained in a `README.markdown` file inside
   the package, but you will probably need to install some or all of the following
   dependencies:

   ```
   # apt-get install -y build-essential irb libmysql-ruby
   libmysqlclient-dev libopenssl-ruby libreadline-ruby mysql-server
   rake rdoc ri ruby ruby-dev
   ```

2. Create a MySQL database and user for the Puppet Dashboard application (use a
   different password):

   ```
   # mysql -uroot

   Welcome to the MySQL monitor.  Commands end with ; or \g.

   Your MySQL connection id is 39

   Server version: 5.1.41-3ubuntu12.9 (Ubuntu)


   Type 'help;' or '\h' for help. Type '\c' to clear the current
   input statement.

   mysql> create database dashboard;
   Query OK, 1 row affected (0.00 sec)


   mysql> grant all on dashboard.* to dashboard@localhost identified
   by 'topsecret';
   Query OK, 0 rows affected (0.01 sec)


   mysql> flush privileges;
   Query OK, 0 rows affected (0.00 sec)
   ```

3. Copy the example `database.yml` file supplied with Puppet Dashboard to reflect these settings as follows:

```
# cd puppetlabs-puppet-dashboard-071acf4
# cp config/database.yml.example config/database.yml
# vi config/database.yml


production:
    database: dashboard
    username: dashboard
    password: topsecret
    encoding: utf8
    adapter: mysql
```

4. Use the included Rake task to build the initial database as follows:

```
# rake RAILS_ENV=production db:migrate
```

How to do it...

1. Start the built-in webserver:

```
# script/server -e production
=> Booting WEBrick
=> Rails 2.3.5 application starting on http://0.0.0.0:3000
=> Call with -d to detach
=> Ctrl-C to shutdown server
[2011-02-21 09:54:32] INFO   WEBrick 1.3.1
[2011-02-21 09:54:32] INFO   ruby 1.8.7 (2010-01-10) [i486-linux]
[2011-02-21 09:54:37] INFO   WEBrick::HTTPServer#start: pid=16570
port=3000
```

Using a web browser, connect to `localhost:3000`

2. You should see the Puppet Dashboard interface, as shown in the following screenshot:

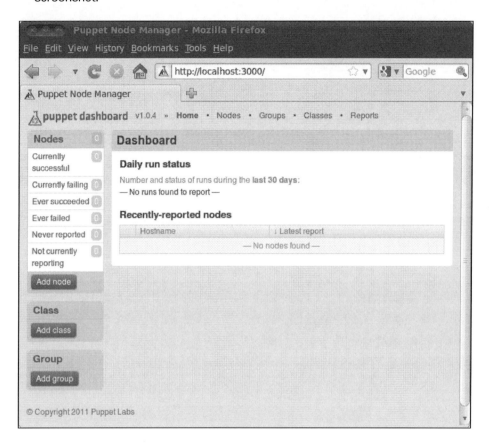

3. You now need to configure your Puppetmaster to send reports to Puppet Dashboard. To do this, add the `http` report type to the `reports` setting in `puppet.conf`:

```
reports = http,log
```

4. Restart the Puppet server to enable the new report.

5. Run Puppet on a node:

```
# puppet agent --test
```

6. Click the **Nodes** link in Puppet Dashboard. You should see a green bar on the graph indicating a successful Puppet run as shown in the following screenshot:

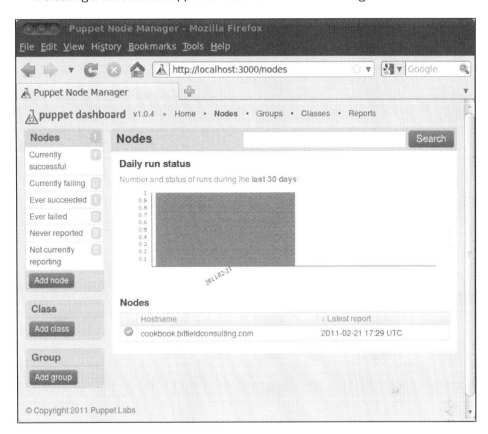

How it works...

When Puppet runs on a node, it sends a report to Puppet Dashboard using the reporting facility. Puppet Dashboard then stores this data and uses it to display graphs and summaries of Puppet activity on all your nodes.

There's more...

You can also use Puppet Dashboard to create new nodes and classes, and control which classes are included on which nodes. In effect, it becomes a web interface for your Puppet manifests so that you can edit them through a web browser rather than having to edit the text files directly. This is an attractive feature, especially if you want people in other teams and departments to be able to manage their own Puppet configurations.

To get this functionality in Puppet Dashboard, you need to configure Puppet to use it as an **external node classifier**; which we'll cover in the section on using an external node classifier to manage nodes.

See also

- ▶ *Generating reports* in *Chapter 2*
- ▶ *Creating graphical reports with RRD* in *Chapter 2*
- ▶ *Using an external node classifier* in this chapter

Using Foreman

Foreman is a web-based Puppet management tool like Puppet Dashboard, but more ambitious. Foreman can manage not only Puppet reporting, nodes and manifest configuration, but also provision new machines for you. If you need to build large numbers of servers automatically, or if you frequently rebuild servers, Foreman will help with this process.

Getting ready...

1. Add the Foreman package repo to your system, following the instructions at
   `http://theforeman.org/projects/foreman/wiki/Installation_instructions`.

2. Install the Foreman package as follows:

   ```
   # apt-get update
   ```

   ```
   # apt-get install foreman
   ```

3. You will be prompted to select a database, so choose `mysql`, `pgsql`, or `sqlite` depending which one you want to use.

4. Install one of the following packages depending which database you selected in the previous step:

   ```
   # apt-get install foreman-mysql
   ```

   ```
   # apt-get install foreman-pgsql
   ```

   ```
   # apt-get install foreman-sqlite3
   ```

5. Copy the file `/etc/foreman/extras/puppet/foreman/files/foreman-report.rb` to your Puppet custom report directory (usually `/usr/lib/ruby/1.8./puppet/reports`) and name it `foreman.rb` as follows:

   ```
   # cp /etc/foreman/extras/puppet/foreman/files/foreman-report.rb /
   usr/lib/ruby/1.8/puppet/reports/foreman.rb
   ```

6. Edit the `foreman.rb` file to set the URL of your Foreman server as follows:

```
# URL of your Foreman installation
$foreman_url="http://cookbook.bitfieldconsulting.com:3000"
```

7. Edit your `puppet.conf` and add the `foreman` report type to the list of enabled reports:

```
[master]
reports = store,log,foreman
```

8. Restart the Puppet server to enable this new report.

How to do it...

1. Start the Foreman server:

```
# /usr/share/foreman/script/server -e production
```

2. Browse to the web interface at the URL you previously set at `http://cookbook.bitfieldconsulting.com:3000`.

   You should see Foreman's initial welcome page as shown in the following screenshot:

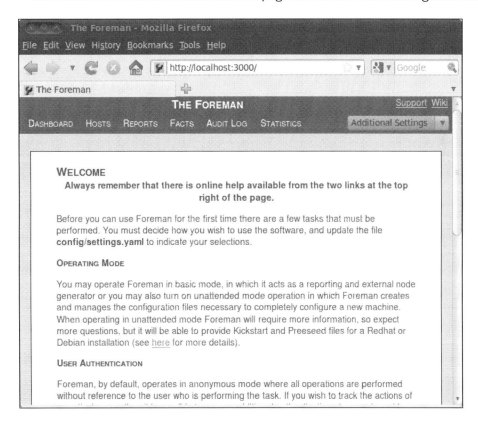

3. Now run Puppet on a client:

```
# puppet agent --test
```

Go to the **Reports** section in the Foreman web interface. You should see a report for the client where you just ran Puppet as shown in the following screenshot:

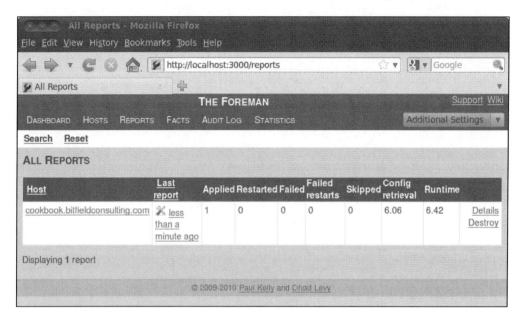

4. Go to the Dashboard page and you will see an **OVERVIEW** of all your clients (just one in this case, but you get the idea).

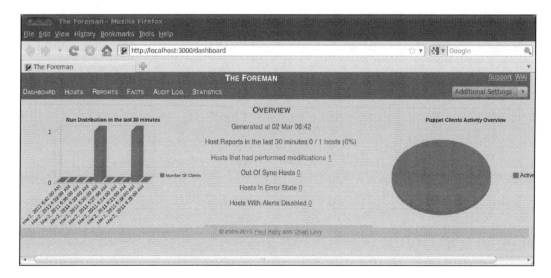

There's more...

We've only touched on the basics of Foreman here. Now that you've got it set up, you can experiment with the different reports, graphs, and other information available in Foreman. These become more valuable when you have many hosts to look after, and want to see statistics about how Puppet is running across the whole network.

The other major feature of Foreman is provisioning: it can use PXEboot and Kickstart to build virtual or physical servers from scratch, sign your Puppet certificates automatically, and run Puppet to bring the machine up to production status. For more information about how to do this, see the Foreman documentation: `http://theforeman.org/projects/foreman/wiki/Unattended_installations`.

> If you decide to use Foreman in production, it's probably worthwhile setting up an Apache virtual host for it rather than using the Webrick server that ships with Foreman. Webrick is useful for testing, but it's not really a production-grade web server.

Using MCollective

The **Marionette Collective** (**MCollective** for short) is a tool for system administration. It can run commands on large numbers of servers in parallel, and uses a broadcast architecture so that you can administer a large network without the need for a central master server or asset database.

Each server runs an MCollective daemon that listens for requests, and can execute commands locally or return information about the server. This can be used to filter the list of target servers. So, for example, you could use MCollective to execute a given command on all servers that match certain criteria.

You can think of MCollective as a complement to Puppet (though it also works fine with Chef and other configuration management systems). For example, your provisioning process for a new node might require firewall changes on other machines, permissions granted on a database server, and so on, which is not very easy to do with Puppet. Although you could automate specific jobs using shell scripts and SSH, MCollective provides a powerful and flexible way to solve this general problem.

Getting ready...

1. MCollective uses the ActiveMQ message broker framework (actually, any STOMP-compliant middleware, but ActiveMQ is a popular choice), which in turn requires Java, so if you don't have Java already installed on your system, install it:

```
# apt-get install gcj-4.4-jre-headless
```

2. Go to the ActiveMQ download page and get the latest stable "Unix distribution" tarball: `http://activemq.apache.org/download.html`.

3. Install the `stomp` gem as follows:

    ```
    # gem install stomp
    ```

4. Download the latest stable MCollective `.deb` packages from: `http://www.puppetlabs.com/misc/download-options/`.

5. Install the packages as follows:

    ```
    # dpkg -i mcollective_1.0.1-1_all.deb mcollective-client_1.0.1-1_
    all.deb mcollective-common_1.0.1-1_all.deb
    ```

6. Download the tarball of the same release from the MCollective downloads page (because it contains an example ActiveMQ configuration file).

7. Edit the MCollective `server.cfg` file:

    ```
    # vi /etc/mcollective/server.cfg
    ```

8. Set the `plugin.stomp.host` parameter to the name of your server (where you're running ActiveMQ):

    ```
    plugin.stomp.host = cookbook.bitfieldconsulting.com
    ```

9. Make the same change in the MCollective `client.cfg` file:

    ```
    # vi /etc/mcollective/client.cfg
    ```

10. Unpack the MCollective tarball and copy the example ActiveMQ configuration into place:

    ```
    # tar xvzf mcollective-1.0.1.tgz
    ```

    ```
    # cp mcollective-1.0.1/ext/activemq/examples/single-broker/
    activemq.xml /etc/mcollective
    ```

11. Edit the configuration file to set the password of the `mcollective` user to the same as it is in `server.cfg`:

    ```
    # vi /etc/mcollective/activemq.xml
    ```

12. Unpack the ActiveMQ tarball and start the server using the following config file:

    ```
    # tar xvzf apache-activemq-5.4.2-bin.tar.gz
    ```

    ```
    # apache-activemq-5.4.2/bin/activemq start xbean:/etc/mcollective/
    activemq.xml
    INFO: Using default configuration

    (you can configure options in one of these file: /etc/default/
    activemq /root/.activemqrc)


    INFO: Invoke the following command to create a configuration file

    bin/activemq setup [ /etc/default/activemq | /root/.activemqrc ]
    ```

```
INFO: Using java '/usr/bin/java'

INFO: Starting - inspect logfiles specified in logging.properties
and log4j.properties to get details

INFO: pidfile created : '/root/apache-activemq-5.4.2/data/
activemq.pid' (pid '3322')
```

13. Start the MCollective server:

```
# service mcollective start

Starting mcollective:    *
```

How to do it...

1. Check that MCollective and ActiveMQ are set up and working by running:

```
# mc-ping

cookbook                                  time=68.82 ms


---- ping statistics ----

1 replies max: 68.82 min: 68.82 avg: 68.82
```

2. If you don't see any results, check that the `mcollectived` daemon is running, and that a Java process is also running for ActiveMQ.

3. Run `mc-inventory` against your machine to see what information MCollective knows about it:

```
# mc-inventory cookbook

Inventory for cookbook:


    Server Statistics:

                      Version: 1.0.1

                   Start Time: Mon Mar 07 11:44:53 -0700 2011

                  Config File: /etc/mcollective/server.cfg

                   Process ID: 4220

               Total Messages: 14

       Messages Passed Filters: 6

             Messages Filtered: 5

                  Replies Sent: 5

         Total Processor Time: 0.8 seconds

                  System Time: 0.47 seconds


        Agents:
```

```
        discovery            rpcutil


    Configuration Management Classes:


    Facts:

        mcollective => 1
```

4. Create a new custom fact for the server by adding the following code snippet to `/etc/mcollective/facts.yaml`:

    `purpose: webserver`

5. Now use MCollective to search for all machines matching this fact:

    `# mc-find-hosts --with-fact purpose=webserver`

    `cookbook`

How it works...

MCollective is a broadcast framework; when you issue a request like `mc-find-hosts`, MCollective sends a message out to all clients asking, "Does anyone match this filter?" All clients that match the filter will send a reply, and MCollective gathers the results and prints them out for you.

You can install a number of plugins and agents for specific tasks (for example, running Puppet). These are installed on the clients, and MCollective handles the communications involved in sending the command out to all matching machines, and collating any results.

There's more...

Even though we've only taken a few steps with MCollective, it's clearly a powerful tool for both gathering information about servers, and executing commands on a list of servers that can be selected by facts. For example, you could get a list of all machines that haven't run Puppet in the last 24 hours. Or, you could take some action on all webservers, or all machines with an `x86_64` architecture.

MCollective itself only provides a framework for such applications. There are a variety of plugins available which do useful things, and writing your own plugins is easy. In this example we'll use the `package` plugin that allows you to query and operate on packages.

Installing an MCollective plugin

1. Clone the MCollective plugins repository from GitHub:

    `# git clone https://github.com/puppetlabs/mcollective-plugins.git`

2. Copy the plugin files into place as follows:

```
# cd mcollective-plugins
# cp agent/package/mc-package /usr/bin
# cp agent/package/puppet-package.rb /usr/share/mcollective/
plugins/mcollective/agent/package.rb
# cp agent/package/package.ddl /usr/share/mcollective/plugins/
mcollective/agent
```

3. Restart MCollective:

```
# service mcollective restart
```

4. Run `mc-inventory` to check that the plugin appears in the list of agents:

```
# mc-inventory cookbook
Inventory for cookbook:

    Server Statistics:
                      Version: 1.0.1
                   Start Time: Tue Mar 08 08:28:29 -0700 2011
                  Config File: /etc/mcollective/server.cfg
                   Process ID: 6047
               Total Messages: 1
       Messages Passed Filters: 1
             Messages Filtered: 0
                  Replies Sent: 0
          Total Processor Time: 0.04 seconds
                  System Time: 0.02 seconds


    Agents:
        discovery          package           rpcutil


    Configuration Management Classes:


    Facts:
        mcollective => 1
        purpose => webserver
```

5. Try the `mc-package` command to verify that it works with the following command:

```
# mc-package status apache2
Do you really want to operate on packages unfiltered? (y/n): y
```

```
    * [ ===========================================================
> ] 1 / 1


cookbook                                    version = apache2-2.2.14-
5ubuntu8.4


---- package agent summary ----
            Nodes: 1 / 1
         Versions: 1 * 2.2.14-5ubuntu8.4
     Elapsed Time: 0.58 s
```

The `package` agent provides a powerful way to check package versions across your whole network, or only on certain machines, and install or update packages as necessary. For more details about this and other MCollective plugins, check the wiki page at: `http://projects.puppetlabs.com/projects/mcollective-plugins/wiki`.

For more information on MCollective, see the main page at: `http://docs.puppetlabs.com/mcollective/`.

Using public modules

"Plagiarize, plagiarize, plagiarize / Only be sure always to call it, please 'research' "
—Tom Lehrer, 'Lobachevsky'

If in doubt, steal. In many cases when you write a Puppet module to manage some software or service, you don't have to start from scratch. Community-contributed modules are available at the **Puppet Forge** site for many popular applications. Sometimes, a community module will be exactly what you need and you can download and start using it right away. In other cases, you will need to make some modifications to suit your particular needs and environment.

If you are new to Puppet, it can be a great help to have some existing code to start with. On the other hand, community modules are often written to be as general and portable as possible, and the extra code required can make them harder to understand.

In general I would not recommend treating Puppet Forge as a source of 'drop-in' modules that you can deploy without reading or understanding the code. This introduces an external dependency to your Puppet infrastructure, and doesn't help advance your understanding and experience of Puppet. Rather, I would use it as a source of inspiration, help, and examples. A module taken from Puppet Forge should be a jumping-off point for you to develop and improve your own modules.

Be aware that a given module may not work on your Linux distribution. Check the README file that comes with the module to see if your operating system is supported.

Getting ready...

1. The easiest way to use Puppet Forge modules is to install the `puppet-module` tool:

```
# gem install puppet-module

Fetching: puppet-module-0.3.2.gem (100%)

****************************************************************
***********


   Thank you for installing puppet-module from Puppet Labs!


   * Usage instructions: read "README.markdown" or run `puppet-
module usage`

   * Changelog: read "CHANGES.markdown" or run `puppet-module
changelog`

   * Puppet Forge: visit http://forge.puppetlabs.com/


****************************************************************
***********

Successfully installed puppet-module-0.3.2

1 gem installed

Installing ri documentation for puppet-module-0.3.2...

Installing RDoc documentation for puppet-module-0.3.2...
```

2. Run `puppet-module` to see the available commands:

```
# puppet-module

Tasks:

   puppet-module build [PATH_TO_MODULE]           # Build a
module for release

   puppet-module changelog                        # Display
the changelog for this tool

   puppet-module changes [PATH_TO_MODULE]         # Show
modified files in an installed m...

   puppet-module clean                            # Clears
module cache for all repositories

   puppet-module generate USERNAME-MODNAME        # Generate
boilerplate for a new module

   puppet-module help [TASK]                      # Describe
available tasks or one speci...

   puppet-module install MODULE_NAME_OR_FILE [OPTIONS]  # Install a
module (eg, 'user-modname')...
```

```
      puppet-module repository                        # Show
   currently configured repository

      puppet-module search TERM                       # Search
   the module repository for a mo...

      puppet-module usage                             # Display
   detailed usage documentation ...

      puppet-module version                           # Show the
   version information for this...


   Options:
      -c, [--config=CONFIG]   # Configuration file
                              # Default: /etc/puppet/puppet.conf
```

How to do it...

In this example, we'll use `puppet-module` to find and install a module to manage the Tomcat application server.

1. Search for a suitable module as follows:

    ```
    # puppet-module search tomcat

    =======================================

    Searching http://forge.puppetlabs.com

    -------------------------------------

    2 found.

    --------

    camptocamp/tomcat (0.0.1)

    jeffmccune/tomcat (1.0.1)
    ```

2. In this example we'll install the Jeff McCune version:

    ```
    # cd /etc/puppet/modules

    # puppet-module install jeffmccune/tomcat

    Installed "jeffmccune-tomcat-1.0.1" into directory:
    jeffmccune-tomcat
    ```

3. The module is now ready to use in your manifests: looking at the source code will show you how to do this.

How it works...

The `puppet-module` tool simply automates the process of searching and downloading modules from the Puppet Forge site. You can browse the site to see what's available at: http://forge.puppetlabs.com/.

There's more...

Not all publically available modules are on Puppet Forge. Some other great places to look are on GitHub:

`https://github.com/camptocamp`

`https://github.com/example42`

Dean Wilson maintains an excellent repository of Puppet patterns, tips, and recipes, at the Puppet Cookbook website: `http://puppetcookbook.com/`.

Using an external node classifier

When Puppet runs on a node, it needs to know which classes should be applied to that node. For example, if it is a web server node, it might need to include an `apache` class. The normal way to map nodes to classes is in the Puppet manifest itself, for example in a `nodes.pp` file:

```
node web1 {
   include apache
}
```

Alternatively, you can use an **external node classifier** to do this job. An external node classifier is any executable program that can accept a node name and return a list of classes for that node. It could be a simple shell script, for example, or a wrapper around a more complicated program or API that can decide how to map nodes to classes.

Getting ready...

1. Set the following variables in your `puppet.conf`:

```
[master]
external_nodes = /usr/local/bin/puppet_node_classifier
node_terminus = exec
```

How to do it...

1. Create this simple example script as `/usr/local/bin/puppet_node_classifier`:

```
#!/bin/bash
if [ "$1" == "cookbook.bitfieldconsulting.com" ]; then
    cat <<"END"
---
classes:
```

```
    - admin::sudoers
    - admin::exim
    - puppet
    - nagios::target

  environment: production
  parameters:
    location: Bitfield HQ
END

else
    exit 1
fi
```

2. Make the script executable:

   # chmod 755 /usr/local/bin/puppet_node_classifier

3. Run Puppet:

   # puppet agent --test

   info: Retrieving plugin

   info: Caching catalog for cookbook.bitfieldconsulting.com

   info: Applying configuration version '1299677816'

   notice: Finished catalog run in 1.19 seconds

How it works...

Puppet calls the script you specify as `external_nodes` in `puppet.conf` and passes the name of the node as the command-line argument. In our example script, we check this argument and if it is equal to `cookbook.bitfieldconsulting.com`, we output a list of classes in the required format for Puppet. Otherwise, the script exits with status 1 (indicating to Puppet that the node was not found).

The script also sets the value of `environment` (see the section on using environments for an explanation of this parameter). The variable `location` is also set to `Bitfield HQ`—this means nothing to Puppet, but the variable will be defined in scope in your manifest, so you could use it to determine DNS resolver settings, for example. You can set any variables you like here.

Obviously, this script is not terribly useful since it just outputs a predetermined list of classes. A more sophisticated script might check a database to find the class list, or look up the node in a hash or an external text file. Hopefully, this example is enough to get you started writing your own external node classifier.

There's more...

One of the major uses for external node classification is to connect Puppet with an LDAP directory. Many large organizations have an LDAP infrastructure, and you can set this up so that Puppet can get information on nodes from the LDAP directory, and other LDAP clients can also get information about the nodes managed by Puppet.

For more information about how to do this, see the "Puppet and LDAP" page at: `http://projects.puppetlabs.com/projects/puppet/wiki/LDAP_Nodes`.

This feature is also used by Puppet Dashboard and Foreman to manage the relationship between nodes and classes via a web interface—they act as external node classifiers.

Creating your own resource types

It's time to get creative. You'll know about various different resource types in Puppet: packages, files, users, and so on. Usually, you can do everything you need to do by using either combinations of these built-in resources, or a custom `define` that you can use more or less in the same way as a resource (see *Chapter 4, Writing Better Manifests* for information on `define`).

However, if you need to create your own resource type, Puppet makes it quite easy. The native types are written in Ruby, and you will need a basic familiarity with Ruby in order to create your own.

Let's refresh our memory on the distinction between **types** and **providers**. A type describes a resource and the parameters it can have (for example, the `package` type). A provider tells Puppet how to implement a resource for a particular platform or situation (for example, the `apt/dpkg` providers implement `package` for Debian-like systems).

A single type (`package`) can have many providers (`apt`, `yum`, `fink`, and so on). If you don't specify a provider when declaring a resource, Puppet will choose the most appropriate one given the environment.

In this section we'll see how to create a custom type to manage Git repositories, and in the next section, we'll write a provider to implement this type.

Getting ready...

1. Enable `pluginsync` in your `puppet.conf`, if you haven't already:

    ```
    [main]
    pluginsync = true
    ```

2. Create a custom module for your plugins and types in your Puppet repository, if you haven't already:

   ```
   # cd /etc/puppet/modules
   # mkdir custom
   ```

3. Within the module, create a `lib/puppet/type` directory:

   ```
   # cd custom
   # mkdir -p lib/puppet/type
   ```

How to do it...

1. Create a file in the `type` directory named `gitrepo.rb` with the following contents:

   ```
   Puppet::Type.newtype(:gitrepo) do
       ensurable

       newparam(:source) do
           isnamevar
       end

       newparam(:path)
   end
   ```

How it works...

The first line registers a new type named `gitrepo`:

```
Puppet::Type.newtype(:gitrepo) do
```

The `ensurable` line automatically gives the type a property `ensure`, like Puppet's built-in resources.

```
    ensurable
```

We'll now give the type some parameters. For the moment, all we need is a `source` parameter for the Git source URL, and a `path` parameter to tell Puppet where the repository should be created in the filesystem.

```
    newparam(:source) do
        isnamevar
    end
```

The `isnamevar` declaration tells Puppet that the `source` parameter is the type's `namevar`. So when you declare an instance of this resource, whatever name you give it will be the value of `source`. For example:

```
gitrepo { "git://github.com/puppetlabs/puppet.git":
    path => "/home/john/work/puppet",
}
```

Finally, we add the `path` parameter:

```
newparam(:path)
```

There's more...

Once you're familiar with creating your own resources, you can use them to replace complicated `exec` resources and make your manifests more readable. However, it's a good idea to make your resources robust and reusable by adding some documentation, and validating your parameters.

Documentation

Our example is deliberately simple, but when you move on to developing real custom types for your production environment, you should add documentation strings to describe what the type and its parameters do. For example:

```
Puppet::Type.newtype(:gitrepo) do
    @doc = "Manages Git repos"

    ensurable

    newparam(:source) do
        desc "Git source URL for the repo"
        isnamevar
    end

    newparam(:path) do
        desc "Path where the repo should be created"
    end
end
```

Validation

You can use parameter validation to generate useful error messages when someone tries to pass bad values to the resource. For example, you could validate that the directory where the repository is to be created actually exists:

```
newparam(:path) do
    validate do |value|
        basepath = File.dirname(value)
        unless File.directory?(basepath)
            raise ArgumentError , "The path %s doesn't exist" %
            basepath
        end
    end
end
```

You can also specify the list of allowed values that the parameter can take as follows:

```
newparam(:breakfast) do
    newvalues(:bacon, :eggs, :sausages)
end
```

Creating your own providers

In the previous section, we created a new custom type called `gitrepo` and told Puppet that it takes two parameters, `source` and `path`. However, so far we haven't told Puppet how to actually check out the repository—in other words, how to create a specific instance of this type. That's where the provider comes in.

We saw that a type will often have several possible providers. In our example, there is only one sensible way to instantiate a Git repo, so we'll only supply one provider: `git`. If you were to generalize this type—say to just `repo`—it's not hard to imagine creating several different providers depending on the type of repository; for example, `git`, `svn`, `cvs`, and so on.

Getting ready...

1. Within your `custom` module, create a subdirectory of `lib/puppet called provider/gitrepo`:

    ```
    # mkdir -p lib/puppet/provider/gitrepo
    ```

2. In the `gitrepo` directory, create a file called `git.rb` with the following contents:

    ```
    require 'fileutils'

    Puppet::Type.type(:gitrepo).provide(:git) do
        commands :git => "git"
    ```

```
    def create
        git "clone", resource[:source], resource[:path]
    end

    def exists?
        File.directory? resource[:path]
    end
end
```

How to do it...

1. Create an instance of your new type somewhere in your Puppet manifest as follows:

```
gitrepo { "https://github.com/puppetlabs/puppet.git":
    path   => "/tmp/puppet",
    ensure => present,
}
```

2. Now run Puppet, and your new type will be loaded and instantiated:

```
# puppet agent --test

info: Retrieving plugin

notice: /File[/var/lib/puppet/lib/puppet]/ensure: created

notice: /File[/var/lib/puppet/lib/puppet/provider]/ensure: created

notice: /File[/var/lib/puppet/lib/puppet/provider/gitrepo]/ensure:
created

notice: /File[/var/lib/puppet/lib/puppet/provider/gitrepo/git.rb]/
ensure: defined content as '{md5}a12870d89a4b517e48fe417ce2e12ac2'

notice: /File[/var/lib/puppet/lib/puppet/type]/ensure: created

notice: /File[/var/lib/puppet/lib/puppet/type/gitrepo.rb]/ensure:
defined content as '{md5}90d5809e1d01dc9953464e8d431c9639'

info: Loading downloaded plugin /var/lib/puppet/lib/puppet/
provider/gitrepo/git.rb

info: Loading downloaded plugin /var/lib/puppet/lib/puppet/type/
gitrepo.rb

info: Redefining gitrepo in Puppet::Type

info: Caching catalog for cookbook.bitfieldconsulting.com

info: Applying configuration version '1299850325'

notice: /Stage[main]//Node[cookbook]/Gitrepo[https://github.com/
puppetlabs/puppet.git]/ensure: created

notice: Finished catalog run in 74.43 seconds
```

Note: due to a bug in Puppet, when you first create your new type, you may need to run `puppet agent` twice: once to load the type definition, and again to actually create the instance. If you see the following message:

```
err: /Stage[main]//Node[cookbook]/Gitrepo[https://
github.com/puppetlabs/puppet.git]: Could not
evaluate: No ability to determine if gitrepo exists
```

you've been bitten by the bug—just run Puppet again and it should work. By the time you read this it may well have been fixed.

How it works...

First we register this as a provider for the `gitrepo` type as follows:

```
Puppet::Type.type(:gitrepo).provide(:git) do
```

When you declare an instance of the type in your manifest, Puppet will first of all check whether the instance already exists:

```
def exists?
    File.directory? resource[:path]
end
```

We implement a method `exists?` that will be called by Puppet to make this check. It returns `true` if a directory exists matching the `path` parameter of the instance.

If `exists?` returns `true`, then Puppet will take no further action. If not, Puppet will try to create the resource by calling the `create` method:

```
def create
    git "clone", resource[:source], resource[:path]
end
```

In this case, the `create` method does a `git clone` on the Git source provided (in the `source` parameter) into the path specified by the `path` parameter.

There's more...

You can see that custom types and providers in Puppet are very powerful. In fact, they can do anything—at least, anything that Ruby can do. If you are managing some parts of your infrastructure with complicated `define` and `exec` resources, you may want to consider replacing these with a custom type. In fact, it's worth looking around to see if someone else has already done this before implementing your own.

Our example was very simple, and there is much more to learn about writing your own types. If you're going to distribute your code for others to use, or even if you aren't, it's a good idea to include tests with it. Puppet Labs has some useful pages on type development: `http://docs.puppetlabs.com/guides/custom_types.html` and `http://projects.puppetlabs.com/projects/1/wiki/Development_Practical_Types`. For information on writing tests to Puppet Labs standards, see `http://projects.puppetlabs.com/projects/1/wiki/Development_Writing_Tests`.

For an excellent, easy-to-follow introduction to type development, see James Turnbull's article "Creating Puppet types and providers is easy..." at `http://www.kartar.net/2010/02/puppet-types-and-providers-are-easy/`.

Dean Wilson also has a very instructive example of a custom type to manage APT sources: `https://github.com/deanwilson/puppet-aptsourced`.

Index

Thank you for buying
Puppet 2.7 Cookbook

About Packt Publishing

Packt, pronounced 'packed', published its first book "*Mastering phpMyAdmin for Effective MySQL Management*" in April 2004 and subsequently continued to specialize in publishing highly focused books on specific technologies and solutions.

Our books and publications share the experiences of your fellow IT professionals in adapting and customizing today's systems, applications, and frameworks. Our solution based books give you the knowledge and power to customize the software and technologies you're using to get the job done. Packt books are more specific and less general than the IT books you have seen in the past. Our unique business model allows us to bring you more focused information, giving you more of what you need to know, and less of what you don't.

Packt is a modern, yet unique publishing company, which focuses on producing quality, cutting-edge books for communities of developers, administrators, and newbies alike. For more information, please visit our website: www.packtpub.com.

About Packt Open Source

In 2010, Packt launched two new brands, Packt Open Source and Packt Enterprise, in order to continue its focus on specialization. This book is part of the Packt Open Source brand, home to books published on software built around Open Source licences, and offering information to anybody from advanced developers to budding web designers. The Open Source brand also runs Packt's Open Source Royalty Scheme, by which Packt gives a royalty to each Open Source project about whose software a book is sold.

Writing for Packt

We welcome all inquiries from people who are interested in authoring. Book proposals should be sent to author@packtpub.com. If your book idea is still at an early stage and you would like to discuss it first before writing a formal book proposal, contact us; one of our commissioning editors will get in touch with you.

We're not just looking for published authors; if you have strong technical skills but no writing experience, our experienced editors can help you develop a writing career, or simply get some additional reward for your expertise.

Zenoss Core Network and System Monitoring

ISBN: 978-1-847194-28-2   Paperback: 280 pages

A step-by-step guide to configuring, using, and adapting this free Open Source network monitoring system - with a Foreword by Mark R. Hinkle, V

1. Discover, manage, and monitor IT resources

2. Build custom event processing and alerting rules

3. Configure Zenoss Core via an easy to use web interface

4. Drag and drop dashboard portlets with Google Maps integration

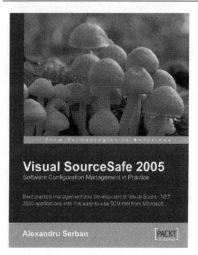

Visual SourceSafe 2005 Software Configuration Management in Practice

ISBN: 978-1-904811-69-5   Paperback: 404 pages

Best practice management and development of Visual Studio .NET 2005 applications with this easy-to-use SCM tool from Microsoft

1. SCM fundamentals and strategies clearly explained

2. Real-world SOA example: a hotel reservation system

3. SourceSafe best practices across the complete lifecycle

Please check **www.PacktPub.com** for information on our titles

Zenoss Core 3.x Network and System Monitoring

ISBN: 978-1-84951-158-2   Paperback: 312 pages

Implement Zenoss core and fit it into your security management environment using this easy-to-understand tutorial guide

1. Designed to quickly acquaint you with the core feature so you can customize Zenoss Core to your needs

2. Discover, manage, and monitor IT resources

3. Write custom device reports to extract, display, and analyze monitoring data

Cacti 0.8 Network Monitoring

ISBN: 978-1-847195-96-8   Paperback: 132 pages

Monitor your network with ease!

1. Install and setup Cacti to monitor your network and assign permissions to this setup in no time at all

2. Create, edit, test, and host a graph template to customize your output graph

3. Create new data input methods, SNMP, and Script XML data query

4. Full of screenshots and step-by-step instructions to monitor your network with Cacti

Please check **www.PacktPub.com** for information on our titles